QUIET SPIDERS OF THE HIDDEN SOUL

D1521416

Ukrainian Studies

SERIES EDITOR
Vitaly Chernetsky
(University of Kansas)

ІЗ ПРІРВ СВІДОМОСТІ

Рання

експериментальна

поезія

Миколи (Ніка) Бажана

За редакцією Оксани Розенблюм,
Лева Фрідмана та Анжеліки Хижньої

QUIET SPIDERS OF THE HIDDEN SOUL

Mykola (Nik) Bazhan's

Early

Experimental

Poetry

Edited by Oksana Rosenblum,
Lev Fridman, and Anzhelika Khyzhnia

Boston
2020

This publication was made possible by the financial support of the Shevchenko Scientific Society, USA from Ivan and Elizabeta Chlopetsky Fund.

This book has been published with the support of the Translate Ukraine Translation Grant Program (Ukrainian Book Institute).

Library of Congress Cataloging-in-Publication Data

Names: Bazhan, Mykola Platonovych, 1904-1983, author. | Bazhan, Mykola Platonovych, 1904–1983. Poems. Selections | Bazhan, Mykola Platonovych, 1904–1983. Poems. Selections. English | Rosenblum, Oksana, 1976- editor. | Fridman, Lev, 1983- editor. | Khyzhnya, Anzhelika, 1970- editor.
Title: "Quiet spiders of the hidden soul" : Mykola (Nik) Bazhan's early experimental poetry / [Mykola Bazhan]; edited by Oksana Rosenblum, Lev Fridman, and Anzhelika Khyzhnya.
Description: Boston: Academic Studies Press, 2020. | Series: Ukrainian studies | Includes index. | Poems in English and Ukrainian.
Identifiers: LCCN 2020011337 (print) | LCCN 2020011338 (ebook) | ISBN 9781644693940 (hardback) | ISBN 9781644693957 (paperback) | ISBN 9781644693964 (adobe pdf) | ISBN 9781644693971 (epub)
Classification: LCC PG3948.B3 A2 2020 (print) | LCC PG3948.B3 (ebook) | DDC 891.7/9132--dc23
LC record available at https://lccn.loc.gov/2020011337
LC ebook record available at https://lccn.loc.gov/2020011338

Cover design by Misha Beletsky.
Book design by PHi Business Solutions.

Academic Studies Press
1577 Beacon Street
Brookline, MA 02446, USA
press@academicstudiespress.com
www.academicstudiespress.com

Contents

Acknowledgements

T his book would not have been possible were it just an anthology of poetry. It owes its existence to another anthology—one comprised of people. Here we acknowledge a diverse crowd, oblivious to borders, time zones, languages, and generations. We thank a group of individuals and institutions that unanimously agreed, and often reassured us, that this book simply had to be written.

We owe a debt of gratitude to Oleksii Darsky, Mykola Bazhan's grandson. We began by seeking his official approval for our endeavor, but what commenced was constant correspondence replete with support and reassurance. We wish to thank Oleksii for his faith in our vision to publish the work of his grandfather in the West, something long overdue.

Alongside Oleksii, we thank Lyudmila Reznikova, the former director of the Mykola Bazhan Literary Memorial Museum in Kyiv. Her effort, work ethic, and time spent in helping us gather and make sense of the arcane and elusive material in this anthology do not conform to any standard system of measurement. At times it felt as if Lyudmila's role in this project had become a part-time job: by sunrise on the East Coast of the United States, we were often in receipt of multi-paragraph emails answering questions we had asked the previous day.

In Ukraine, we were also supported by the knowledge and resources of Yaryna Tsymbal at the Institute of Literature, Academy of Sciences of Ukraine. We are grateful for our collaboration with Taissa Sydorchuk at the Omeljan Pritsak Memorial Library, the National University of Kyiv-Mohyla Academy, the staff at Vernadsky National Library of Ukraine, Department of Periodicals, and thank the Mykola Bazhan Museum in Kyiv for their ongoing support. A special thanks to Natalia V. Kostenko, formerly of the Institute of Linguistics at Kyiv National University, for her expertise, her human insight, for taking phone calls at her home, and for supporting our efforts.

We would also like to acknowledge the community of scholars and friends in North America. They appeared and reappeared in sync with our needs, with answers and questions, advice, constructive criticism, and morale boosts. In no particular order: Alexander Cigale, Oksana Maksymchuk, Alexander Motyl, Boris Dralyuk, Irina Mashinski, Maria Genkin, Val Vinokur, Olena Jennings, Markian Dobczansky, Oleh Ilnytzkyj, and Oleh Kotsyuba. To the institutions and their staff that helped us unearth the texts, often inside the so-familiar paradox of that which is hidden in plain sight, hidden by a system and regime which needs no introduction here: Olha Aleksic (Ukrainian Collection, Harvard University Library) and James Kominowski (Elizabeth Dafoe Library, University of Manitoba). To Rick Carroll and Max Shterngel who nurtured this endeavor from its most nascent stage to this very minute, fueled by the conviction (as you are probably beginning to notice, a slightly contagious conviction) that this work needs to be done.

For their roles as academic advisors to our project: Vitaly Chernetsky (Center for Russian, East European & Eurasian Studies, University of Kansas), Mark Andryczyk (Ukrainian Studies Program, Columbia University), Myroslav Shkandrij (Slavic Studies, University of Manitoba), and Amelia M. Glaser (Literature, University of California—San Diego). Vitaly started as a collegiate proponent of the project when it was in its most nascent and formative state. After approaching Academic Studies Press, we found him there again, and this time we were able to present a more developed and mature monster, which he continued to help us tame and cultivate. Myroslav, Amelia, Svetlana Lavochkina, and Ostap Kin (Zimmerli Art Museum, Rutgers University) are among the team of translators in this anthology but, like others, they have worn many hats and appear in different roles as we called upon them throughout this work.

To our team of editors, proofreaders, and the watchful and vigilant, making sure through countless hours of pro bono labor that nothing stood out of place and everything stood in its place. For their pages upon pages of commentary, often regarding a single word or line in a poem or essay, until the collective could come to a consensus, for their attention to the detail of detail. To Anzhelika Khyzhnya, who tirelessly worked with the writers and translators on the intricacies of the Ukrainian language (often a necessarily difficult, nuanced, and wonderfully bizarre idiom) with her expertise and flexibility. To Eugene Ostashevsky, Graeme McGuire (our resident Graemarian), Eric Maroney, Jon Frankel, and Anya Krushelnitskaya for spending countless hours doing the very opposite, lending us eyes unattuned to Ukrainian, but so very attuned to English language and literature and to the needs of our readers. To Jurij Karpenko (Prague Education Center) for his generous donation for the cover design of our book.

To our team of translators and writers for being part of the journey and taking their turns at the wheel. Last and most, to those closest to us for their patience and for ensuring that we continued to function in the day-to-day while we labored at that which we hope, and intend, to be timeless.
Thank you all.

Lev Fridman
Oksana Rosenblum

Preface

When Lev and I first met sometime in February 2018 to discuss Mykola Bazhan, we could not have known what would eventually emerge from those fragmentary and tentative discussions about publishing a small book of Bazhan's early poetry in English translation. Right now you are holding in your hands the simultaneously improbable and inevitable product of that work: a snowball of inspiration rolling down a mountain of effort and support.

Lev came to this project through an emotional encounter with Bazhan's gut-wrenching poetic response to the Babyn Yar massacre, having compelled a group of translators to work on a poem called "Iar" (Ravine, 1943), and was awed by the poet's efforts to document the horrors that occurred on his native soil. I, on the other hand, emerged from three months' work on the translation of Bazhan's long poem "Rozmova serdets'" (Heart-to-heart conversation, 1929), and realized that I had become completely engrossed in the intensity of the emotions and dreamlike quality of the text that transformed my understanding of this—as I used to think of him before—conventional poet. I kept wondering why, having studied Ukrainian poetry of the 1920s–1930s in the past, I had never heard of this oeuvre, filled with the overwhelming internal monologues of a lyrical hero, who in the first part of the poem finds himself stuck in a building-coffin structure: "Arching over me/The building lifts, like a maddening hearse. The floors, immobile and silent coffins/Are stacked on top of one another."[1] This feeling of being stuck epitomized the situation in which an entire generation of Ukrainian writers, poets, and artists in general found themselves toward the end of the 1920s. Furthermore, Bazhan's poetry, the trajectory of which encompassed various movements and creative platforms, was far from conventional, eclectic in style, and not easy to categorize.

Our selection of Bazhan's early poetry took into account a few seemingly simple principles: we wanted to showcase the work that is lesser known, more

---

1   Quoted from this volume.

experimental, and speaks to the sensibility of the contemporary reader. With that being said, Bazhan's work is known for its linguistic complexity, so there is nothing simple about it, which might be one of the reasons why this kind of a collection has not been put together before. Despite continued interest in Bazhan's life and work in Ukraine, he has received little attention in the West, and it is our humble hope that this book will fill in this gap.[2]

Our anthology includes poems from the three early Bazhan collections: *Simnadtsiatyi patrul'* (*The Seventeenth Patrol*, 1926), *Riz'blena tin'* (*The Sculpted Shadow*, 1927), and *Budivli* (*Edifices*, 1929). It also includes translations of Bazhan's important long poems, written in 1929–1930: "Getto v Umani" (Ghetto in Uman'), "Hofmanova nich" (Hoffmann's night), and "Sliptsi" (Blind bards). Additional material is represented by the book of both prose and poetry *Zustrich na perekhresnii stantsiï: rozmova tr'oh* (Meeting at the crossroad station: a conversation among the three, 1927), which contains a polemical exchange between three leading poets of the time: Mykhail' Semenko, Geo Shkurupii, and Mykola Bazhan. *Zustrichi* sheds light on Bazhan's creative thought process behind his collection *Budivli*.

The rationale behind publishing the originals in Ukrainian is that up until now there has been no collection of Bazhan's early work. One has to scout various Ukrainian and North American libraries in order to find the poems, quite a few of which are scattered among journals and almanacs of the 1920s. Because of the rarity of some of Bazhan's early poems and collections, such as *Riz'blena tin'* (*The Sculpted Shadow*), there has been confusion among scholars of Bazhan's work as to the content of each particular poetry collection, as well as with the dating of the poems. As a result, some poems have been mistakenly assigned to collections to which they did not belong. This anthology consolidates this material and clarifies the confusion.

In addition to creating the critical apparatus for the early works of Bazhan, clarifying the content of the collections and dates of the poems, the translation process itself represents a new milestone in the process of expanding Bazhan's literary canon in both Ukrainian and English. Only a few of Bazhan's poems from the 1920s and early 1930s have previously been published in English.[3]

---

2   See Aheieva, *Vizerunok na kameni. Mykola Bazhan: zhyttepys (ne)radians'koho poeta* (*Pattern on a stone. Mykola Bazhan: a chronicle of a [non-]Soviet poet*) (Lviv: Vydavnytstvo staroho leva, 2018).

3   "Hofmanova nich" (Hoffmann's night) appeared in *Kenyon Review* 2, no. 3 (1980): 35–40, in a translation by Bohdan Boychuk and Mark Rudman. "Getto v Umani" (Ghetto in Uman') appeared in *Agni* 52 (2000): 217–220, in a translation by Michael M. Naydan.

His poetry has been described as dense, rich, and syntactically complex. His vocabulary is unusually varied, even for a poet of this caliber. It is no wonder that contemporary readers of Bazhan have to reach for numerous dictionaries and encyclopedias, as well as post their inquiries on Facebook forums.

The translators' essays that supplement almost every chapter of the book were conceived as experimental pieces, as a common ground for testing out various ideas about the process of translation itself. Inevitably, every translator has their own approach. Some are more literal, while others prefer to wander off into unknown territory and take risks by conveying the emotional component of the poetry, rather than its literal meaning, in the target language.

We know that not every poem and its translation in this anthology will resonate with the reader, yet we hope that everyone finds something here that presents Mykola Bazhan's early creative output from an unexpected angle.

A few words about the title of our book: it comes from Bazhan's 1929 poem "Hoffmann's Night," a tribute to Romanticism and early Modernism. The strikingly dark imagery of the poem speaks volumes about the role of the unconscious in the creative process, something that Bazhan must have been acutely aware of:

Наказую я привидам-словам:
Із прірв свідомості, з найглибших людських ям
Ви павуками тихими вилазьте!

I order the word-ghosts
To creep out from the deepest manholes of the mind,
Like quiet spiders of the hidden soul![4]

Oksana Rosenblum

"Krov polonianok" (The blood of captive maidens) appeared in *Hundred Years of Youth: A Bilingual Anthology of 20th Century Ukrainian Poetry*, ed. Olha Luchuk and Michael M. Naydan (Lviv: Litopys, 2000).

4   Translated for this book by Svetlana Lavochkina.

The Ukrainian Avant-Garde and Its Roots: The Poetics of Mykola (Nik) Bazhan

HALYNA BABAK

In his nomination of Mykola Bazhan for the 1970 Nobel Prize,[1] Omeljan Pritsak, the founder of the Harvard Ukrainian Research Institute, proposes Bazhan's early period—his most controversial and stylistically diverse—as crucial for understanding the nature of his poetic talent. It is the works of Bazhan's first literary decade, ranging from his debut publication in 1923 to a panegyric for Stalin in 1932, that secured him a place in Ukrainian Soviet literature.[2] Pritsak especially singles out Bazhan's second poetry collection, *The Sculpted Shadow*, and

---

1   The nomination was doomed from the very beginning because of the political realities of that time. Mykola Bazhan refused to send the bibliography of translations of his poems needed for the nomination because he knew too well how dearly he would have to pay for it if it came to pass.

2   Mykola Bazhan, "Rura-marsh" (Ruhr-March), *Bil'shovyk*, May 17, 1923, 10. Mykola Bazhan, "Liudyna stoït' v zorenosnim Kremli" (A man stands in the star-bearing Kremlin), in Mykola Bazhan, *Poezii* (Saratov: Ukrvydav CK KP(b)U, 1943).

also such poems as "Edifices," "Ghetto in Uman'," "Hoffman's Night," and "Blind Bards." For Pritsak, Bazhan's poetry of the 1920s represents the European experimental style. But at the same time he stresses that it is deeply rooted in the late seventeenth-century Ukrainian Baroque tradition,[3] "with its profusion of grotesque emblematic details, extended metaphors, often enigmatic metonymies, and an approach which is at the same time furiously sensual and icily detached."[4]

The poet himself emphasized the dichotomy between the avant-garde and Baroque in his work. In 1927 Bazhan wrote: "I love the Zaborovs'kyi Gate and the Dniprel'stan.[5] I love organic and robust culture, and Ukraine produced such culture only once: the culture of feudalism, the culture of Mazepa. Now it'll have it the second time: the culture of proletariat and the culture of building a socialist society."[6] The two architectural symbols of the radically opposing styles that Bazhan names are Dniprel'stan, part of the Dnipro hydroelectric station, which had just been started in 1927, and the former main entrance to Saint Sophia Cathedral in Kyiv, Zaborovs'kyi Gate, one of the most vivid examples of Ukrainian Baroque. He thereby indicates the two poles of his poetics. On the one hand, he is a member of the avant-garde; on the other, from the mid-1920s he turns to the Baroque tradition and to philosophical epic poems. The coexistence of these different stylistic approaches is demonstrated in his two earliest poetry collections.

Bazhan's first Futurist book *The Seventeenth Patrol* (1926) was an attempt to pay tribute to the revolutionary years; it consequently required decisive gestures and new forms of expression. However, his second collection *The Sculpted Shadow* (1927) struck a completely different tone in addition to that of experimentalism: its speaker tries to develop an understanding of life with all its contradictions. The same philosophical orientation can be detected in the poems Bazhan wrote in the late 1920s and early 1930s. They are marked by accumulating images that are perceived as separate and chaotic, but together the poems uncover the very essence of things through the objectification—both in the sense of focusing on concrete objects or details, and in the sense of refraining

---

3   For the Ukrainian Baroque, which flourished during the Hetmanship of Ivan Mazepa (1639–1709), see Giovanna Brogi Bercoff, "Plurilinguism and Identity: Rethinking Ukrainian Literature of the Seventeenth Century," in *Ukraine and Europe: Cultural Encounters and Negotiations*, ed. Marko Pavlyshyn et al., 45–72 (Toronto: University of Toronto Press, 2017).

4   Omeljan Pritsak Memorial Library, Archival Collection, National University of Kyiv-Mohyla Academy, collection 10, file 983, pages 101–118.

5   *Brama Zaborovs'koho*. More can be found at http://www.encyclopediaofukraine.com/display.asp?linkpath=pages%5CZ%5CA%5CZaborovskyGate.htm.

6   All translations are from the current volume, unless otherwise specified.

from personal emotion—of the sensory world.[7] The initial chaos, divided and solidified by the description of disparate objects, is perceived by the reader as a sequence of fragments, built frame by frame in the manner of montage, conveying the complexity of the artistic experience.

Thus, objectification and montage become the main techniques that connect avant-garde with Baroque aesthetics in Bazhan's poems of the late 1920s. In broader terms, these principles may be said to characterize European art and literature of the 1920s in general: the emergence of Surrealism and Neue Sachlichkeit from Dada, and of Constructivism, Bauhaus, and other forms of engineering-oriented art from Cubism and Futurism. The employment of these techniques also indicates an understanding of art and literature as autonomous spheres, governed by their own laws, as the focus shifts to the formal aspects of a literary work. The ontological autonomy of art was a foundational tenet of the Russian Formalists and, a bit later, of the Anglo-American New Critics. Both movements developed as a reaction to the older literary history schools that considered literary work only as a product of the author's personality, status, or attitudes toward their own social reality.

In his essay "Art as Device" (also translated as "Art as Technique"), published 1917, Viktor Shklovsky, one of the founders of Russian Formalism and its main proponent, considered the complexity of artistic form as the main principle of defamiliarization or estrangement, which is also a "way of experiencing the process of creativity."[8] If avant-garde technique defamiliarizes the object by dividing it into parts and reshuffling them, then Baroque technique is avant-garde avant la lettre in its desire for asymmetry, logical leaps, semantic and rhythmic shifts, conjunction of distant ideas, and its ambition to surprise. Hence concretization of detail and, at the same time, the transition from linear connections to juxtaposition and montage are features common both to avant-garde and Baroque. Later in his 1931 essay "The Golden Land" Shklovsky wrote: "People of our time, people of intense detail are people of the

---

7   This could be compared to the destruction of the lyrical "I" in Marinetti's Futurist manifestos, Pound's principle of "Direct treatment of the 'thing,'" or William Carlos Williams's dictum "no ideas but in things." See Paolo Tonini, *I manifesti del futurismo italiano 1909–1945* (Gussago: Edizioni dell'Arengario, 2011); Ezra Pound, "A Retrospect," in *Literary Essays of Ezra Pound,* ed. and introd. T. S. Eliot (London: Faber and Faber, 1954), 3–14; William Carlos Williams, *Paterson,* ed. Christopher McGowan (New York: New Directions Publishing, 1995).

8   Viktor Shklovsky, *Theory of Prose,* trans. and ed. Benjamin Sher (Illinois: Dalkey Archive Press, 1990), 6.

Baroque. ... The Baroque, life of intense details, is not a vice, but an attribute of our times."[9]

It is no coincidence that T. S. Eliot, in his shaping of the principles of modern poetry, appeals to the English Baroque tradition. In his famous essay "The Metaphysical Poets" (1921), along with ascribing a new level of significance to early modern English poetry, he concludes "that poets in our civilization, as it exists at present, must be *difficult*. ... The poet must become more and more comprehensive, more allusive, more indirect, in order to force, to dislocate if necessary, language into his meaning."[10] In another essay "Hamlet and His Problems" (1919), Eliot provides a more precise formula: "The only way of expressing emotion in the form of art is by finding an 'objective correlative'; in other words, a set of objects, a situation, a chain of events which shall be the formula of that particular emotion; such that when the external facts, which must terminate in sensory experience, are given, the emotion is immediately evoked."[11]

Bazhan's definition of poetry appears in his 1927 manifesto "Put On Your Glasses." Although he calls it "revolutionary materialism," his idea is similar to those of both Eliot and Shklovsky: "To properly see things, browse, and touch them—means to be unlike the impressionists. To touch things that are material and objective—means to differ from the Expressionists. To not contemplate, not photograph them—means to differ from the naturalists. To be a revolutionary materialist."[12] The same overt objectification becomes the foundation of modern aesthetics, and is also effective in Bazhan's poetry of the late 1920s, where it is given the task of defamiliarization.

Bazhan was thirteen years old during the October 1917 revolution. This partly explains the romantic perception of the events in his first poetic collection *The Seventeenth Patrol*, published under the name Nik Bazhan.

In 1921 Bazhan set out from Uman' to study in Kyiv. From the beginning of the February Revolution until the final establishment of Communist rule in

---

9   Viktor Shklovsky, *Gamburgskii schet. Stat'i—vospominaniia—esse (1914–1933)* (*The Hamburg reckoning. Articles—memoirs—essays*), ed. Aleksandr Galushkin (Moscow: Sovetskii pisatel', 1990), 444.

10   T. S. Eliot, "The Metaphysical Poets," in *Selected Essays*, 3rd ed. (London: Faber and Faber, 1951), 287.

11   T. S. Eliot, "Hamlet and Its Problems," in *The Sacred Wood* (London: Methuen, 1921), 87–94.

12   Mykola Bazhan, "Odiahnit' okuliary" (Put on your glasses), *Bumerang. Zhurnal pamfletiv* 1 (1927): 25. My translation.

1920, Kyiv was controlled by various powers, changing hands fourteen times. In the spring of 1920, the city suffered a terrible famine. Still, this hardship and turmoil did not stop an intense whirlpool of literary life. Among the first to appear in the literary arena were the Futurists, headed by Mykhail' Semenko. The history of Ukrainian Futurism began as early as 1914, when Semenko invented "Quero-Futurism" (Searching-Futurism) and published his collection *Daring*, containing the manifesto "Myself."

The manifesto challenged the most canonical of Ukrainian poets, Taras Shevchenko, who for Semenko symbolized the rustic backward Ukrainian culture of the nineteenth century. Semenko called upon Ukrainians to "burn *The Kobzar*," Shevchenko's main poetry collection. The text caused a large debate among the intelligentsia, primarily because the Romantic poet was perceived not only as poet but as liberator, prophet, and messiah. Although inspired by Italian and Russian precedents, this gesture was much stronger than Marinetti's call to "burn libraries and museums" or the Cubo-Futurist command "to throw Pushkin, Dostoyevsky, Tolstoy, and others off from the ship of modernity."[13] Of course, Pushkin and Shevchenko were the main representatives and symbols of their national literatures. But the difference is that Pushkin, unlike Shevchenko, was a poet of an imperial, multinational Russia. Shevchenko, on the other hand, had been installed as a symbol of Ukrainian national liberation during his lifetime. At this point, further development of Ukrainian Futurism was interrupted by World War I.

At the end of the 1910s the Futurist movement in Ukraine began gaining more power, pushing earlier Symbolist practices into the background. The demands of Communist ideology to destroy the old "bourgeois" world and build the new "proletarian" society were to a certain extent consistent with the Futurist vision of art. Therefore, after the revolution the avant-garde movement saw itself as the righteous art of the new proletarian class.

Here it would be helpful to introduce the term "Late Futurism" to help define some versions of 1920s Futurism. The term "Late Futurism" can be applied to avant-garde groups and movements in those national literatures which either never had the first phase of so-called "High Futurism" (in the prewar period) or in which this phase was not original or quickly aborted. We can see examples of

---

13 Filippo Marinetti, "The Foundation and Manifesto of Futurism," 1909; "Slap in the Face of Public Taste," 1912. See also Tonini, *I manifesti del futurismo italiano 1909–1945*; S. Dzhymbinova, ed., *Literaturnye manifesty ot simvolizma do nashykh dnei* (Moscow: XXI vek—Soglasie, 2000), 142.

Late Futurist movements in Poland and Slovenia.[14] "Late Futurism" arises as a more mature form of the radical avant-garde and—this is very important—as an artistic consciousness that is much closer to national traditions.

Ukrainian Futurism started its quick development after World War I and 1917, at the time when the main European Futurist movements began to transform. Whereas prewar Italian and Russian Futurisms were anarchic and anti-establishment, especially anti-state, after the war both movements tried to position themselves as the artistic arms of their respective regimes. In 1922, former Russian Futurists formed a new organization, LEF (Left Front of the Arts), and no longer called themselves "Futurists." Furthermore, after the war, Italian Futurists started to support the fascist movement, and embraced the state after Mussolini's "March on Rome" in October 1922. In Western literatures, nationalism and communism were the two paradigms between which "Late Futurism" played its brief role.

As for Ukraine, the development of a separate Futurism was minor before the war and interrupted by it. The period from 1918, when Semenko came back to Kyiv, until about 1922, can be described as Late Futurism. At that time, Ukrainian Futurism was one of the vocal factions offering competing visions of artistic form and social function in the initially dynamic Soviet environment. But in the early to mid-twenties, political pressure began to distort and dilute avant-garde aesthetics. The mechanism of "social demand" played a substantial role in literature: it empowered the creation of works that fit into state discourse.

It was in 1921 that Semenko invented "Pan-Futurism"—a "post-art of the future" that aimed to synthesize the achievements of all experimental movements in art. In terms of its theory and artistic practices, "Pan-Futurism" s was close to Constructivism, even though the followers still called themselves "futurists" or "pan-futurists". Bazhan joined the Association of Pan-Futurists (Aspanfut) that same year. As he later explained in his memoirs:

> By the time I moved to Kyiv, I had already become a full-scale "leftist," and so I did not join the Neoclassicists[15] but instead went to meet up with Mykhail'

---

14 See Nina Kolesnikoff, "Polish Futurism: Its Origin and the Aesthetic Program," *Canadian Slavonic Papers* 18, no. 3 (1976): 301–311; Marijan Dović, "Anton Podbevšek, Futurism, and Slovenian Interwar Avant-garde Literature," *International Yearbook of Futurism Studies* 1 (2011): 262–276.

15 The Neoclassicists (from the word "neoclassicism." In Ukrainian: *neoklasyky*) was a group of Ukrainian poets as well as literary critics and theorists of Ukrainian Modernism in the 1920s. Unlike other groups, they had no organized structure. Their works were characterized by aestheticism, an appeal to Greek and Roman themes and plots, and an interest in the formal

Semenko. Semenko persuaded me and Iurii Ianovs'kyi to move to Kharkiv.
... He discovered us all. He supported us and helped us to get settled.[16]

Bazhan's other mentor was the avant-garde director Les' Kurbas. Kurbas, the leader of *Berezil'* theatre, was one of the most outstanding figures in the Ukrainian arts:

> When he [Kurbas] came to Uman' with his theatre lab, I read him Tychyna's "Like Harps, Like Harps." He was stunned. ... Tychyna and, of course, Mayakovsky: these were my first teachers. I happened to get hold of Mayakovsky's "150000000" in Uman', and this book greatly influenced me. ... When I moved to Kyiv, I used to visit Kurbas quite often, and I followed Berezil' theatre all the time. I really felt the influence of expressionism through the plays of Berezil'. ..."[17]

Apart from Kurbas, the influence of Vladimir Mayakovsky and German Expressionism can be discerned in Bazhan's first poetry collection *The Seventeenth Patrol* (1926), which includes twenty-four poems written during the years he spent in Kyiv. The poems are clearly identified with Futurist poetics: they aim to affirm the heroic pathos of the revolutionary years, and feature sound polyphony, sophisticated metaphors, pronounced emotion, and asymmetric rhythm. Bazhan plays with the formal and semantic aspects of word-creation, capitalizes on the nuances of meaning, and searches for new techniques to effect dynamism.

Perhaps unexpectedly for a Futurist, the poet appeals to traditional songs and ballads, but he fills them with unusual content. For example, the poem "Trooper's Song" (1925) reflects the author's perception of the revolutionary years. What it lacks in plot development it makes up for in revolutionary and romantic pathos. As Red Army guards leave for a battle, figurative sound patterning evokes the clanking of steel stirrups. The reader is meant to be immersed in the atmosphere of the battle and to experience the ringing of weapons and the smoke of the battlefields:

---

aspects of literature. From the mid-1920s, Marxist critics accused them of formalism. The main representatives of this movement were Mykola Zerov, Maksym Ryl's'kyi, Pavlo Fylypovych, Mykhailo Drai-Khmara, and Iurii Klen. See http://www.encyclopediaofukraine. com/display.asp?linkpath=pages%5CN%5CE%5CNeoclassicists.htm.

16 Nataliia Kostenko, "Razgovory s poetom" (Conversations with the poet), in *Vospominaniia o Mykole Bazhane* (*Memories of Mykola Bazhan*), ed. Nina Bazhan and Evgeniia Deich (Moscow: Sovetskii pisatel', 1989), 272.

17 Ibid., 271.

The troopers set off, their horses were neighing
(Soft steady clanking of stirrup steel).

Original:

Бійці виїжджали і коні іржали
(**Стр**имано в **стр**еменах **ст**аль дзвенить).

The motif of self-sacrifice in support of the revolution appears in Bazhan's poem "Imobe of Galam" (1924). The poem uses the fight against colonialism in the French colonies for its thematic framework. Surrounded by "exotic" nature, a black slave named Imobe rises against his European oppressors. Bazhan's original again employs sound patterning, this time to convey the atmosphere of tension against the backdrop of a mystical night:

When in the papyrus sedge
                        birds scream aghast
And the sky is congealed
                        in a clot of black musk,
A knight
            of the old Maghreb faith
                        prowls in the wildwood.

The reader is not provided with any context or details, but the poem functions as a manifesto for fighting a violent social order. As a consequence of this kind of work, *The Seventeenth Patrol* was highly praised by critics. One of them wrote: "The thing is, Bazhan does not make you wander through the watery prairies of boring lyricism, instead he immediately captures your attention with the plot."[18]

As a Futurist, Bazhan also carried out linguistic experiments which, however, were not included in any collection. For example, "Hops of Green Legs" (1924) offers examples of semantic *zaum*:[19]

---

18 Ihor Shakhivets', "Mykola Bazhan, '17-i Patrul'" (*The Seventeenth Patrol* by Mykola Bazhan), *Kul'tura i pobut* 14 (1926): 8. This is a review of Bazhan's *The Seventeenth Patrol*.

19 *Zaum* (Rus.: *zaum'*, also *zaumnyi iazyk* [trans-sense language]) was the most radical expression of the new concept of poetry proclaimed by the Russian Futurists in their manifestos. According to this concept, the word had to be treated and perceived "as such," a phonetic entity possessing its own ontology. *Zaum*, therefore, is an experimental language which consists of neologisms that are rich in sound but devoid of any conventional meaning. See

The hops of green legs lull me,
of bodies, tulle.
O, one who eyes in the evening
the shimmering shingles of waves.

Original:

Мене зелених ніг,
тіл тюль люля хміль.
О, хто зазирає ввечері на зорі
в хвиль сльотну толь?

Such semantic shifts attempt to communicate the *mood* of night. The poem replaces sense with sound. The author uses a purely avant-garde strategy of creating an image by emphasizing impulsive forms of utterance.

In 1925, Semenko's Pan-Futurists settled in Kharkiv, which from 1919 was the capital of Soviet Ukraine. Having moved there as well, Bazhan found himself at the epicenter of Ukrainian cultural and artistic life, where most of the literary groups and publishing houses were concentrated. *Berezil'* moved to Kharkiv in 1926. Bazhan befriended the future film director Alexander Dovzhenko, who worked as a magazine illustrator there. The poet also encountered the avant-garde artists led by Vasyl' Iermylov, who had collaborated with Russian Futurists Velimir Khlebnikov and David Burliuk. Vladimir Mayakovsky also frequented the city. Kharkiv in the 1920s lay at an intersection of Ukrainian and Russian cultures.

A new period in Bazhan's artistic development began in 1926. In his search for a suitable cultural paradigm, he turned to the Ukrainian folklore tradition as well as to classical forms. This turn testified to an ideological discrepancy between Semenko and Bazhan. Bazhan's avant-garde strategies—unlike those of Semenko or Geo Shkurupii—never entailed ideological gestures against the national literary canon.[20] He became a member of the more

---

Gerald Janecek, *Zaum: The Transrational Poetry of Russian Futurism* (San Diego: San Diego State University Press, 1996).

20   In 1925, Semenko published his complete collection of poetry in one volume (1910–1922) provocatively titled *Kobzar'*. In 1930, Geo Shkurupii published his unfinished novel *A Tale of the Poet Taras Shevchenko's Bitter Love* in the journals *Zhyttia i revoliutsiia* (the first three parts) and *Nova generatsiia* (another two parts).

aesthetically conservative literary group VAPLITE that same year.[21] Headed by Mykola Khvyl'ovyi, this organization adopted Bolshevik policy in matters of literature. VAPLITE advocated for the creation of a new Ukrainian literature, which should be oriented towards the best examples of West European writing. VAPLITE also emphasized the professional status and qualifications of the writer. It did not recognize the participation of its members in any other literary organizations, which caused problems for Bazhan who did not break his cooperation with Semenko.

In 1927, the Pan-Futurists published the collection *Meeting at the Crossroad Station*, subtitled *A Conversation Between the Three*, that contained poems by Mykhail' Semenko, Mykola Bazhan, and Geo Shkurupii, as well as a prosaic fragment with the same title. Here, Bazhan presented such classical stanza poems as "The Blood of the Captive Maidens" and "The Night of Zalizniak," as well as "Heart-to-Heart Conversation," which he signed with his own name rather than his Futurist pen name Nik. This gesture itself indicates a transition to new aesthetic and ideological positions. In the prose section, the authors expressed their visions of contemporary literature and of their further participation in the Futurist movement. Here Bazhan said that he had lost faith in Futurism, with its ideal of art for the masses and by the masses, and turned instead to the elite culture of Ukrainian Baroque:

> Okay, I'd admit it: I've laid down my arms. I stopped dreaming about new forms of art that are a thousand times more influential, robust, majestic than the old ones. I stopped believing that tomorrow, or the day after tomorrow, pocket-size, chamber, domestic art (like in the collocation "domestic cattle") will be supplanted by new art of mobs, streets, demonstrations, and uprisings.

Such a decision could have been dictated not only by the artistic search of the poet, but also by domestic politics.

By the mid-1920s, revolutionary enthusiasm gave way to feelings of confusion and uncertainty among Ukrainian intellectuals, as they reacted to the policies of the Soviet state. On the one side, there was the policy of *korenizatsiia*

---

21 VAPLITE, an acronym of *Vil'na akademiia proletars'koï literatury* (*Free Academy of Proletarian Literature*), was an organization of Modernist writers founded in 1925 by Mykola Khvyl'ovyi. In subsequent years, Maik Iohansen, Oleksa Slisarenko, Iurii Ianovs'kyi, Pavlo Tychyna, Mykola Bazhan, Oleksandr Dovzhenko, and other cultural figures joined the group.

(nativization), which aimed to strengthen the Communist regime in the national republics by promoting the local population into larger governing bodies. On the other, the Bolsheviks introduced the NEP, or New Economic Policy, which was more market-oriented and aimed to foster the economic development of the country. While the policy of Ukrainization was perceived positively and stimulated the flourishing of Ukrainian culture in the 1920s, the NEP was criticized by the left wing of the Communist Party and was seen by its representatives as an unpleasant, temporary necessity. The split directly affected the ideological climate of literary life. Some of the literary groups tried to maintain the "leftist" approach to literature and show their "usefulness,"[22] while others assumed an increasingly loyal attitude to the party's general line. As a consequence, from the mid-1920s the Pan-Futurists were criticized by both party authorities and other literary groups, including VAPLITE.

Another heated polemic concerned the ideological and aesthetic principles of Ukrainian national art and its accomplishments. In the course of the so-called Literary Discussion of 1925–1928, initiated by Mykola Khvyl'ovyi, the question of the content of Ukrainian proletarian literature became an object of focus. The fact that more than a hundred writers and critics participated in the polemics may indicate its relevance. The discussion centered on some of Khvyl'ovyi's statements in a series of pamphlets from 1925–1928. Khvyl'ovyi mainly argued against didactic literature as well as low-quality, mass-market literature, and for the professionalization of writers as an educated elite: "First, the new art is being created by workers and peasants. On condition, however, that they be intellectually developed, talented, people of genius."[23]

From the second half of the 1920s, the intellectual vector of discussions changed: the question of the content of national literature was articulated with a more sharply politicized tone. Khvyl'ovyi called for Ukrainian literature to "flee as quickly as possible from Russian literature and its styles."[24] He argued that

---

22 From 1924, *Aspanfut* was reorganized as the Association of Communist Culture (AsKK or Komunkul't). The main aim was to introduce art to the masses. The Futurists saw themselves as "a political body on the Third Front and as a State Planning Committee (GOSPLAN) through cultural production" (quoted in Mykhail' Semenko, "Tsentr, iacheiki komunkul'ta," *Gong komunkul'ta* 1 [1924]: 4–5). Also see Oleh S. Ilnytzkyj, *Ukrainian Futurism, 1914–1930* (Cambridge, MA: Harvard Ukrainian Research Institute, 1997), 111–133.

23 Mykola Khvyl'ovyi, "On Satan in a Barrel …," in *The Cultural Renaissance in Ukraine: Polemical Pamphlets, 1925–1926*, ed. Myroslav Shkandrij (Edmonton: University of Alberta, 1986), 54.

24 Mykola Khvyl'ovyi, *Mykola Khvyl'ovyi. Tvory v 5-kh tomakh* (Mykola Khvyl'ovyi: Works in five volumes), ed. Hryhoriy Kostiuk (Toronto: Smoloskyp, 1983), vol. 4, 315.

"Russian literature has weighed down upon us for centuries as master of the situation, as one that has conditioned our psyche to play a slavish imitator. ... Our orientation must be towards Western European art, its style, its techniques."[25] These views drew the attention of party authorities. In April 1926, Joseph Stalin sent a special letter to Lazar Kaganovich, who was the first secretary of the Communist Party of the Ukrainian SSR. In his letter Stalin stated that "a wide movement for Ukrainian culture among the Ukrainian public has begun and is growing in Ukraine."[26] He continued: "this movement, led by non-Communist intelligentsia, can manifest itself at the local level as an attempt to alienate Ukrainian culture and the Ukrainian society from all-Soviet culture, to reveal itself in the manner of struggle against Moscow as a whole, against the Russians, against Russian culture and its highest achievement—Leninism."[27] Khvyl'ovyi was accused of Ukrainian nationalism, and VAPLITE was dissolved in 1928.

Bazhan later recalled of his participation in VAPLITE that "I was not orthodox. I kept close to Oleksa Slisarenko, Iurii Smolych, Iurii Ianovs'kyi. ... We were rather cosmopolitan. But most of us did not take part in the literary clashes."[28] The word "orthodox" here is used in the sense of an aesthetic orthodoxy, under which the poet was meant to be faithful to a particular literary group. However, echoes of literary discussions are evident in Bazhan's poems from the period, such as "The Blood of the Captive Maidens," "The Road," "An Autumn Road," "Heart-to-Heart Conversation," and "Hoffmann's Night." For example, "The Blood of the Captive Maidens" (1926) is a poetic transformation of Khvyl'ovyi's conception of an "Asiatic Renaissance." Khvyl'ovyi prophesied a spiritual rebirth in then-backward Asian countries, which, he claimed, were fated to wrest cultural primacy from the West: "It has to appear, the Asiatic Renaissance, because the idea of Communism stalks like a specter not so much over Europe as over Asia; because Asia, realizing that only Communism will liberate it from economic slavery, will utilize art as a factor in the battle."[29] Interestingly, it is Soviet Ukraine that Khvyl'ovyi locates the birthplace of the Asian Renaissance. Correspondingly, Bazhan's poem depicts the rape and impregnation of the "fair Ukrainian captive woman" by the Mongol conqueror. The

---

25 Mykola Khvyl'ovyi, "Apologists of Scribbling," in ibid., 222.

26 Iurii Shevel'ov, introduction to *Mykola Khvyl'ovyi. Tvory v 5-kh tomakh*, by Mykola Khvyl'ovyi, vol. 4, 16–17.

27 Ibid.

28 Kostenko, "Razgovory s poetom," 274.

29 Mykola Khvyl'ovyi, "About Copernicus from Friborg ...," in Shkandrij, ed., *The Cultural Renaissance in Ukraine*, 67.

mixing of blood allegorically indicates not only the genesis of Ukrainian people but also Khvyl'ovyi's utopian conception: "But through the centuries the off-spring's managed to preserve/That ancient blood inside its knotty veins."

Bazhan's second poetry collection *The Sculpted Shadow* (1927), which included this poem, testifies to a new period of his development. Its uncertainty, hesitation, and a minor, elegiac mood stand in sharp contrast to the sublime and affirmative intonations of the early heroic ballads and songs. It is surprising that such a great change in the author's artistic views could happen within a year. The poet gives preference to sonnets and verses with a clear strophic structure. The sonnets "Fern," "Lovage," and "Love Potion" show a Modernist desire to reconstruct lost truths by turning to Ukrainian traditional culture, folklore, and Slavic legends. However, Bazhan employs conventional narrative as a pretext for Modernist concretization, disjunction, formal innovation, and a lack of obvious personal emotional involvement. For example, in the sonnet "Lovage," a man goes to war and leaves his pregnant lover. The child dies afterwards: "And in the hut, the newborn will emit a short-lived cry." In this way the poet hints that the newborn was killed shortly after the birth, as would befit a child resulting from an extra-marital affair. The situation is so archetypal that the woman has no name. Normally, the protagonists of such a traditional plot rouse sympathy and compassion, but the poet transfers the reader's attention to language itself. The easily reproducible classical scheme allows for a great deal of linguistic improvisation and lets Bazhan show the very process of creating the text. He plays with unexpected comparisons and the symbolic meanings of colors ("blue umbra," "pink traces"). The irony of the title is revealed only at the end. According to folk beliefs, lovage, a common herb, protects the home and represents love and concord: "Rue buds will bloom and lovage stems will sprout." This "objectification" of the story exposes Symbolism as an observer rather than a participant in life.

Symbolism and Romanticism are also drawn upon in the cycle composed of "Autumn Path" and "The Road." Working against its archetypal motif of the journey of life, "Autumn Path" surprises by projecting a feeling of alienation and despondency onto postrevolutionary reality. The dramatic bifurcation between dream and reality provokes a feeling of confusion and disappointment. This private experience is articulated publicly and is felt as a matter of public significance: "Whom can I offer the pain of my little mornings,/my miserable and useless exhaustion?" Non-Futurist feeling is buttressed by non-Futurist, classical prosody. The poem consists of a sequence of eight-line iambic stanzas tending towards octaves. However, at the end of it all the speaker tries to throw away doubt and disappointment in the name of the Communist ideal, because "there are no words of disbelief on the flag of the Commune!" The final couplet, serving as a conclusion, sharply—and perhaps not entirely convincingly—contrasts with the pessimistic intonation of the whole text: "The fog settles. Lights are shining/The lights are far away. A distant, happy road." The poem attempts to throw away the "ghosts of romanticism" in order to affirm socialist reality, but makes a respectable case for Romanticism—and for hesitation—in the process. Critics hated this change in Bazhan's internal trajectory. For example, the poet Yakiv Savchenko lambasted the book: "M. Bazhan, who has recently written poetry full of revolutionary energy, with a clear phrasing of social problems, now copies neo-classical poetry, mainly Ryl's'kyi, wandering in the shaky fogs of his own vague feelings."[30] Indeed, Bazhan did greatly value Maksym Ryl's'kyi.

The late 1920s saw Bazhan at a "breaking point."[31] Seemingly directing a spotlight at the inner self, he tried to harmonize universal values with the ideological demands of the new regime. Hence dualism, bifurcation, and uncertainty haunt the poems of that period. In his masterpieces—"Heart-to-Heart Conversation" (1928), "Edifices" (1929), "Hoffmann's Night" (1929), "Ghetto in Uman'" (1929), and the unfinished poem "Blind Bards" (1931)—Bazhan achieves a new complexity in structure, semantics, and rhythm. Notwithstanding his interest in classical forms, Bazhan works with avant-garde techniques and employs montage, contrast, grotesquery, metaphorical complexity, and "objectification" as literary devices. His poetry acknowledges the coexistence of different artistic paradigms. He creates both Futurist (see "Foxtrot" or "Elegy for Circus Attractions") and allegorical poems.

As for their subject matter, the poems of the late 1920s are ideologically and philosophically concerned with the establishment of the new socialist world. The triptych "Edifices," which gave the title to Bazhan's third poetry collection, published in 1929, describes three architectural structures characteristic of three epochs: the Middle Ages; the Cossack Hetmanate; and the Soviet era. The poem interprets national history lyrically with metaphors that symbolize the respective epoch, contrasting the past with modernity. The poem's montage bears traces of Constructivism and Expressionism in its imagery.

---

30 Iakiv Savchenko, "Zanepadnytstvo v ukraïns'kii poezii" (Decay in Ukrainian Poetry), *Zhyttia i revoliutsiia* 2 (1927): 165. See Andrii Bondar, "Poema M. Bazhana 'Sliptsi' iak tekst-vyklyk: sproba teoretychnoho modeliuvannia" (M. Bazhan's poem "Blind Bards" as a text-challenge: an attempt at theoretical modeling), *Suchasnist'* 12 (1998): 70.

31 See Bondar, "Poema M. Bazhana," 70.

The first part of the triptych, "Cathedral," presents a Gothic cathedral as the embodiment of human suffering and torment. However, along with a metaphorically rich description of the Gothic style, the poem also emphasizes the suffering of the people who built the cathedral for the "glory of the feudal lord":

> And they fell,
>> and clawed their way forward under the vault,
> Those bodies without arms, and arms without bodies,
> With mouths half torn apart.

In the second part of the poem, "Archway," Bazhan portrays the Zaborovs'kyi Gate, the Baroque main entrance to Saint Sophia Cathedral in Kyiv, by again contrasting civilizational achievement with the oppression that made it possible. The richness of architectural ornaments and the lush details common to Baroque style disguise the true function of the gates, because

> no one opened the generous arch
> To let through prisoners captured
>> in conquered states.

The poet likens the construction of the gate to sexual intercourse between a man and a woman, while the arch itself is compared with a female breast. This juxtaposition of the sacred and the profane is characteristic of the Baroque, a technique which the poet explicitly calls "raunchy" (*khtyvyi*).

The third part of the poem, "Building" ("Budynok"), is the most expressive because great architecture is here for the first time not predicated on slavery. Bazhan finds delight in the music and rhythm of the focused work of a free people: "The iron is beaten, the beautiful brass bent/In the rolling muscles of men's arms." The author depicts socialist reality as better and more progressive than previous historical epochs.

Together with "Edifices," the poem "Heart-to-Heart Conversation" (1928) constitutes another of the central text-allegories of the book. Its background is the social and political atmosphere of the late 1920s in Soviet Ukraine. The reader overhears echoes of the Literary Discussion of 1925–1928, and of the anticipation of new political changes (the Ukrainization policy and the NEP were abolished in 1928). Bazhan's deep psychological discomfort again manifests itself in dual structures and an attitude of inner ambivalence. The author takes the position of a fellow traveler, which was common for many intellectuals.[32] He makes great efforts to adhere to Communist ideals, but at the same time experiences doubts. The poem offers another example of how private sentiments are converted to public forces by publication. Back in 1928, Bazhan found the courage to speak of doubts common to his time.

"Heart-to-Heart Conversation" appears to be a phantasmagoria in the form of a dialogue between the protagonist and a mysterious figure in an "old blue uniform," which signifies participation in the governance of the Russian Empire. Curiously, this specter of prerevolutionary Russia, given in opposition to the "new" socialist reality, is in fact an alter ego of the main character. At the same time, pre-revolutionary Russia is portrayed as backward, dirty, drunken, and religious: "In foreign dumps, like a starving dog,/Your Rus' expired." In this context, the conjuring up of Dostoyevsky ("Dostoyevsky with his withered arms"), who symbolizes not only the old regime, but also uncertainty, becomes clear. Dostoevsky did not fit into the framework of official Marxist literary criticism, as he opposed the violent methods of the revolutionary struggle and preached Christianity. Consequently, the dead novelist was vilified at the time and his works were no longer printed. The dismissive term *dostoevshchina* was bandied about to denote the confusion, mental instability, and wallowing in suffering that is inherent to Dostoyevsky's characters. Bazhan himself strikes a critical, or perhaps self-critical, pose: "Obviously, the poem had an internal intention. It was a protest against *dostoevshchina*, which was common not only among the Russian but among the Ukrainian intelligentsia as well. The ghosts followed me up the stairs to the attic. They had to be fought against."[33] Yet the poem's perception of imperial Russia strangely concords with that of Mykola Khvyl'ovyi, who urged Ukrainian literature to "run away from Moscow" as "the center of an All-Union Philistinism."[34]

The central image-symbol of the poem is a heart. It appears "chewed-up," "screaming," or "crumbled," as if it were the organ itself that is suffering. On the other hand, it is a heart given to the revolutionary idea, where it serves as a "trophy" and "honorary banner." At the end of the poem, the lyric subject chooses to break the two-faced heart, and the "night guest" disappears like a ghost at the dawn of a new era. Thus, the protagonist makes up his mind and decides to be faithful to the revolutionary ideals.

---

32 The term *fellow traveler* (also *poputchik* [one who travels the same path]) was invented by Lev Trotsky to identify those indecisive intellectuals, who were sympathetic to the Communist regime, but were not the formal members of any organization.

33 Kostenko, "Razgovory s poetom," 275.

34 Ibid., 228.

The conflict between a talented artist and his surroundings reappears in "Hoffmann's Night," which is not part of *Edifices*, although it organically fits into the scope of the collection's aesthetic and philosophical problems. When it was published in 1929, the poem provoked controversy and even animosity with its ideological implications, the author's detached manner of narration, and lack of clear standpoint. Choosing the German romantic writer E. T. A. Hoffmann as his protagonist, Bazhan displays an interest in the irrational and unconscious—features that are typical of Hoffmann's Romanticism as well as early Modernism. Consequently, the text again reads like a phantasmagoria. Its events take place in a Berlin tavern, where Hoffmann and his friends, the members of the literary circle The Serapion Brethren, probably met in 1815. Located in a cellar, the tavern is depicted as a place of debauchery, chaos, and mysticism. Grotesque and naturalistic descriptions associate it with hell, while the main character is likened to Mephistopheles. These analogies let the author launch into his main theme: the company of drunkards does not empower the spirit of the true artist. Hence the negative depiction of the most important character, who ruins his talent: "It's here that for thousands of hours and thousands of nights/The spiteful Amadeus drinks and guffaws."

In another poem "Ghetto in Uman'," published separately in 1929, Bazhan raises the question of the historical perspectives of the Jewish people. In the USSR in the late 1920s, the the idea of national self-determination for the Jews was considered unacceptable, since the prevailing view was that they should assimilate with other nationalities. The author's criticism is, on the surface level, directed at the phenomenon of ghettos, such as had existed in Uman' since the city's foundation in the seventeenth century. But what is in fact being critiqued is ethnic or national separatism in general—in the case of the city's Jews, no matter whether separatism it is enforced by others or by themselves. Even though the city is not named in the body of the poem, the author signals it by referring to Maksym Zalizniak, a leader of the Koliivshchyna rebellion, who destroyed the Jewish community in the Uman' in 1768.[35]

Bazhan draws an ambivalent analogy between the hilltop city and Mount Zion. On the one hand, this makes the history of the Jewish community in Uman' stand for the tragic history of the entire Jewish people, with Maksym Zalizniak's pogrom associated with the autos-da-fé of the Inquisition and the

---

35 Koliivshchyna, a peasant and Cossack rebellion in Right-Bank Ukraine in 1768, was also characterized by violence towards Roman Catholics, Poles, and Jews, and culminated in the massacre of Uman'.

First Crusade, and perhaps even with the burning of the Temple by the Babylonians and the Romans:

Zion is burning—above it an unwavering and unmerciful flame
Has arisen for centuries,
Whether the fire of twisted Torquemada,
Or the sharp tongues of the Rhine's bonfires,
Or the sweeping, unkempt and treacherous storms
Of Zalizniak's desperate gang. ...

On the other hand, Bazhan *also* calls for the burning of "Zions," which he perceives as symbols of Hasidic fanaticism (the poet even names them "Hasidic Sodom" and "the burial pit of faith's orgasm") and relics of the past:

Not all your paths, Israel,
Lead to defamed Zion, to execution and despair!
Do not sleep, Israel!

Such an appeal could provide us with more than one interpretation. In the poet's historical context, the call "to burn Zions" suggests a vision of the future of the Jewish people as not separate but, on the contrary, fully integrated into the family of progressive nations that makes up socialist humanity. Bazhan therefore opposes religion, represented by the Hasidic fanaticism that led to the creation of self-imposed ghettos and made integration into general society impossible. "Religious stupor" and "ruthlessness of faith" are the remains of the "old world," but "Your future is born on other fields,/exhausted, defamed people!" Yet the poem can, in addition, be seen as taking aim at nationalist—rather than religious—separatism. At least by implication, one may overhear in it a critique of the Zionist movement at a time when it offered a vision for secular Jews that competed with the Soviet one—a vision in which Jews would have a separate state rather than become integrated into the socialist world. The logical development of this argument, however, also implies a critique of any nationalism, including a Ukrainian one.

The idea of the representation of a truly modern Ukrainian national identity, constructed on the historical phenomenon of *kobzarstvo*, plays a crucial role in one of Bazhan's early masterpieces, the poem "Blind Bards." The poem remained incomplete, and just two parts of it survive—"Odklynshchyna" (1930) and "At the Fair" (1931). Bazhan's quest for a new artistic form and way to engage with the ideological context of the late 1920s takes shape here, as is evident in the thematic intersection of "Blind Bards" with his other compositions from this period—"Heart-to-Heart Conversation," "Edifices," and "Hoffmann's Night."

The plot of the poem concerns the ritual of initiation (or, more specifically, the ritual of "release" known as *odklynshchyna* in *kobzar* terminology) of a young bard who intends to join a kobzar guild.[36] According to custom, the young bard has to learn the art of kobza from a master for three years and three months; and after an initiation ritual he is permitted to lead a vagrant life playing kobza and asking for alms. The heart of the second part of the poem is a dialogue between the young aspirant and an old, blind kobzar. In this conversation, they discuss the role of the singers and their art in society.

Bazhan rejects the Romantic view of kobzarstvo that had taken hold in Ukrainian literature by the time the poem was written. From the beginning of the nineteenth-century National Revival, the Romantics saw kobzars as the exclusive keepers of oral tradition, folk wisdom, and consequently national identity. Bazhan adheres to this perspective; the blind bard in the poem is undoubtedly the one who sees more than the sighted:

> O, blind guide
>> look sharply and lead
> The crowds that are blinder than you!

However, the author also takes up the other side of this phenomenon as well. Kobzars are not simply moral authorities: they are also human beings, who can be weak, make mistakes, and even abandon their talent. The heated discussion in the first part of the poem starts when the young kobzar addresses a kobzar guild. The author depicts the feasting blind bards in a naturalistic and satirical manner:

> What's preserved in your songs
>> and what's in your hearts?
> For these desperate lechers
>> just carry their stomachs like kobzas?

---

36 Kobzar guilds (Kobzars'kyi tsekh) were professional groups of kobzars and lirnyks, which existed from the seventeenth century on in the territory of contemporary Ukraine. The guilds ceased to exist during the Soviet period.

Bazhan called his work "a historical poem in four parts."[37] Yet the histori-cal background (the late eighteenth to early nineteenth century) appears only at the end of the second part and has little significant meaning. The author is interested in more than a specific period. The interaction between the young bard and the blind bards takes place at a fair, that is, at a *market*—a place where items are bought and sold by means of the exchange equivalence facilitated by money. But in "Blind Bards", Bazhan reflects upon the high social and symbolic capital of talent, rather than ordinary market trade where the value of goods is reckoned in terms of price.

By the time of "Blind Bards," early modernity's Romantic attitude to cul-tural activity, with its cult of genius, had been replaced by a more pragmatic, bourgeois approach, according to which the artist or writer was just another producer. Bazhan strongly opposes this perspective from a socialist standpoint, thus departing from a now outdated Romanticism. Yet in the Soviet period, the artist was expected to be an "engineer of the human soul."[38] That is why Bazhan regards the revival of the artist's special status important: the bard is a vital part of the new socialist society. The young bard asks:

> So give me an answer, passerby. …
> Will I,
> Ever in shame, haul my doubt around the world's market?

Of course, this poem is not only about the historical phenomenon of kobzarstvo and the challenges that kobzars faced at the time of writing. "Blind Bards" also reveals two major strategies used by Bazhan in his work. The first is artistic; the second is cultural-ideological. The intentionally sophisticated lan-guage of the poem, comprised of professional jargon and archaic dialects, is not used by the author in order to imitate forgotten, even nonexistent languages. Its aim is to make understanding the poem *difficult*, or, after Viktor Shklovsky,[39]

---

37   Nataliia Kostenko, "Komentari, prymitky do rozdilu 'Poemy,'" [Comments, notes to the chapter "Poems"] in *Mykola Bazan. Vybrani tvory v dvoch tomach* [Mykola Bazhan: select-ed works in two volumes], vol. 1, ed. Dmytro Pavlychko (Kyiv: Ukrains'ka entsyklopediia, 2003), 579.

38   This expression was applied to writers and other cultural workers by Joseph Stalin in 1932. See Kornely Zelinsky, "Odna vstrecha u M. Gorkogo (Zapis iz dnevnika). Publikatsya A. Zelinskogo" (One meeting with M. Gorky (Note from the diary). Published by A. Zelinsky), *Voprosy literatury* 5 (1991): 144–170.

39   Viktor Shklovsky, *Theory of Prose*, trans. and ed. Benjamin Sher (Illinois: Dalkey Archive Press, 1990), 6.

to *defamiliarize* its subject. In other words, Bazhan takes a typically modernist position: one must speak about modernity using perplexing language in order to prompt the reader to rethink modernity and its reality. This puts him fully in step with the great European and American modernist poets of the 1920s and 1930s, such as Yeats, Eliot, and Pound.

Bazhan's second strategy appeals to the cultural and ideological context. Kobzarstvo was known as one of the cornerstones of the Ukrainian national cultural identity. While building a new national culture within the ideological framework of Soviet Ukraine, Bazhan attempts to reassert the unconditional cultural value of Kobzarstvo with the help of defamiliarization. The polemic between the young and old bards manifests the tension, even struggle, between the two ways of representing Ukrainian national culture—the "old" and the "new." This is probably why Bazhan did not complete the poem. The very possibility of developing a new voice for Ukraine's national culture was destroyed by the imposition of the Stalinist regime's cultural policy in the early 1930s.[40]

Ironically or not, Bazhan's early poetry ends with an ode to Joseph Stalin "A Man Stands in the Star-Bearing Kremlin," published in 1932. Bazhan adopts Socialist Realism, necessary at the time for those who wished to continue to live and publish. This aesthetic turn took place during a period of increasingly harsh ideological scrutiny of artists and their work. In 1931 the Russian literary critic Aleksei Selivanovskii published a crushing article titled "Where M. Bazhan is Heading," in which he accused the poet of being a "fellow traveler":

> We can add Bazhan to the group of authors, whose creativity passed by the socialist revolution in silence, even though he should have become a fully competent master of the subject. Bazhan, especially in his recent poetry, seems to be beyond politics. ... Yet we would like to get a better sense of Bazhan's *poputnytstvo*, its roots, state, and possible prognosis as to its development.[41]

This attack was dictated by the general policy of the party: from the end of the 1920s onwards, both the national project and all the theories that competed with Marxism gradually ground to a halt. As a result, the diverse and

---

40 For a more detailed analysis of the poem, refer to George G. Grabowicz's essay "A Spectral Text" in this volume.

41 Oleksii Selivanovs'kyi [Aleksei Selivanovskii], "Kudy priamuie M. Bazhan" (Where M. Bazhan is heading), *Krytyka* 4 (1931): 41, 45.

multilayered Soviet culture of the 1920s was replaced by a more monolithic culture. In 1934, the Union of Soviet Writers was created and Socialist Realism was proclaimed as the only form of literature permitted in the USSR. This led to the "breaking" of those artists who had to choose between reforming in order to "play" by established rules or else becoming the victims of the regime. Already in the early 1930s, Mykola Bazhan's work had started to change drastically. In order play the role of a Socialist Realist writer, the main requirement was glorifying socialist "reality" in a style that was comprehensible to the masses, and therefore abandoning one's avant-garde past.

The 1930a were some of the most tragic in the history of Ukraine: Stalin's purges of Ukrainian intelligentsia, which began in 1930 and reached their apogee in 1937,[42] were followed by the mass starvation that the dictator forced on the republic—the Holodomor—in 1932–1933. In these years of violence, social upheaval, and near-complete totalitarian rule, it was impossible to oppose the Communist Party and defend the interests of a national culture. This period of Ukrainian culture is also known as the "Executed Renaissance"—a term that was invented by literary critic Iurii Lavrinenko to describe the generation of Soviet Ukrainian writers and artists of 1920s who were wiped out by Stalin's regime.

Even though Mykola Bazhan became a captive of his age, we cannot underestimate his poetic genius, which was fully manifested in his ability to rejuvenate the Ukrainian literary tradition and his attempt to establish a new model for the further development of the national literature. Certainly, the avant-garde—with its experimentalism, playfulness, and audacity—provided him with the poetic freedom to produce his masterpieces of the late 1920s: his unique writing flourished in the context of Ukrainian Futurism (and its Baroque roots) while, however, remaining outside the framework of any movement. A construction of poetic reality with a focus on objects became the common feature of Bazhan's poetry. Despite its avant-garde techniques, metaphorical complexity, and creative debt to a Ukrainian literature and folklore largely unknown outside the country, the philosophical scope and universality of his lyrics place him among the great world writers.

---

42 The first fabricated trial of the so-called Union for the Liberation of Ukraine (Spilka Vyzvolennia Ukraïny) took place in 1930 in Kharkiv. Forty-five Ukrainian intellectuals were convicted of anti-state activities. See Volodymyr Prystaiko and Yuriy Shapoval, *Sprava "Spilky Vyzvolennia Ukraïny." Nevidomi dokumenty i fakty* (Kyiv: Intel, 1995).

BIBLIOGRAPHY

Bazhan, Mykola. "Odiahnit' okuliary." *Bumerang. Zhurnal pamfletiv* 1 (1927): 25.

———. "Liudyna stoït' v zorenosnim Kremli" (A man stands in the star-bearing Kremlin). In Mykola Bazhan, *Poezii.* Saratov: Ukrvydav CK KP(b)U, 1943.

———. "Rura-marsh." *Bil'shovyk*, May 17, 1923.

Bondar, Andrii. "Poema M. Bazhana 'Sliptsi' jak tekst-vyklyk: sproba teoretychnoho modeliuvannia." *Suchasnist'* 12 (1998): 70.

Brogi Bercoff, Giovanna. "Plurilinguism and Identity: Rethinking Ukrainian Literature of the Seventeenth Century." In *Ukraine and Europe: Cultural Encounters and Negotiations,* edited by Marko Pavlyshyn, Giovanna Brogi Bercoff, and Serhii Plokhy, 45–72. Toronto: University of Toronto Press, 2017.

S. Dzhymbinova, ed. *Literaturnye manifesty ot simvolizma do nashych dnei.* Moscow: XXI vek— Soglasie, 2000.

Dović, Marijan. "Anton Podbevšek, Futurism, and Slovenian Interwar Avant-Garde Literature." *International Yearbook of Futurism Studies* 1 (2011): 262–276.

Eliot, T. S. *The Sacred Wood.* London: Methuen, 1921.

———. *Selected Essays.* London: Faber and Faber, 1951.

Ilnytzkyj, S. Oleh. *Ukrainian Futurism, 1914–1930.* Cambridge, MA: Harvard Ukrainian Research Institute, 1997.

Janecek, Gerald. *Zaum: The Transrational Poetry of Russian Futurism.* San Diego: San Diego State University Press, 1996.

Khvyl'ovyi, Mykola. "Apologists of Scribbling." In *The Cultural Renaissance in Ukraine: Polemical Pamphlets, 1925–1926,* edited by Myroslav Shkandrij, 169–225. Edmonton: University of Alberta, 1986.

———. "On Satan in a Barrel …" In Shkandrij, ed., *The Cultural Renaissance in Ukraine,* 43–54.

Kolesnikoff, Nina. "Polish Futurism: Its Origin and the Aesthetic Program." *Canadian Slavonic Papers* 18, no. 3 (1976): 301–311.

Kostenko, Nataliia. "Razgovory s poetom." In *Vospominaniia o Mykole Bazhane.* Compiled and edited by Nina Bazhan and Evgeniia Deich. Moscow: Sovetskii pisatel', 1989.

———. "Komentari, prymytky do rozdilu 'Poemy,'" [Comments, notes to the chapter "Poems"]. In *Mykola Bazan. Vybrani tvory v dvoch tomach* [Mykola Bazhan: selected works in two volumes], vol. 1, edited by Dmytro Pavlychko (Kyiv: Ukrains'ka entsyklopediia, 2003), 579.

Omeljan Pritsak Memorial Library. Archival Collection, National University of Kyiv-Mohyla Academy. Collection 10, file 983, 101–118.

Pound, Ezra. "A Retrospect." In *Literary Essays of Ezra Pound,* edited and introduced by T. S. Eliot, 3–14. London: Faber and Faber, 1954.

Prystaiko, Volodymyr, and Yuriy Shapoval. *Sprava "Spilky Vyzvolennia Ukraïny." Nevidomi dokumenty i fakty.* Kyiv: Intel, 1995.

Savchenko, Iakiv. "Zanepadnytstvo v ukraïns'kii poezii." *Zhyttia i revoliutsiia* 2 (1927): 165.

Semenko, Mykhail'. "Tsentr, iacheiki komunkul'ta." *Gong komunkul'ta* 1 (1924): 4–5.

Shakhivets', Ihor. "Mykola Bazhan '17-i Patrul'.'" *Kul'tura i pobut* 14 (1926).

Shevel'ov, Iurii. Introduction to *Mykola Khvyl'ovyi. Tvory v 5-kh tomakh,* vol. 4, edited by Hryhorii Kostiuk, 7–67. Toronto: Smoloskyp, 1983.

Shklovsky, Viktor. *Gamburgskii schet. Stat'i – vospominaniia – esse (1914–1933)*. Edited by Aleksandr Galushkin, 443–446. Moscow: Sovetskii pisatel', 1990.

———. *Theory of Prose*. Edited and translated by Benjamin Sher. Illinois: Dalkey Archive Press, 1991.

Tonini, Paolo. *I manifesti del futurismo italiano 1909–1945*. Gussago: Edizioni dell'Arengario, 2011.

Williams, William Carlos. *Paterson*. Edited by Christopher McGowan. New York: New Directions Publishing, 1995.

Zelinsky, Kornely. "Odna vstrecha u M. Gorkogo (Zapis iz dnevnika). Publikatsya A. Zelinskogo" (One meeting with M. Gorky (Note from the diary). Published by A. Zelinsky), *Voprosy literatury* 5 (1991): 144–170.

Collections

Сімнадцятий патруль/
The Seventeenth Patrol
(1926)

Translator's Essay

Jumping the Corral Fence

SVETLANA LAVOCHKINA

A translator's first encounter with a Ukrainian Futurist poem is like the first eye contact between a gaucho and a wild horse. A stallion from Mykola Bazhan's artistic prairies is always hot-blooded, and the only way for the whisperer to tame it is to learn its ways, its lithe anatomy and its wayward rhythms, to fathom its instincts and imitate its movements. Only then would the horse deign to be harnessed in the stiff halter of English grammar and braced with the stirrups of the rigid English syntax. How much pressure will the poem bear before jumping the fence and leaving the bruised translator on the ground in the white dust of her notebook corral?

I've had the simultaneous privilege, and the ordeal, of more or less "taming" two poems for a race through the English-speaking world—"Trooper's Song" and "Imobe of Galam" from *The Seventeenth Patrol* collection. The two poems are very different, although both focus on war themes, unfurling Bazhan's virtuosity of the poet as chameleon.

"Trooper's Song" is a mini-epic within a marching chant, a Greek amphora painting come alive. Like the *Iliad*'s heroes, the warriors are on horseback but, as befits the Red Army Guards in the 1917–1921 Civil War, wear a Bolshevik combat uniform, "cowhide coats" and *papakhas*, high karakul sheep hats "over their brows." They are armed with rifles and revolvers. Like Homer, the narrator relishes in the righteousness of the proletarian army's cause:

> You are now avengers,
> Avengers for your next of kin,
> For your lacerated brothers,
> For your sisters raped.

"Trooper's Song" is etched in sharp, concise commands and put into the fire to harden into the harsh laws of the war:

> Don't ask for the way,
> Go over the corpses.
> Spur your heart
> And tighten your belt!

Any signs of weakness are nipped in the bud, be it fatigue or longing for "kids and a woman": "Troopers don't sleep on a vigil"; "Now you must learn different love though:/For seven copper slugs in your revolver!" The commander's spell echoes Lady Macbeth steeling herself for murder: "Unsex me here,/And fill me from the crown to the toe topful/Of direst cruelty!"[1]

Whatever the historical period, warfare is a binary system: yes—no, love—hate, death—survival, victory—defeat. "Trooper's Song" is firmly embedded in the marriage of black and red. The foreground figures and the background settings swap colors as the day passes: bloodred soldier shapes ("their cowhide coats reek of blood") against the black background ("the disturbed peace of black woods"); black soldier shapes—red background ("bitter and rusty smoke of the field").

The language of the poem is so basic, the words so short, that the translator easily falls in step with a ready-made Anglo-Saxon vocabulary. The English equivalents are found effortlessly, and even alliterative elements can be rendered almost verbatim:

> The troopers set off, their horses were neighing
> (Soft steady clanking of stirrup steel),
> The smoke in the field was bitter and rusty,
> The horses' lips drooled in spear grass strands.

Yet, the simplicity of the vocabulary is contrasted with pace of the meter, jinking from two to five feet, often changing in a flurry within one stanza—iambus pace, amphibrach or dactyl canter, trochee trot, anapest gallop, racing towards the finish line, where the polarities finally merge in the ecstasy of double self-annihilation: "we could die *twice*" for "black coal, for dark bread; we could die once again for those toil-blackened hands."

---

1   *Macbeth*, 1.5.38–43.

If in "Trooper's Song" the narrator orders readers about as if they were soldiers under his command, in "Imobe of Galam" they are not participants in a heroic epic but, rather, spellbound contemplators of a battle scene painted by a Pan-Futurist crossbreed of Miró, Dalí, and Gauguin. We are torn out of our temperate comfort zone of steppes, fields, and forests and teleported to the West Africa of the late nineteenth century, into the eerie night of a Senegalese slave uprising against the French colonialists:

> When in the papyrus sedge
> > birds scream aghast
> And the sky is congealed
> > in a clot of black musk,
> A knight
> > of the old Maghreb faith
> > prowls in the wildwood.

Wind, desert, night are animate beings, shocking and enthralling in their monstrosity: "Like a hungry hyena,/The wind sucks the Sahara sand"; "Night fell on the Sahara Desert,/Hauled its heavy womb through the sand."

"Imobe of Galam" teems with vocabulary beyond the daily usage in Europe: *baobab, tam-tam, bayou, spahi, mitrailleuse, gris-gris, marabou*, to name just a few words: Bazhan relishes in cross-hatching an exotic palette of words into bizarre arabesques. In Ukrainian, the poem reads like a foreign-language text. The Futurist extravagance of the meter, unlike in "Trooper's Song," does not convey velocity gracefully framed in strict rhyme. This poem is an intricately cut gem—immovable like the consciousness of a people still too "backward" to awake for the "real (Russian!) revolution" of the "Trooper's Song." Although the proletarian poet empathizes with the Senegalese, the way he introduces them betrays his inadvertent view of them as his inferiors: the local women are reduced to the "black vapors" or "wineskins" of their breasts; the insurgent hero is seen as a gladiator in an arena—the spectacle-thirsty audience both admires his audacity and savors his death.

Written almost a hundred years ago, "Imobe of Galam" would be declined by contemporary publishers for racism and chauvinism, while "Trooper's Song" would be suspect for its glorification of violence. It is a razor-thin line for the translator to balance between loyalty to the original, in which case the poems would jump the corral fence of modern protocol, and allow a modern Western reader to approach these poems without pangs of conscience. Yet, the gaucho has stayed in the saddle so far and hopes for a lucky ride along the Anglophone tracks.

ПІСНЯ БІЙЦЯ

Бійці виїжджали, і коні іржали
(Стримано в стременах сталь дзвенить),
А дим терпкий у полі, а в полі дим іржавий,
І слина з кінських губ—немов ковильна мить.

Дібровою загін бійців поїхав,
Підковами клепали коні путь,
І лязк шабель, і брязкіт піхов
У тиші чорній чуть.

Насували на лоба папахи,
Ковтали піль міцний, солодкий дух,
І порохом робучі руки пахнуть,
І кров'ю засмердівсь ялозений кожух.

Ось один похилився. Я знаю: ти мариш
Про дітей і про жінку якусь.
Полюби ж, полюби, товаришу
В барабані сім мідних куль!

Бійцям не можна спать на варті,
Плекать утому на лиці.
Чого ж то будуть варті
Такі бійці?

Ви—месники тепер за них,
Ви месники єсте
За братів розтерзаних,
Згвалтованих сестер.

Бережіть, бережіть і гордіться
Найменням суворим своїм,
Найменням червоногвардійця
І прапором бойовим!

TROOPER'S SONG

The troopers set off, their horses were neighing
(Soft steady clanking of stirrup steel),
The smoke in the field was bitter and rusty,
The horses' lips drooled in spear grass strands.

The squadron rode through a forest,
The path punched with horses' hooves.
The clangor of sabers, the clatter of sheaths,
Disturbed the black peace of the woods.

They pulled their *papakhas* over their brows,
They swallowed thick dust, inhaled strong sweet fumes.
The workers' hands smell of gunpowder,
Their cowhide coats reek of blood.

One trooper stooped. You're dreaming, I know:
Your kids and a woman.
Now you must learn different love though:
For seven copper slugs in your revolver!

Troopers don't sleep on a vigil,
Your face is no place for fatigue.
Or else, what kind of a trooper
Would you be?

You are now avengers,
Avengers for your next of kin,
For your lacerated brothers,
For your sisters raped.

Hold dear, be proud of your title,
The title of the Red Army Guard—
A stern, austere vocation,
And cherish your battle flag!

Коли ворожий почуєш постріл,
Рушницю,—й на коня!
Подивися на обрій просто,
Поганяй!

Крізь гони, крізь гони
Боєць помчить.
Лічи патрони,
Ран не лічи!

Не питай дороги,
Хоч трупом ляж!
Серце—в остроги,
Розкрий патронташ.

Хай вітер в вічі,
Умри—не стій!
На кожній стрічі
Стрічаєм бій.

Команд не ждіте!
Хто став—пристрель!
Розкраюь вітер
Сотні шабель.

І ми двічі умерти змогли б
За чорний вугіль, за чорний хліб;
За чорні натруджені руки
Ми двічі умерти змогли б.

1925

When you hear the enemy shooting,
Grab your rifle, mount your horse!
Just have a look at the skyline—
Urge on!

Through furrows, through furrows
The trooper is racing.
Count your bullets,
Don't count your wounds.

Don't ask for the way,
Extinguish your selfhood.
Spur your heart
And tighten your belt!

Eyes to the wind,
On every encounter
Look war in the face!
Death's better than sloth!

Don't wait for commands.
We shoot those who linger!
The wind is slashed up
By hundreds of swords.

We could die twice
For black coal, for dark bread;
We could die once again
For those toil-blackened hands.

Translated by Svetlana Lavochkina

ІМОБЕ З ГАЛАМУ

Коли в папірусах
            злякано зойкнуть птиці
І чорним мускусом згусне небо,
В гущавині лісу
            ховається лицар
Старовинної віри Магреба.

В небо зорі вп'ялися, мов краби,
В землю намулом вгрузла тьма.
А під листям рудих баобабів
Розцвітає очей емаль.

Імобе з країни Галаму.
І з ним тисячі чорних рабів
В ніч повстання і зойків тамтама
Іржавий набили карабін.

То не на плесі кричить марабу
Не жінки б'ють в бурдюк грудей,
То тамтам дає вість рабу,
Понуро зітхає й гуде.

В ніч повстання, жалоби і згаги
В очереті ворушиться негр,
І не знають білошкірі спагі,
Чому кров'ю пустеля тхне.

В ніч повстання, жаги і жалоби
Місяць верхів'ям бананів гравсь,
І підповз чорний раб Імобе
Під білявий французький блокгауз.

Не здригнулась земля Галаму,
Очеретом не хитнувся Сенегал,
Тільки вітер сухими губами
Жовтавий пісок лигав.

IMOBE OF GALAM

When in the papyrus sedge
                              birds scream aghast
And the sky is congealed
                              in a clot of black musk,
A knight
          of the old Maghreb faith
                              prowls in the wildwood.

The stars claw the sky crab-like,
The silt of dusk squelches the earth,
And in the ruddy baobab shade,
Glazed buds of eyes burst into blossom.

Imobe from the Land of Galam
And with him, thousands of slaves
On the riotous night, to the bawls of tam-tam,
Loaded a rusty carbine.

It's not marabou calling in bayou,
Nor women slapping their wineskins of breasts,
It's the tam-tam sending news to the slave,
Dreary sighs become blasts.

Anguished night of upheaval and yearning,
In the reeds, a black shape's astir.
The white-skinned *spahi* can't fathom
Why the desert is reeking with blood.

Thirsty night of woe and upheaval,
Moon-ruffled banana tree tops,—
And a Senegal slave named Imobe
Skulked under the whitish French fort.

The Land of Galam didn't shudder,
Senegal calm in the reeds,
Only the yellowish sand dunes
Munched by the dry-lipped wind.

Тільки вітер пісок Сахари,
Мов голодна гієна, ссе;
Вії солдатів набрякли від марев,
І останній випито абсент.

Рвуться уста солдатів піснею,
Німіє в кутку холодний маузер.
Хто порою пізньою
Вийде за ворота блокгауза?

А в Сахарі вітер мне гам,
В Сахарі вітер сичить.
Роз'ятрено чорними ночами
Хрумтливі дюни уночі.

Шепче
      присмерк бананових дерев,
Все ближче
      плеще
         гуща
            трав ...
А коли в небо вдарив рев,
Вартовий прокинувся зуав.

Гей, вітре, на чотири боки дми,
Зойком дюни злякай Сенегала!
В спагі серце спухло між грудьми.
Спагі серце ввірвалось і впало.

Брязкотливий язик мітральєзи
Черево тьми перебоєм розсік.
Кривавих зір розцвітає безліч
Під тамарисками, на ранішній росі.

Засіяним кров'ю лобом
Негр в намул зелений вріс.
О, на бронзових грудях Імобе
Не дзвенять старовинні грі-грі.

Like a hungry hyena,
The wind sucks the Sahara sand,
Swollen and dazed soldiers' eyelids,
They'd swilled their last absinthe.

The cold Mauser numb in the corner,
Soldiers' lips are frazzled with songs,
Whoever would leave the blockhouse
At these short hours of the morn?

And in the Sahara Desert, the wind is mauling the din.
Over the Sahara Desert, the searing hiss of the wind.
Crackly dunes chafed to blisters
By the night of the rebels' feet.

The dusky
            banana tree whisper.
Ever closer,
            the grass thicket
                        swash …

The sky was hit by the howl,
And the warden *zouave* woke up.

Hey you wind, blow your rose full blast,
Scare the Senegal dunes with your screams!
In the *spahi* chest, *spahi* heart bloated and throbbed,
The *spahi* heart leapt out and dropped.

The rattling *mitrailleuse* tongue
Slashes the womb of the night,
Scarlet myriads of stars are in blossom
In tamarisk dawn, on the dew.

His forehead peppered with blood,
Imobe sank in green silt.
Oh on his bronze-colored chest,
No amulet tinkling gris gris!

І на Сахару упала ніч,
Зашаруділа по пісках важким черевом.
Здригнувся Імобе й захлинувся в багні,
Де спіткнулося скорчене дерево.

Стогоном небо розкраяв,
З стегон ночі підповз вий гієн.
Це для тебе, Галаме, чорний краю,
Імобе в пісках гниє!

Весною знов пахне бамбули
І грудей жіночих чорний чад,
І серце Галама про все забуло
І все віддало своїм ночам.

В ніч бамбули, кохання й жадоби,
Млосний, згадає хто,
Як мухи повзли в Імобів
Роздертий, кривавий рот?

Не один Імобе
          серце в дюни виклав
І в іклах папірусів згнив,
Щоб виклик
        збудив незвиклий
Жорстке шепотіння пісків.

Бути негру
        самому
              самумом,

Бути негру не рабом, а бійцем,
І повстання багряним шумом
Вдарити блокгаузу в лице.

1924

Night fell on the Sahara Desert,
Hauled its heavy womb through the sand,
Imobe choked in the mire,
Where the crooked tree fell.

Slashing the sky with its groaning,
Hyena howl crept from the night's thighs,
For you, the dark Land of Galam,
Imobe decayed in the mire!

Spring smells of baobab blossoms,
Black vapors of women's thighs,
The heart of Galam is forgetful,
Abandoned in dark night's trance.

Lusty night of baobab blossoms,
Indolent, will they recall
The flies swarming in Imobe's mouth,
Bloodstained and torn?

It wasn't only Imobe
        who left his heart
                in the dunes,

Decayed in the fangs of papyrus,
for a weird alarm
      to wake up
           the harsh hiss of the sand.

Let the Senegalese
           become simooms,
Let Imobes be warriors, not slaves.
Let the purple roar of upheaval
Punch the blockhouse in the face.

Translated by Svetlana Lavochkina

Різьблена тінь/
The Sculpted Shadow (1927)

Translator's Essay

Mykola Bazhan's
The Sculpted Shadow:
Echoes of Acmeism

AMELIA M. GLASER

Mykola Bazhan published his book *Riz'blena tin'* (*The Sculpted Shadow*) in 1927.[1] This was his second book of poems, and marked a shift in form for the twenty-three-year-old poet. Up to that point, Bazhan had been associated with the Ukrainian avant-garde, publishing Futurist-influenced poems in his late teens. Oleh Ilnytzkyj has observed that in this early period, Bazhan's poetry drew upon a broad variety of forms: he "wrote trans-sense poetry and made extensive use of free verse."[2] At the same time, he was experimenting with ballads, sonnets, and even agit-prop.[3] In *The Sculpted Shadow*, his work conjures sublime, Romantic, images of the Ukrainian landscape. Bazhan's resistance to categorization, like his resistance to perfect metrical consistency, is one of the strengths of his poetry. George Luckyj, who has favorably compared Bazhan to the more popular Sosiura, struggles to name Bazhan's style: "Futurism? Expressionism? Baroque? Romanticism à la Hoffmann?"[4] Bazhan's 1920s work, indeed, does not look quite like the poetry of his contemporary Ukrainians. It is all the harder to characterize his style given that Bazhan soon shifted toward Soviet-aligned poetry, dedicating an ode to Stalin in 1932.[5] What we find in the poems of *Riz'blena tin'*

---

1   Mykola Bazhan, *Riz'blena tin'* (Kharkiv: Knihospil'ki, 1927).
2   Oleh S. Ilnytzkyj, "Mykola Bazhan: Six Unknown Poems," *Journal of Ukrainian Graduate Studies* 7 (1979): 20–33, 20–21.
3   Ibid.
4   George Luckyj, *Ukrainian Literature in the Twentieth Century: A Reader's Guide* (Toronto: University of Toronto Press, 1992), 39.
5   See Galyna Babak, "Teksty Mykoly Bazhana 1920–1930-kh rr.: mizh avangardom ta sotsrealizmom" (MA thesis, Charles University, Prague, 2014); George Luckyj, "Bazhan, Mykola,"

is a meditation, grounded in physical reality, on the individual's relationship to the passage of time.

Both the form and imagery of Bazhan's poems of the late 1920s suggest a relationship between time and matter, reminiscent of Henri Bergson's conception of consciousness as dependent on memory.[6] The landscape, as well as the dirt, stone, and brick of the ground jog the persona's memory about the recent past. Formally, "Autumn Path" is an irregular sonnet. The long poem consists almost entirely of eight-line stanzas in iambic verse, alternating between pentameter and hexameter. The A-B-A-B-A-B rhyme scheme concludes with a rhyming couplet. However, Bazhan resists a perfectly consistent form, inserting, for example, one anomalous seven-line stanza midway through the poem that drastically varies the number of iambic feet; and in the second half of the poem, he shortens many of his lines to iambic tetrameter. The meter mirrors the disillusionment Bazhan describes in the poem itself, with its barren landscape and the disembodied memories of the still-recent civil war. The assertion, in the last stanza, that "There are no faithless, desperate words/ on your flag, on the flag of the Commune!" hints at doubt about the revolution. Indeed, some critics at the time viewed *Riz'blena tin'* as dangerously nationalist and insufficiently pro-Soviet.[7] "Autumn Path" was not republished after 1927.

The variance in Bazhan's rhyme scheme, which includes numerous slant rhymes and internal rhymes, further softens the meter, highlighting rather the images of a barren landscape. Bazhan's rhymes often illuminate contractions. In the closing couplet of the first stanza of "Autumn Path" we find: "I tuga skriz', i bachu tugu tu-zh/V porozhnikh iamakh zsherkhnulykh kaliuzh" ("And everywhere sorrow, there, too, the same sorrow/In the wrung-out puddles' empty pits."). Here, the rhyme between *tu-zh* ("the same") and *kaliuzh* ("puddle") emphasizes the return to the barren path described in the opening stanza. However, equally important to Bazhan's line is his repetition of sound. The repetition of *tuga* ("sorrow") is mirrored in the shortened form of the same word, *tu-zh* ("that sorrow"). In the eight four-line stanzas of another

---

in *Columbia Dictionary of Modern European Literature*, ed. Jean Albert Bede and William Benbow Edgerton (New York: Columbia University Press, 1980), 56.

6 See Henri Bergson, *The Creative Mind: An Introduction to Metaphysics*, trans. Mabelle L. Andison (New York: Dover, 2007).

7 See O. Levada, "Notatky pro tvorchist' Mykoly Bazhana," *Radians'ka literatura* 7 (1933): 206, cited in Luckyj, *Literary Politics in the Soviet Ukraine, 1917–1934*, 123.

poem, "Indistinct Sound," Bazhan adheres to a stricter rhythmic and rhyming scheme than we find in "Autumn Path." Here, the lines follow an A-B-A-B rhyme scheme in iambic pentameter, and yet Bazhan's occasional disruptions of the line stand out all the more because of the expected meter, adding to the rising discomfort in a poem where a "whistling whisper" at night combines the regular change of seasons with the violence of men overpowering women in a whorehouse.

To accurately place Bazhan within East European Modernism, it is worth looking not only to his fellow Ukrainian-language poets, but to contemporary poets and thinkers across languages. His poetics in this decade might be fruitfully compared to that of Nikolai Gumilev and his fellow Russian Acmeists. The Ukrainian Futurists and Russian Acmeists alike disdained the ethereal spirituality of the Symbolists. Bazhan, in particular, throughout *Riz'blena tin'* anchors his poetics of memory in concrete, physical reality. The natural world, for Bazhan, is intimately tied to the human world, and like the road that is crushed by warhorses in "Horseshoe," in "Indistinct Sound" the life of the poetic persona is "thoroughly crushed" ("moe zhyttia protoptano use") in the city, "here, underfoot, on this cold brick" ("tut, na tsii kholodnii tsehli"). Like the Acmeists, who emphasize concrete "building" and human agency in time, Bazhan sought, with his "Sculpted Shadow," to give substance to memory. He would continue in this vein in his subsequent book *Budivli* (Edifices, 1929). His repeated emphasis, in "Autumn Path," on the "trace" of war visible on the faces of veterans is not only a comment on the generation that has been through the revolution, but also on the physical markings of time:

> Бо не зітерти вічний слід
> Жорстоких і натхненних літ.
> (For you can't erase the eternal trace
> of those cruel and inspired years.)

In this concern for the human trace in history, we hear an echo of Osip Mandelstam's assertion in his 1909 "Given a Body" (Dano mne telo), asserts that the individual's "Beloved pattern can't be erased" ("Uzora milogo ne zacherknut'").

The subsequent poem in *The Sculpted Shadow*, "Horseshoes," also suggests commonalities with Mandelstam, who had published "Nashedshii podkovu" (The Horseshoe finder) in 1923. Mandelstam compares life to the physical matter that preserves the traces of time:

Конь лежит в пыли и храпит в мыле,

Но крутой поворот его шеи

Еще сохраняет воспоминание о беге с разбросанными ногами,—

(The stallion lies in the dust and snorts in its lather,

But the sharp articulation of its neck

Still conserves the memory of its gallop, its legs ascatter—)[8]

The poet, for Mandelstam, is, to cite Gregory Freidin, "the 'lucky charm' fragment of a once magnificent racing steed."[9] As Jacques Ranciere has formulated, Mandelstam's horseshoe is "the last metonym of Pindaric ode to the glory of Olympic victories … but destined hereafter to be a door ornament or archeological remnant."[10] The poet and horseshoe finder "Blows the dust from it/And polishes it with wool, until it shines" ("Sduvaet s nee pyl'/I rastiraet ee sherst'iu, poka ona ne zablestit).[11] Bazhan's "Horseshoes," like his "Autumn Path," relates history to substance. Stones, ground to dust by hooves, are compared to the trampled human heart and the dust of human thought. Bazhan's hooves, like Mandelstam's, mark the gradual dissolution of the poetic "I." The poem opens with warhorses—signs of both classical antiquity and the civil war—and quickly dissolves into "The melting, drizzling workday hour."

The melting, drizzling workday hour—

I wanted to love it, but couldn't,

And golden memories blow the dust of thoughts.

What remains is a painful memory of past greatness.

The Mandelstamian echoes in Bazhan's poems of the mid-1920s are not surprising. Mandelstam, who had spent time in Kyiv in 1918–1919, had a pronounced influence on his contemporary Ukrainian poets.[12] Bazhan's consistent

---

8   Osip Mandelstam, "He Who Found a Horseshoe," trans Alex Cigale, *New England Review* 34, nos. 3–4 (2014): 131–133. I have slightly revised the translation.

9   Gregory Freidin, *A Coat of Many Colors: Osip Mandelstam and His Mythologies of Self-presentation* (Berkeley: University of California Press, 1987), 8.

10 Jacques Rancière, *The Flesh of Words: The Politics of Writing* (Stanford: Stanford University Press, 2004), 40.

11 Mandelstam, "He Who Found a Horseshoe," 131–133.

12 Miron Petrovs'kyi discusses Mandelstam's meeting with, and influence on Ukrainian poets, including Tychyna and Ryl's'kyi in *Gorodu i miru: Kievskie ocherki* (Kyiv: A+C, 2008), 255, 268.

use of iambic meter further suggests his similarity to the Acmeists, who viewed iambs as a means of entering the European poetic tradition. Gumilev's 1913 "Iambic Pentameter" (Piatistopnye iamby) is an autobiographical poem that inserts the poetic subject into the context of classical mythology and is written in the eponymous meter. Mandelstsam wrote admiringly of the French iambic tradition. Iambs, which create the basis for Ukrainian syllabo-tonic verse dating back to Kotliarevs'kyi's *Eneïda*, simultaneously evoke the foreign and the local in Bazhan's verse. The result is a book of poems, composed in the years following the Ukrainian Civil War, that are uniquely local while universally legible.

In my translations, I have privileged Bazhan's imagery above all else. Given the importance of form to Bazhan's portraits of memory, I have also sought, wherever possible, equivalent alliterative sound in English, and have offered end rhymes (usually imperfect rhymes) and internal rhymes where possible to give a sense of Bazhan's form, while avoiding a suspiciously dominant rhyme in the English. I have preserved a sense of Bazhan's iambic meter wherever possible.

Amelia M. Glaser

ОСІННЯ ПУТЬ

Осіння путь, і мряка пелехата.
Рипить понад шляхом старий понурий дуб,
І листя дня, зів'яле та латате,
Прослалось стріхами обідраних халуп;
І край села ми сіли зачекати
На вітром звалений, грабовий голий слуп.
І туга скрізь, і бачу тугу ту ж
В порожніх ямах зшерхнулих калюж.

В полях туманних бився у тривозі
Холодний день, і жаль, хоч в душу стрель,
На серце впав. Ішли ми по дорозі
Серед пустельних і сумних земель.
Торохкотів далеко дядько десь на возі,
Спухав туманом лан забутих конопель.
І вітровіння скрізь, і вітровіння те ж
Між пальцями похудлими оцих знайомих меж.
Звідкіль прийшли такі вітри старечі,
До нас вони прийшли відкіль?
Загасить темний і холодний вечір
І радости останню горіль.
На мрій моїх похилі, журні плечі
Ляга важкий і стозапеклий біль.
І розкриває крила, й поринає в льот
Суворий вітер гніву, гніву і скорбот.

Я в криках вітру чув далеку сурму бою,—
Та крок бойців хвилює далечінь,
Бо дика квиль вітрів проносить наді мною
Недавніх літ ще не забуту тінь.
Не втамувать стисканнями спокою
Душі стривожених тремтінь,
Коли згадаю я, і бачу я, що ось
Струміння диму з вітром заплелось.

AUTUMN PATH

Autumn path, misty coat of fog,
A dismal oak groans overhead,
The leaves of day have faded, fall,
Wide, wilted leaves obscure a crumbling shed
We sat at the edge of the village, awaiting
The wind-blown hornbeam tree, its trunk naked,
And everywhere sorrow, there, too, the same sorrow
In the wrung-out puddles' empty pits.

On foggy fields the cold day fought,
And the grief in my heart was so deep
I could have shot my soul. We walked
Through that deserted sorrow-scape
Far off, the rumble of an old man's cart,
A long-lost hemp field swelled with fog
And wind was all around, the selfsame wind
Between the skinny fingers of those boundaries we knew well.
Where did these elderly windstorms blow in from?
How did they get to us?
To extinguish the dark and frigid night,
And whatever joy was still burning.
On the hunched, mournful shoulders of my dreaming
There settles a pain—heavy and hardened,
And the hard wind of anger—of anger and sorrow,
Opened its wings and plunged into flight

I heard in the windscream the trumpet of battle,
And soldiers' footsteps stir the expanse,
For the wind's wild moaning brings to me
Those recent years' unforgotten shadows.
You can't appease the soul's frightened tremble
Even with the clasp of calm,
When I remember, and I glimpse
The smoke stream, braided with this wind.

Це—дим боїв, і дим жорсткий пожарищ,
Коли степи гули прибоями атак,
Коли напружено у ребра серцем вдариш,
І серце,—відданий товариш,
Не знає слова: переляк,
і ти ідеш, і серця зламок твій
Набито захватом, як порохом—набій.
А ось тепер лиш вітер коливає

У серці порослі уже достиглих туг,
Та в далеч стелеться і тягнеться без краю
Доріг розімкнений ланцюг.
Іду, іду й не помічаю,
Що тьма й туман росте навкруг,
Що на полях голодних достига
Порожня осінь і нудьга.

Кому ж цей біль моїх маленьких ранок,
Моїх мізерних непотрібних втом?
Я хочу днів, щоб знов підводивсь ранок,
Мов кінь з розламаним хребтом,
І стяг нездоланих тачанок
Знов загорівся за горбом,
Бо не зітерти вічний слід
Жорстоких і натхненних літ.

Я знаю: літ сліда не стерти,
Минулих літ, проведених в бою;
Величніх літ боїв і смерти
З сердець не стерти колію,
І на лиці людей тепер твій
Слід радісно й побожньо пізнаю,
А слід цей—рана або шрам,
Або конвульсій машкара.

This smoke is from battles, this smoke is from blazes,
When steppes rumbled with the first attacks,
When your heart beats hard against your ribcage,
And your heart, that devoted comrade,
Doesn't know the word for fear,
and you go, and your lump of heart
Is loaded with awe, like a loaded gun.
But now only the wind trembles here.

The grief in my heart has grown ripe and big
And the open chain of roads expands
And continues on, infinite
I walk, walk without observing
That darkness and fog grow all around,
That empty autumn and yearning
Are ripening in this hungry ground

To whom can I offer my little morning pain,
My miserable, useless exhaustion?
I want days, where morning rises
Like a horse with a broken spine
And the flag of unconquered machine gun carts
Are again lit up against the hills,
For you can't erase the eternal trace
Of those cruel, inspired years.

I know you can't erase the trace,
Made by years, bygone years, at war;
Great years of battle, years of death,
You can't clear your heart of these tracks,
Now, joyfully, piously, I recognize
Your trace on people's faces,
For this trace is either a wound or a scar,
Or else a convulsive mask.

Вдивляюся в таке тремтіння,
Зів'ялих губ чіткий, тривожний змах.
І бачу загравне цвітіння
У глибоко закопаних очах.
В чола похилене склепіння
Той трепіт б'ється, наче птах.
О, ні! Не кожному дано
Носити днів святих клейно.

Вже не бренять шляхи, і в далеч вже промчали
Зухвалих коней дикі табуни,
А я відстав, на мене не чекали,
Тепер-же спробуй, здогони,
І накажи, щоб не мовчали
Ці переорані лани.
Ні, то пройшло, і мариш, як ідеш
Про час покошених пожеж.

Ляга туман. Ревуть далекі луни.
Суворі луни хмурих піль.
Мотузкою в'яжи свої подерті струни,
У зашморга в'яжи свій непотрібний біль.
На прапорі твоїм, на прапорі Комуни
Немає слів зневіри і знесиль!
Ляга туман. Вогні цвітуть.
Вогні далекі. Дальня, щасна путь.

ПІДКОВИ КОНЕЙ

Відстукали копита коней бойових.
Серця—в мозиль, каміння—в пил зітерши,
І я прийшов, прийшов уже не перший
Слідами втоптаних доріг.

Слідами втоптаних доріг
Прийшов, спізнившись і відставши,
І стрів, хоч знаю—не назавше,
Буденний час мигички та відлиг.

I look close at this trembling, into the clear,
Discomforting stroke of faded lips
And I see the flowering sunset
In these sunken eyes,
Which—bird-like—throb a beat,
Into the forehead's sloping vault.
Not everybody gets to wear
These saints' day stigmata!

The paths no longer resonate,
The wild, brazen herds have galloped off.
And I stayed back, they didn't wait.
Now to hurry and catch up
To command this tilled earth
Not to be quiet.
No, that's gone, and you dream as you go,
Of the time of those smothered fires.

The fog settles. Distant echoes rumble.
Harsh echoes from fields of gloom.
Braid your frayed strings into cords.
Twist your useless pain into a noose.
There are no faithless, desperate words
On your flag, on the flag of the Commune!
The fog settles. Lights glow.
The lights are far away. A distant, happy road.

Translated by Amelia M. Glaser

HORSESHOES

War horses' hooves once pounded.
Hearts into callouses, stones into dust,
And I wasn't the first who followed
The footsteps on those trampled roads.

The footsteps of those trampled roads,
I followed, beginning long after,
And I met, though I knew it wasn't forever,
The melting, drizzling workaday hour.

Буденний час мигички та відлиг
Я полюбити хтів, і полюбить не зміг,
І куряву думок знов згадка золота жене,

І б'ється в розуму незборений поріг
Невпинний плин думок моїх,
Й густою кров'ю серце навантажене.

НІЧНИЙ МОМЕНТ

Ніч, як труп на шибениці, терпне,
Рвучи пуповину з днем.
І промінь карявий на брукові вмер пнем,
Жовтим, трухлявим пнем.

Мево лякливе, проціжене й злібне.
Вгинаючись в ями, тече.
Заб'ється в конвульсіях, стане і зблідне.
Вчепившись в камінне плече.

Вітер пручається й злякано ловиться
В пальцях рвучких верховіть.
І, захлинувшись на мент, прохрипить,
Наче в горлі сухому сукровиця.

І не зводить лихтар ллятих кров'ю очей,
І зімнеться пітьма в чорну грудку,
І тужливо ударять в якусь проститутку
Пухирі її в'ялих грудей.

І прогуде, і напружено спиниться
Хрипкий, як повія, дзвін.
Тільки вітер клекоче і піниться
Біля брудних вітрин.

Тільки тіні повзуть незакінчені,
Цвіт неуважний лихтарних бруньок.
Тільки вереск тихії жінчині
Та чийся прискорений крок.

The melting, drizzling workaday hour—
I wanted to love it, but couldn't,
And golden memories blow the dust of thoughts.

The unstoppable stream of thoughts
Floods over the threshold of reason,
Thick blood filling my heart.

Translated by Amelia M. Glaser

A MOMENT IN THE NIGHT

The night, like a corpse on a gibbet, grows numb,
Tearing the navel cord with a day.
A twisted ray died on the cobblestones
Like a stub, a yellow, rotten stub.

A timid, sieved, wicked fog,
Wriggling into the pits, flows,
It convulses, stops and turns pale,
Clinging on the stone shoulder.

The wind resists and fearfully
Stalls in the fingers of the impetuous crowns.
And, after a brief choke, rasps
As if it has a lymph in a dry throat.

And the lantern keeps its raged eyes on,
And the darkness shrinks into a black clod,
And the lumps of its sluggish breasts
Mournfully hit a random prostitute.

And the husky voice of the bell
Horns and intensely holts.
Only the wind gurgles and spumes
Near the dirty showcases.

Only the pendent shadows crawl,
Careless blossom of lanterns' buds.
Only the quiet woman's shriek
And someone's rapid pace.

І там, де ліхтарнеє мево,
Мов коріння рослин, заплелось,
Спинилась повія дешева,
Ще в шубі розстібнутій хтось.

Тільки вулиці втомлені й змучені,
Тільки площі почути змогли б
Голодні слова проститутчені
Про трипер, кохання і хліб ...

У шелестах тихих, в хитаннях невловних
Стане тінь моя, стане і далі мине
Задурманить мене, заполонить мене
Тривога ночей невимовних.

НЕЯСНИЙ ЗВУК

Неясний звук, далекий звук у млі,—
То обрії черкає ніч осіння.
Встає в шорохкім шамотінні
Туман із мокрої землі.

То ніч бреде, і тіні міста бродять,
Лякливі тіні кішл і тайних бурдіїв,
І лихтарі мінливим цвітом сходять
Міських огнів, болотяних огнів.

То черепки огнів розбризкали пиварні
По цеглі площ, холодній і слизькій,
Де мева лихтарів, сильвети незугарні
Іще не спроданих повій.

Осіння ніч, незрівняна й нестерпна,
Прийшла, о місто, в сховища твої,
А десь гаї ще марять жовтим серпнем.
І золотом гілля іще бринять гаї.

And where the lantern's looming
As if the plants' roots are intertwined,
A cheap prostitute stopped
with someone in an unbutton mantle.

Only the tired and weary streets,
Only squares could hear
The prostitute's hungry words
About tripper, love and bread ...

In the quiet rustle, in the subtle wavering
My shadow stands still, it stands and passes by.
The unspeakable anxiety of the nights
Makes me drunk and enchants me.

Translated by Yuliya Ilchuk

INDISTINCT SOUND

Indistinct sound in the haze, a distant sound
The autumn night etches a horizon,
And in a whistling whisper it rises,
The fog from the wet ground.

The night is roaming, city shadows roam,
In the slums—a brothel's frightening shadows,
Lanterns leak their multicolored glow,
City lights, will-o'-the-wisps.

The breweries splashed out shards of fire
On the bricks of the plaza, slippery and cold,
Where the blaze of the lanterns
Casts the ugly silhouettes
Of prostitutes still unsold.

The autumn night, incomparable, unbearable,
Came, O city, into your vault,
And somewhere, wooded groves still rave of yellow August,
And branches in the groves still chime with gold.

Та ні, хай спогади прибиті й полеглі
Осінній вітер пилом рознесе,
Бо ось лиш тут, на цій холодній цеглі
Моє життя протоптано усе.

Бо тут шумлять розпатлані пиварні.
Де труться серед стін пісні хрипкі людей.
Але цілунками не стулять п'яні парні
Шаршавий рот, голодний рот ночей …

І дзвонять лихтарі, і верески біргалок.
І ще темніший, ще бридкіший льох,
Де б'ється у руках жіночих тіл кавалок …
—Іди-но, стерво, вип'ємо удвох …

Глибока ніч, і ось достотна осінь
Останній лист достука на панель,
А ти стоїш не продана ще й досі
У сутіні мовчазних будівель …

ПАПОРОТЬ

Мов карб старий,—цей місяць білозір,
Мов сни старі,—ці хмари білопінні.
І бачу я: в незнаному тремтінні
Поганська ніч лягла на чорний бір.

Снується дим опівнічних офір.
Несуть жерці на слані рядна лінні
Німим богам свої дари уклінні:
Важучий мед і соковитий сир.

Поганська ніч—таємний час оман.
Пливе з озер мережаний туман
І духмяніють папороті трутні.

І вихожа на росяний майдан
Весільне коло молодих древлян,—
Слов'янських зельних піль веснянки незабутні.

But no, let these memories dry out and die,
Let the autumn wind carry them off like dust,
Only here, underfoot, on this cold brick
My life has been thoroughly crushed.

For they rumble in this disheveled cellar,
People's hoarse singing mingles between these walls.
But drunken boys' kisses can't cover over
The rough mouth, the hungry mouth of nights.

And the lanterns ring, and the beerhalls are screaming.
And that abyss is ever more repugnant, ever darker,
Where, struggling in someone's arms, a lump of female body,
Come on, bitch, let's drink together …

Deep night. And this is truly autumn,
The last leaf hits the pane,
And you, unsold, are still standing
In the dusk of silent buildings …

Translated by Amelia M. Glaser

FERN

This bog-star moon is like an ancient trove,
These white and foamy clouds—ancient dreams.
I see the pagan night in restless twitch
Descend to shroud the pitch-black grove.

The curling smoke of midnight sacrifice.
Priests carry gifts to their silent gods.
They put pellucid honey, mellow cheese
On cloths of linen with a pious bow.

The pagan night, the secret time of daze.
From lakes, approaching wafts of lacy haze,
The toxic ferns exude their heady scent.

Here comes onto the dewy village square
A merry wedding circle of young Drevlians:
The vernal Slavic fields resound with ageless carols.

Translated by Svetlana Lavochkina

КРОВ ПОЛОНЯНОК

Б'є космогрудий кінь копитом на припоні.
Кипить на дні подовбаних барил
Солодке молоко розпалених кобил.
Пахілля пахнуть, дикі та солоні.
Войовники так сплять, що смерти не почули б,
І нерухомо на землі лежить
Узор карбований могутніх верховіть,
Мов левня мускулястий тулуб.

Додолу хиляться рясні кущі багаття
І дим струною в небозвід зіперсь.
Рвучи нитки ялозеного шмаття,
Немов квічена брость, так гнеться повна персь.
У добру вільгість, в плідний піт
Зарошено тіла вкраїнських ясних бранок,
І рот розтерзано, і проросте на ранок
В дівочих черевах їдкий монгольський плід.

Ростуть роки, одвічний цвіт отав,
І в сайдаках сердець зотліли стріли згадок,
Та кров стару століттями нащадок
У ґудзуватих жилах схороняв.
І любимо слова важкі, мов чорний дим
Зловіщих ватр, що сяяли татарину,
Викохуємо кров тугу і міцно зварену
І просторінь—безмежну царину
Вітаєм серцем круглим і простим.

ЛЮБИСТОК

З-під вій—блакитна тінь, ознака нестеменна,
Й рожевий слід на грудях де-не-де,
А він стромив вже ногу у стремена
І кінь баский вже гривою пряде.

THE BLOOD OF CAPTIVE MAIDENS

Tethered firmly, the Curly paws the ground with his hoof.
The sweet milk of fiery mares
Seethes in the bottoms of chiseled barrels.
Scents, salty and feral, perfuse the air.
Warriors sleep as if already dead,
And on the ground there spreads
The notched design of mighty treetops,
Like a lion's muscular trunk.

Luxuriant bushes of bonfires cant to the ground,
A stream of smoke braced against the sky.
Tearing at the threads of greasy rags,
Like a shoot bearing blooms, a breast reveals its fullness.
Well moistened, in a fecund sweat,
Thus were bedewed the captive bodies of fair Ukrainian girls.
The maw's been rent, and come the morn there'll sprout
A Mongol's noxious fruit inside the maidens' wombs.

Years wax, the timeless bloom of aftermath,
And shafts of memories have long decayed inside the quivers of hearts,
But through the centuries the offspring's managed to preserve
That ancient blood inside its knotty veins.
We love words ponderous like the sooty smoke
Of premonitory bonfires that for the Tatar glowed,
This blood we cosset, dense and vigorously boiled,
And greet the vast expanse—a boundless field—
With a heart simple and full.

Translated by Roman Koropeckyj

LOVAGE

Blue umbra fell around her eyes, a fateful sign,
Pink traces here and there on her breasts.
But he already put his foot into the stirrups,
His restless steed is shimmying its mane.

Лишилася сама, коханка безіменна,
І дивиться на путь, де курява паде.
Одного вечора, як праця цілоденна
Кінчиться геть, дитину приведе.

Та прокричить не довго немовля,
І лиш в садку, де скопана земля,
Розквітне рута й проросте любисток.

Вона ж сапатиме поля
Й сама не знає, відкіля,
Від кого день і ніч чекає тайних звісток.

РОЗМАЙ—ЗІЛЛЯ

I

Порожня ніч землі туману й трясовиці,
Мов моторошний цвіт відьомський, розцвіта,
І струшена з небес на дно студне криниці
Тріпочеться зоря, як риба золота.

Гниллям й пліснявою запахли луки ниці
І по труських ланах прослалась пишнота
Розпалених пісень безстидної плідниці
Про незносиму скорб, що назва їй—цнота.

Де мерехтить в сирих туманах улоговин,
Пахнот вільгох, солодкмлоких повен,
Той перелесний цвіт, таємний цвіт тирлич,

Хитнувши оситняг, причалив тихо човен.
Дівочий спів стає блажен і снажнокровен
В передчутті нічних і виблаганних стріч.

He left his nameless lover all alone.
She looks along the path veiled in the sinking dust.
One evening, when her day-span grind is done,
She will bring forth a child.

But in the hut, the newborn will emit a short-lived cry,
And in a forlorn garden, on that patch of disturbed ground,
Rue buds will bloom and lovage stems will sprout.

By day, she'll till the fields the same way as before,
By night, she'll weep: she won't know
From whom she yearns to hear the secret tidings.

Translated by Svetlana Lavochkina

LOVE POTION

I

The hollow earthy night, awash with fogs and spells,
Enfolds its haunted core, like a bewitching bloom.
The star dropped from the sky into the secret well
Flickers its goldfish tail down in the icy gloom.

The meadows wear a veil of damp and musty smells.
Amid the rippling fields, a woman softly croons.
Her song is like a moan: it shamelessly declares
That chastity's a pain to be forgotten soon.

Where in the moist ravines sweet milky moons are swelling,
A ghostly flower blooms, elusive and compelling—
A secret herb that has a potent bitter root.

The boat drifts to the bank, the slender reeds are swaying
The song grows full of need and longing. It's foretelling
Encounter in the dark, the end of long pursuit.

II

Опівночі земля застугоніла
І сілует їздця відбився у ріці.
Спинився нагло кінь. Повисла піна біла
На садженім сріблом, коштовнім ремінці.

Кінь замордований, та постать міцнотіла
Упертіш хилиться на шитім сідельці.
Козак стиска міцніш гаптовані удила
В своїй порепаній, натрудженій руці.

Немов кривий танець нічних хмільних потвор
Заплівсь у витворний, вигадливий узор,—
Над лісом підвелись дівочі співи кличні.

Зійшов з коня козак, і заблудивсь у млі,
Де в дивній тишині проходять по землі
Мовчазні тіні, мляві і величні.

III

Кінчається ночей вільготних половіння
І круглих зор достиг багатий урожай.
В чарованих гаях ти, дівчино, чекай
Собі ядерного і чистого насіння.

Мов келих пінявий, пролялось через край
Ярких, жаждивих снів солодке шумовиння.
Роздерла на грудях намист своїх плетіння
І гостю странному докинула розмай.

Віддала всю любов забрати в ярий свид,
Упавши на моріг, розкривши плідні чресла,
На запашній землі п'ючи росу і піт.

А потім підвелась, пішла і їй у слід
Покірлива луна, мов марний дар, понесла
Прощальний тихий клич і дальній стук копит.

II

At midnight came the sound of hurried hoofs approaching.
The river briefly caught the rider's silhouette.
The horse abruptly stopped and stood, its round haunches
And heaving sides all glistening with sweat.

Its handsome rider turned his head, intently watching
For something hiding in the dark ahead.
Dismounting, with his hand he gripped the reins beset
With gems and silver, marked with careful notching.

The girl's enticing voice came calling from the copse.
The writhing twisting words were interlaced like ropes,
Like the distorted limbs of monstrous night-time dancers.

The Cossack left his horse and stepped into the mist,
Where great lethargic shapes in silence coexist,
And slowly walk the earth, and sigh, and yield no answers.

III

The nights are nearly ripe and ready for the taking.
Go to the sacred grove, and gather, while you wait,
The heavy luscious fruit, the finest seed of fate,
Take in these precious gifts to quench your eager aching.

The longing from the dreams remained when she awakened.
A bubbling chalice spilled, when she prepared her brew.
He drank his fill—and yet, his thirst and yearning grew.
She pulled her blouse aside: he saw her necklace breaking.

She gave him all her love down in the wooded hollow:
The breath of pungent earth has filled her naked breast,
They mixed their sweat and dew with needy urgent moves.

When she got up to go, only the echo followed.
It carried, like a gift left by her midnight guest,
A farewell call and then the drumming of the hooves.

Translated by Iryna Shuvalova

ДОРОГА НЕСХОДИМА

I

Нехай слова мої жмаковані і куці.
Та інших слів я не знайшов.
У рік дев'ятий революцій
Ось тільки трохи про любов.

Бо очі зламано у муці
І розпанахано кривавий рота шов.
Я на любовному позбиваному луці
Так змучено й невпевнено пройшов.

Замало днів ішли ми поруч,
Замало сном ми марили одним.
Шляхом розірваним своїм

Ти йдеш наліво, я—праворуч,
І встане мрії нестворенний дим
Над половінням молодим.

II

Завіяно огні чужих, незнаних станцій.
Примружено й пригашено огні.
То нерозрадна путь лягла моїй коханці.
То неминучий шлях лягає і мені.

Ми йтимемо вночі, ми маритимемо вранці,
І знатимемо ми одні,
Що захлинемось в лихоманці
І в лихоманковому сні.

Мов пил до ніг, маріння ті
Впадуть, і знаю—на путі,
Як радість більшую, нестиму

Тебе, зів'ялу і бліду.
І так невтомлений пройду
Кохань дорогу несходиму.

THE INFINITE ROAD

I

My words may be tangled and terse,
They're the only words I have.
Nine years of Revolution,
Here's just a bit about love.

For my eyes have been tortured and broken,
And my bloodied mouth, torn at the seam.
Upon this beaten love-field
I walked, uncertain and drained.

Few were our days walking side by side,
Few were the dreams that bound us.
We part ways on the mangled road.

So you go left, and I'll go right,
And the unformed smoke of dreams
Will rise over early crops.

II

Unfamiliar stations' lanterns,
Are buried, flickering and dim.
An unhappy path lies before my lover.
An inevitable road lies before me, too.

We will walk at night. We will dream in the morning,
And we alone will know
That we're destined to drown in this fever,
And in this feverish dreaming.

Dust-like, all these dreams will sift
To our feet, and I know, along the way
Like a joyful load, I'll carry

You, wilted and pale.
And tireless, I'll carry on
Along that infinite love-road.

III

Коли серця на кор-іню розхитано,
Що оповім коханці я моїй?
З усіх кутків душі позмітано
Любови порох золотий.

Та не розкривано й не читано
Таємний зошит мій і твій.
Потворно й складно позаплітано
Неясного чуття сувій.

Але чіпати не посмій
Неторкнутий і нерозкриваний
Таємний зошит її і свій.

Навіщо зміст той несподіваний
Тобі і їй?

IV

Печальних птиць вечерній перельот
Накине тінь і зникне за полями,
І поповзуть смеркові тихі плями
Мохами теплими закурених болот.

Рожевий кетяг зор розкинеться над нами,
Немов солодкий і достиглий плід.
Цей непомітний, ніжний перехід,
Що ніч сполучує із втомленими днями.

Втомились дні. Мов зайвий епізод,
Забуто всі маленькі міста драми:
Естраду і панель, мансарду і фокстрот.

Снагу сухих, неповних насолод,
Бо ж у часи вечірньої нестями,
Хіба не квітне нам ще візерунок цнот?

III

When hearts are shaken to the core,
What tale shall I tell my lover?
I've swept each corner of my soul
Clean of love's gold powder.

Yet, still unread, still unrevealed
Is our secret notebook—mine and yours.
It's hideously tangled, confused—
Our scroll of ambivalence.

Only, never disturb
That untouched, still unopened
Secret notebook—hers and yours.

What use are its startling contents
To you and her?

IV

The evening flight of grieving birds
Will cast a shadow, pass beyond the fields,
The quiet stains of dusk will crawl across
The smoky swampland's tepid moss.

A pink bundle of stars will spill on us,
Like fruit, sweet and ripe.
This tender, inconspicuous passage
Connects exhausted days with night.

Exhausted days. Like pointless affairs,
These petty city dramas, all forgotten:
The stage, the striptease, garret, foxtrot.

The strength of dry, unfinished pleasures.
For in the night's euphoric hours,
Couldn't our innocence still flower?

Translated by Amelia M. Glaser and Bohdan Pechenyak

Будівлі/Edifices (1929)

ДОРОГА

Ретельно тіні складено в штахети,
І над пустелищем степів,
Як хвіст скаженої комети,—
Огонь рахманних вечорів.

Упали тіні гострі осторонь,
Чіткіш лягли риски гілок,
Перехилившись в темну просторінь
Кущі здичавілих зірок.

Іду, й дороги переламані,
Гнучись, плазують із-під ніг.
Так важко на жорстокім камені
Класть лінії твердих доріг.

Так важко на жорстокім камені
Шляхів вирізьблювати грань.
Невже і справді заважа мені
Дорога зустрічей і тиха путь прощань?

Дорого зустрічей і тиха путь прощань,
Людська дорого,—просто стелься,
Відбивши на холодних рельсах
Огні ночей і дотики світань.

І кожному іти тобою,
Людська дорога меж і мір,
І тягнуться над головою
Сліди скривавлених сузір.

І знатиму, куди іти,
І терени, що проходитиму.
Людському захвату неситому
Невже не вистача мети?

Не всі серця дадуться хробаку,
Не всі шляхи у круг закуто,
І проросте зелена рута
На жовтому піску.

THE ROAD

Shadows are neatly stored on the fence,
And over the wasteland of the steppes
The fire of the tranquil nights
Is like the tail of a raging comet.

Sharp shadows dropped aside,
Shades of the branches fell more clearly,
The shrubs of the feral stars
Leaned forward over the dark wasteland.

I walk, and the broken paths
Crawl at my feet, coiling.
It is so hard to pave the lines
Of the firm roads on the ruthless stone.

It is so hard to carve the facets
Of the paths on the ruthless stone.
Will they really hinder me—
The road of encounters and a quiet passage of farewells?

The road of encounters and a quiet passage of farewells,
The human road, just spread,
Refracting night's lights and dawn's touches
On the cold rails.

And everyone will take you,
The human road of verges and measures,
The traces of the bloodstained constellations
Are stretching over the head.

I will know where to go,
And the thorns that I will pass
Will it be enough of purpose
For an insatiable human rapture?

Not all hearts will give up to the worms,
Not all roads will be shackled into a circle,
And a green rue will sprout
On the yellow sand.

Translated by Yuliya Ilchuk

НІЧНИЙ РЕЙС

Ю. Я.

Підноситься зневажливо рука,
І щерблене перо, неначе шпага,
                    гнеться,
І пада, зломлений, в покресленій
                    чернетці
Рядок, мов щогла неструнка.

Та напина вітрила плавні строф,
Скрипить холодним тросом літер
Вітер
Вишуканих катастроф.

Шукання катастроф, і мандрів, і натхнень—
Утіха всіх утіх, розрада всіх розрад.
Хай спинається твій патетичний фрегат,
Фрегат патетичних пісень,
Що чує крізь шторми, і ночі, і тьму,
Стенувшись з корми до носа,
Що судилось йому,
Простяглися йому
Мужні мандрівки матроса.
Рівні та прості
Лягли на морях
Дороги матроські,
Як шрами од шпаг.
Тінь неспокійна й крилата
Корсарського злого фрегата
Морями облудними буде пливти,
Струмітиме хмуро повз чорні борти
Вітер одвертий солдата,
Вітер хоробрих людей,
Що кричить альбатросом між рей,
Тугий, як дуга арбалета,
Прямий, як удар стилета,
Шершавий, як іржа
Корсарського ножа.

A NIGHT CRUISE

The hand is raised in spite,
And the chipped quill bends
                     like a spade,
The line falls apart, in the cross-outs
                             of a rough draft,
Like a misaligned mast.

You fill smooth sails with floating strophes,
The wind screeches in the cold towrope of letters
The wind
Of exquisite catastrophes.

The quest for catastrophes, and journeys, and inspirations,
Delight of all delights, and pleasure of all pleasures.
Let your wretched frigate stall,
The frigate of wretched songs,
Heard through the storms, and nights, and darkness,
Making the ship shudder from stern to stem,
What befell her sent her on
Mariner's masculine journeys.

Smooth and simple
The sailors' pathways stretch
Along high seas, like scars
Made by spades.

The winged and unquiet shadow of
This sinister corsair frigate
Will sail the treacherous seas,
The clear martial winds
Will blow darkly along the black boards,

The wind of brave men,
The wind that screams like
An albatross between the masts,
Taut as the bow of a crossbow,
Straight, like a dagger's stab, coarse, like rust
On the corsair's knife.

Рубай же ланцюги,
Зривайся із причалу,
Бо не в чорнильницях фрегат
                    шукає шквалу,
Бо ти, як муж і войовник,
В часи смертельного авралу
І компасу,
І серцю
Метнутись не даси убік.

МОЄМУ ДРУГОВІ

Затулиш вікна і зачиниш двері,—
Твоя пора.

Беззвучно б'ються на папері
Сухі істерики пера.
Безжаліса немилосердна гра
Із серцем й словом в перегони,
І божевільний пульс агоній
В химерних вивертах пера.

Так, поетичний гастроном,
Не помічаєш, як росте рік,
Нотуєш в захваті істерик
Убогі рими, серця тухлий жом,
І намагаєшся вотще
Знайти безодні в плоскім слові
І воззвеличувать іще
Любов плохеньку, і серце тще,
Й життя у сірім піджакові.

Cut the chains,
Break the moorings,
Because it is not in the inkwell where
The frigate seeks
                    its squall,
For you, as a man and a warrior,
In the hour of mortal alarm,
You shall not let the compass,
                        and the heart

Leave your side.

Translated by Roman Turovsky

TO MY FRIEND

Shut the windows and lock the doors,—
Now it is your turn.
The dry hysterics of the quill
Convulse on paper, in silence.
A ruthless, heartless game of chase
Between the heart and the word,
And the manic pulse of agonies
Fills the quill's chimeric twists.

So, as a poetic gastronome,
You take no notice how the year grows,
You notate in your hysterical delight
The squalid rhymes, the heart's rotten pulp,
In fact, you try in vain
To find an abyss in a flat word,
While glorifying also
A mediocre love, and a small heart
And life contained in a gray tweed jacket.

В порожніх перевулках туги
Ти заблудився в присмерки бліді.
Пливуть неясні виднокруги,
Неначе круги по воді.
І кров повз серце проплива,
І не зникає з синіх губ ця
Схолола посмішка крива,—
І мій любимий, мій безсилий друг,—
В огидний зашморг самогубця
Зав'язується сам твій чорний виднокруг.

І гнилокровий, і мізерний смуток
Роня кінець твого пера,
Коли в шинках, у колі проституток
Шукаєш правди і добра.
В порожніх перевулках туги
Ти заблудився в присмерки бліді.
Пливуть неясні виднокруги,
Неначе круги по воді.

ФОКСТРОТ

Дугою вигнувшись, дає струна тупа,
Немов краплині, впасти чорній ноті,
І ось улесливо з оркестру накрапа
Мелодія в розбещеній скорботі.
І люди йдуть, згинаючись в фокстроті,
Ламаючись у нерухомім па.

І скрипалі бліді помалу
З скрипок опуклого бокалу
У залу, як в тремкий сосуд,
Переллють прелюд.
Забився в похоті прелюдній
Німий фокстрот, цей крок собак,
Цей акт одвертий, акт прелюдний,
Цей неймовірний акт.

You've gotten lost in pale dusk
In empty alleyways of yearning.
The vague horizons float around
And away like ripples on water.

And so the blood will float past the heart,
And this chilled and crooked smile
Will not come off the blue lips,—
And, my beloved and powerless friend,—
Your black horizon will tie itself
Into the gruesome noose of suicide.

The miserly rancid-blooded sorrow
Will drown your pen's nib,
When in the taverns, surrounded by whores
You sit in search of Truth and Good.
You have gotten lost in the pale dusk
In the empty side streets of yearning.
The faint horizons float around and away
Like ripples on water.

Translated by Roman Turovsky

FOXTROT

Bent in an arc, the blunt string lets
A black note fall, like a teardrop,
And the melody unctuously drizzles from
The band, in some perverted grief,
And the people go on, bent in foxtrot,
Collapsing in an immobile pas.

The pale fiddlers, drop by drop,
Pour the prelude
From the jars of violins into
The trembling vase of the music hall.
The mute foxtrot wriggles in a prelude of lust,
This sincerity, this foreplay,
This implausible act of lust.

Шматуй же крок, труси людей ти,
Кохання механічний знак!
Уже на чорнім горлі флейти
Заходи́в худий борлак.
Струна, як бич, пече банджо,
І стогнуть скрипалі,
Щоб звук хитавсь, як в жилі жовч,
Як ртуть в гарячім шклі,
Щоб, враз упавши з висоти,
Запавсь, зім'явсь, зігбавсь,
Щоб роззявлялися роти,
Роти голодних павз.
І захлинувсь астмічний такт,
Що рве, як рану, рот.
Цинічний акт, прилюдний акт,—
Розчавлений фокстрот.

Ах, солодійництво примар
В розгойданому мюзік-холі!
Віолончелі стегна голі,
І хтиві талії гітар,
І жирний ляпас підошов,
І крок кривий, як корч.
Ну, що ж,
                   така людей любов,
Випростана сторч!
Хитаючись, любов іде,
До рота влипши ртом.
Любов людей, любов людей
Трусить животом,
Животом і клубами,
                         губами ботокуда,
Губами, мов окравками
                         скривавлених лахміть.
То, поспішаючи, стенографують люди
Каракулями шімі свою коректну хіть.
У стоккато шуму шімі,
Спотикатись в шумі шімі,
Це—любов.
Ось така ти в шумі шімі,
У строкатім шумі шімі
Ти—любов!

Break up the pace, shake up the dancers,
You, mechanical sign of love!
A sharp Adam's apple already crawls
Beneath the black throat of the flute.

The string sparks up the banjo, like a whip,
And fiddlers moan away,
To make the sound swing, like gall swings in the veins,
Like mercury in a hot glass tube.
Fallen from great height
Caved, rumpled, crumpled,
To make jaws drop,
To open the mouths of hungry pauses.
And so chokes the asthmatic beat,
Which tears the mouth up, into a wound,
A cynical act, an act of foreplay,—
A foxtrot trampled.

Oh, malting of ghosts in the swaying music hall!
The cello's naked thighs,
And lusty waistlines of guitars,
The fatty slaps of the shoe soles,
And the pace curved like a seizure.
So, no matter,
Such is human love, stuck out, erect!
Swaying, love walks on, mouth stuck To mouth,
The human love, the human love
Shakes its belly, shakes
Bellies and clouds and lips of a Botokude,
The lips, edged in bloodied rags.

So, hurriedly people stenograph
Their desires in shimmying curlicues.
Shimmying in this staccato clamor,
Stumbling in this clamorous shimmy,
This—is love.
Such are you in this shuffling shimmy,
In this striped shimmying shuffle,
Love you are!

Translated by Roman Turovsky

ЕЛЕГІЯ АТРАКЦІОНІВ

Із чорного стебла баска
сівба важких басів,
і флейти метушня баска
на рині голосів.

Різкий плижок, зухвалий скік,
сухий, як дріб, галоп,
і флейт одчай, цих флейт баских,
над ямами синкоп.

Крутися, світ, крутися, цирк,
крутися, карусель!
І гостроверхий фейєрверк
злітає над усе ...

І день—у смерк, і ніч—у смерк,
і серце—нічичирк.
Крутись, скажений фейєрверк,
Крутись, скажений цирк!
І око юрб проколоте
на шпагах тисяч ламп.
Крутись, прокляте коло те ...
Такт!
Темп!

Чи довго прокрутишся так тут,
невже не впадеш,
невже?
Кожен вигиб і темпу, і такту
віддрукує капельмейстерський жест.

ELEGY FOR CIRCUS ATTRACTIONS

From the little black stem of the bass
comes the heavy basses sowing,
and the fluttery fuss of a flute
in the gutter of voices flowing.

A quick hop, a daring leap,
a gallop as dry as a drumroll
and these flutes' trills of despair
above the pits of the syncope.

Spin, world, spin, circus,
spin, o carousel!
And a sharp-edged firework
flies up above it all.

Day—into dusk, and night—into dusk,
and the heart stays mute.
Spin, insatiable fireworks,
spin, insatiable circus!

And the eye of the crowd is pierced
by the blades of a thousand lights.
Spin, you damned circle …
To the beat!
To the tempo!

How long will you keep on spinning?
Won't you fall,
won't you?
Every twist of the tempo, of the beat
engraved by the conductor's gesture.

Віддрукує і занотує:
стій!
На кожну ноту, на ту є
карб
свій.

І пізнаєш уперту математику
пароксизмів захвату і журб ...
Товаришу,
друже,
братику—
в кожного є свій карб.

Кожному ноту нажебрано,
і іншої буть не могло б,
і рипить між іржавими ребрами
серця сухий суглоб.

    Серце! Крутися, хитайся,
    хитайсь, вигинайсь шкереберть!
    Із губ акробата-китайця
    струмочком сповзає смерть.

    Захлинувся ковтками конвульсій,
    завертівсь на блискучій косі,
    і зчепилися в спільному пульсі
    серця
    усі!
    Горло горбом напнеться,
    втнеться крик,
    як звисне, мов флаг, із трапецій
    чорний людський язик.

Скрикне тоненько панійка ...
Тоді націляйся й лети,
в зойки розпачливі, паніко,
зімни їхні голі роти!
Слину і сльози виточи,
губи в гримаси зміси!
Розгойдались, мов трупи на ниточках,
голоси.

Engraved and noted:
stop!
Every note, each one has
been
marked.

And you'll come to know the unyielding mathematics
paroxysms of excitement and despair …
Comrade,
Friend,
brother—
everyone has been marked.

Everyone's scrounged for their note,
and each got just the one destined,
and the dried-out joints of the heart
go on creaking midst ribs that are rusting.

> Heart! Whirl, wobble,
> wobble and clamber and bend!
> Death slides down in a little stream
> from the lips of a Chinese acrobat.
>
> Choking on gulps of convulsions,
> spinning on bright shining spit,
> and clutched in a shared pulse
> of the heart
> —everyone!
> The throat will warp into a hump,
> the scream will halt in place,
> when it hangs, like a flag, from the trapeze—
> the black tongue of human speech.

A lady will shriek out piercingly …
Then panic takes aim and flies
into their heartbreaking howls,
crumpling their naked mouths!
Grind up the spit and tears,
whisk lips into grimaces!
They're swinging like corpses on threads,
the voices.

Translated by Ostap Kin, Ainsley Morse, and Mykyta Tyshchenko

БУДІВЛІ

I

СОБОР

У тіні пагорків, процвівши потаймиру,
Звучить колона, як гобою звук,
Звучить собор камінним Dies irae,
Мов ораторія голодних тіл і рук.

Встає огонь святобливої готики,
Як ватра віри,
               як стара яса,
І по-блюзнірському піднеслись в небеса
Стрілчасті вежі—
                   пальців гострих дотики.

Рукою обійми холодні жили твору,
І дай рукам своїм німим
Піднести серце власне вгору
На грановитих списах рим.
Щоб в очі скнарі темних веж
Заглянуло воно,
                  мов дзвін сухий, забилось.
І тінь впаде із пальців веж, як стилос,
І почерку її на серці не знесеш.

Немов кістляві й люті пута,
На серце ляже слів важкий узор.
Залізом,

EDIFICES

I

CATHEDRAL

Having secretly blossomed in the shadow of hills,
A column resounds, like the note of an oboe,
A stony *dies irae* echoes in the cathedral
Like an oratorio of hungry bodies and arms.

The fire of gothic faith rises.
A bonfire of belief,
      an ancient salvo,
And blasphemously pierces the heavens
with arrow-like spires—
     fingers sharp to the touch.

Embrace with your arms the work's cold veins,
And allow your silent arms
To raise up high your heart
On angular lists of rhymes,
So that it might peer into the stingy eyes of dark spires
And beat,
   like a dry bell.
Then a shadow, like a stylus, will fall from the spires' fingers,
And you will not endure its mark on your heart.

Like bony, cruel fetters
A heavy verbal pattern will press upon your heart.

The cathedral's ominous tale was forged
Of iron,

полум'ям,

      єлеєм,

            кров'ю

                    куто

Зловіщу повість про собор.

Як в захваті баданних юрм,
У скреготі зубів
            і скреготі граніту,
Мов смертний спів,
         мов клич одчайних сурм,
Щоб пломеніти і гриміти,

Вставав собор на славу феодалу,
Яскриня віри,
        кішло прощ,
І на лункі тарелі площ
Вже дзвін його упав помалу,
Мов мідний шаг,
       офіри мідний шаг.
Так в католицьких височлих руках
Бряжчать разки з пахучого сандалу.

На дзвін не йшли,
          а плазували лігма
Раби та блазні, дуки й королі;
І роззівлявсь собор,
         немов солодка стигма
Безвольної й самітної землі.

І падали,
      і дерлись під склепіння
Тіла без рук, і руки, що без тіл,
Роти, розірвані навпіл,
В камінну бистрину вплітали голосіння.

І як худа стріла, злітав над ними вгору,
Як рук голодних гостроверхий сніп,
Натхненний корабель собору
У фанатичнім, виснаженім сні.

fire,
      holy oil,
           and blood,
When in the rapture of straining hordes,
With a gnashing of teeth
          and grinding of granite,

Like a death song,
       like the call of desperate bugles,
The cathedral arose to glorify the feudal,
To flame and thunder.

It was a cave of faith,
       a home for pilgrims,
And on the saucer of its sonorous site
The sound of its bell fell slowly,
Like a bronze coin,
       a coin of sacrificial offering.
Rosary beads of fragrant sandalwood
Rattled in thin Catholic hands.

They did not approach the bell,
       but crawled, prostrate,
Slaves and jesters, dukes and kings,
While the cathedral opened up,
       a sweet stigma
Of the helpless and lonely earth.

And they fell,
       and clawed their way forward under the vault,
Those bodies without arms, and arms without bodies,
With mouths half torn apart
As they wove their lamentation into the stony rapids.

And there flew high above them, like an emaciated arrow,
Like the movement of the starved sharp-topped wheat sheaf,
The inspired ship of the cathedral
In a fanatical, exhausted dream.

Крутилися роки в похмурій веремії,
Та не згасали, щоб ізнов блищать,
Вогні готичних яросних багать
На щерблених мечах і косах Жакерії,

Бо уставав собор—гнобитель і захисник,
Юрби благання і юрби прокльон,
Й готичний розцвітав трилисник,
Мов хрест, мов квіт, мов псалма і мов сон.

II

БРАМА

У грі нелюдській,
в справі неприродній,
Потрясши ланцюги прикрас,
Важкою зморшкою напнувся владний м'яз,
Обняв краї спокійної безодні.

Підніс,
        як пожаданний келих,
Широку браму в вишину,
Широку браму, грішну і земну,
Мов круглий перстень на руках дебелих.

І творчий хист,
            що не втомивсь,
                        не вистиг,
Снопи принадних зел на камені поклав,
Як груди дів,
            гарячих і нечистих,
У шпетних ігрищах уяв.

Так щедро кинув семенасту брость,
Як звик на ложе кидати коханку,
Що зна любовний піт,
                важких запліднень млость,

The years spun by in somber confusion.
Yet the fires of the frenzied gothic pyres
Never died out, but repeatedly revived
In the Jacquerie's notched swords and scythes,

Because the cathedral always rose up, as oppressor and defender,
The crowd's entreaty and its curse,
And the gothic tri-leaf bloomed,
Like a cross, a flower, a psalm, and a dream.

II

ARCHWAY

In an inhuman game,
               an unnatural business,
Shaking its decorative chains,
An imperious muscle tensed into a heavy crease,
And embraced the limits of quiet endlessness.

It raised,
         like a long-desired glass,
A wide archway high above,
A wide archway, sinful and earthly,
Like a round diamond ring on a plump hand,

And the creative skill
              that had not waned,
                       or died,
Placed sheaves of enticing herbs onto the stone,
Like the breasts of girls,
              hot and impure,
In an imagination's perverted games.

It spread generously the seed-covered branch,
The way it threw onto its bed a lover
Who knew passion's sweat,
              the swoon of heavy impregnation,

I ситий сон,

         і спрагу на світанку.

На брості—квіт,

на брості—квіт, мов око

Розпаленого самкою самця

Ще тих століть,

         коли в серця

Вливалась пристрасть хтивого барокко,

Що плинула з віків старого лабіринту,

Що поєднала іздаля

Вкраїнських брам рясне гілля

З вільготними акантами Корінту.

I той акант—не лавр

         на голові державця,

I брами щедрої ніхто не розчиняв,

Щоб бранців пропустить

         з подоланих держав,

Бо шлях звитяг крізь браму не прослався.

То брама пристрасті пригнобленій і лютій

Старих століть.

         Одягнені в шарлат,

Тоді здвигав свої дзвіниці злотокуті,

Мов пишні бунчуки,

         бундючний гетьманат.

Тоді, немов тремкий вінець,

На масне волосся степу

Поклав церкви свої Мазепа,

Поет,

     і гетьман,

         і купець;

Тоді, програвши гру одчайну,

Навчився бігати назад

Мазепин білий кінь, оцей Пегас без стайні,

Безхвостий Буцефал

         прийдешніх гетьманят.

Женіть того коня,

Satiated sleep,
>   and daybreak's thirst.

On the branch is a flower,
>   a flower, like the eye
Of a male inflamed by a female
In those distant centuries,
>   when hearts
Filled with the passions of a covetous baroque
Issuing from age-old labyrinths,
That from afar seemed to combine
The abundant leaves of a Ukrainian arch
With the moistness of Corinth's acanthus.

That acanthus was not a laurel
>   on a sovereign's head,
And no one opened the generous arch
To let through prisoners captured
>   in conquered states,
Because a victory path did not pass through the arch.

It was an arch dedicated to the oppressed and furious passion
Of ancient centuries.
>   Clothed in purple,
At that time the haughty Hetmanate
Erected gold-covered bellfries
Resembling proud Cossack standards.
At that time, like a quivering wreath
On the steppe's sleek hair,
Churches were erected by Mazepa,
The poet,
>   and Hetman,
>   and merchant.
At that time, the desperate gamble was lost,
And Mazepa's white horse learned to run in retreat,
A Pegasus without a stable,
The tail-less Bucephalus
>   of future weakened Hetmans.
Drive off that horse,

хода його хай втихне!
Мов списа ржавого,
дзвіниць ламайте тінь!
І мовкнуть дзвони,
дзвони з-під склепінь,
Бо серце наше більшеє за їхнє!

III

БУДИНОК

Немов веселка, викута в гамарні,
Уже нагнувсь над домом віадук,
Але ще юрбами навколо ходить гук,
Стає в стовпи громохкі й незугарні.

Стовпи громохкі. Палі риштувань.
Підойми зігнуті. Поламані домкрати.
Кипить могутніх будувань
Гарячий бунтівничий кратер!

В'їдається у степ
цупка робота та,
Як смерч, поставлений донизу головою.
Трясе рівниною, і двигає горою,
Мов аркуші, шари земні горта.
І вибуха, як постріл, рух,
Розряд міцних натуг.
Тут
Буяє труд.
І пруг
ляга на пруг,
І кут
ляга на кут,
Луна іде навкруг
Споруд.

Ідуть потужні голоси,
Як лави невгамовні,

let its pace be hushed!
Break the shadow of bellfries,
like rusty spears!
The bells grow silent,
those bells from under vaults,
Because our heart is bigger than theirs!

III

BUILDING

Like a rainbow forged in a smelter,
The viaduct already leans over the house,
But all around dense noises still come
From reverberating and uncomely pillars.

Uncomely pillars. Piles of scaffolding.
Bent cranes. Broken winches.
The boiling hot rebellious crater
Of mighty construction!

That firm work
eats into the steppe,
Like a tornado, standing on its head,
It shakes the plain, moves the mountain,
Turns layers of earth over like leaves of paper.
Movement explodes, like a burst from a gun,
The release of strong tension.
Here
Labor takes flight.
And strip
covers strip,
Corner
covers corner,
Echoes circle
structures.

Powerful voices flow
In irrepressible waves,

І відгукаються баси
Тяжкої електровні,
Де на моторах, з-під щіток,
Між нафтових калюжок,
Повзе, закручуючись, ток,
Немов стальний остружок.
Наллявши сяйва в склянку ламп,
Він в'є свою спіраль
Від паль
До дамб,
Від дамб
До паль,
Кваплячись у даль,
Де хаос ям і хаос куп
Піску й рудої ржі,
Де на твердий, упертий шруб
Нагвинчуються етажі.
Колонки електричних гроз
В дротах прогримотіли,
І лопає тривалий трос.
Як лопаються жили.
І смерчі звуків випряда
Оскаженіла хуга,
То крутиться мерщій труда
Велична центрифуга.
Обертається мерщій,
Луна на гони й гони
По рейках гомінких колій,
Як вагонетки, гонить.
Копають степ, свердлять масив
І закладають тут же
Не арки брам, а дула димарів,
І кратери споруджень.
Зубами чорними зубил
Рубають ромби брил,
Бетон громадять в кучугури,
І пахне, як озон, їдкий металу пил,
І котяться важкі акорди сил,

And bass notes respond
From the heavy electrical station,
Where over machines, under brushes,
Among oil puddles,
Channeled metal creeps, twisting
Like steel shavings.
Its brilliance lights the glass of lamps,
As it weaves its spiral
From pillars
To dams,
From dams
To pillars,
Hurrying into the distance,
To the chaos of pits,
Mounds of sand and reddish rust,
Where layers are wrapped around
A hard stubborn screw.
On small columns electrical shocks
Thunder in wires,
And the strong cable bursts,
Like a vein.
A tornado of sounds spins out
From an enraged snowstorm.
This is labor's fast-whirling
Mighty separator.
It turns rapidly,
Sending echoes for miles,
Like wagonettes
Along sonorous rail tracks.
Digging the steppe, drilling into the massif,
They prepare
Not archways, but smoke stacks
And craters for buildings.
They use the excavator's black teeth
To chop massive rhomboids of earth,
They pile up mounds of concrete.
And the acrid metal dust smells of ozone,
And heavy powerful chords

Широких спин і мускулястих тіл
З залізної клавіатури.
Залізо б'ють і гнуть прекрасну мідь
В горбатих м'язах руки чоловіка.
Як марш нечуваних століть,
Над землею гримить,
Над старою землею гримить
Будування висока музика.
І стогне степ,
          і стугонить країна,
Стальна запінена турбіна
Електростанцій вікових.
І рухається день, як верств одвічний здвиг,
І другий день уже чекає черги,
Бо кожен день—як вибух і як штурм,
Шалений марш напружень і енергій,
Салют,
          і сальва сурм,
             і виклик,
               і алярм.

РОЗМОВА СЕРДЕЦЬ

I

Труський, як лихоманка, дощ.
Осіння ніч, їдка та чорна.
І б'ється на квадратах площ
Людина й тінь її потворна.
Ідуть вони. Спокійні. Вдвох.
Плекають впевненість глибоку,
Що десь дано їм аркушик підлог,
Де вільно ставити
          крапки сухого кроку
І не боятися
          крапок над власним «і,»
Писать собі, читать собі свій вирок,
В брудний конверт
          брудних кватирок

Created by broad shoulders and muscular bodies
Roll from the iron keyboard.
The iron is beaten, the beautiful brass bent
In the rolling muscles of men's arms.
Like a march of never-before-heard centuries
The great music of construction
Thunders above the earth,
Above the old earth.
And the steppe groans,
           and the country rumbles,
Like the frothy steel turbine
Of everlasting electrical stations.
The day moves on, like a passed mile stone,
And already another day awaits its turn,
Because every day is like an explosion and onslaught,
A frenzied march of exertion and energy,
Of salutes,
      bugle calls,
           challenges,
              and alarms.

Translated by Myroslav Shkandrij

HEART-TO-HEART CONVERSATION

The rain comes burning down, on an acid
Autumn night, like black pitch.
A human figure dances with its ugly shadow
Punching across the squares of a chessboard
Each brooding on a deep conviction
That somewhere lies a naked floor
Inviting them to stamp
              their dry steps down
Fearless dots
        On top of "i's,"
To write, to read one's own verdict
While the filthy envelopes
             of dirty windows

Сховавши свідчення свої.
В смердючому, в плескатом конверті
Заховано слова дрібних тремтінь та мук.
І пані Вічності, шановний пані Смерті
Заадресовано до їхніх власних рук.
І так лежать листи,
                        життя малі цидулки,
І руситься над площами сльота,
І розбігаються в усі кінці провулки,
Немов рядкипредсмертного листа.
Я теж іду.
                        І ось уже я вдома:
Хрещатик, № 50.
Я зупинився. Постать невідома
Заходить теж сюди
                        і не верта назад.

На сходах пахне цвіль і сеча,
І купи тьми гниють в кутку.
А я несу на утлих плечах,
Як чадну лампу, голову важку,
І серця виссаний кавалок,
І тіло втомлене своє,—
І наді мною дім встає,
Мов божевільний катафалок.
На нього мовчки і без руху
Кладеться поверхів труна,
І гостро колеться на скалки тишина,
Струмком тонким снується біля вуха.
Всі двері замкнено.
                        Опущено фіранки.
У скриню запхнуто злигодну тишу й мир.
І на шнурку метляється пухир
Налитоїріденьким світлом склянки.
По сходах щойно хтось пройшов,
Бо чую судорожний подих,
І шамотню широких підошов,
І як шуршить об стінку одяг.

Hide their testimonies.
Those flat stinking envelopes
Preserve the quivering words of torture,
Addressed to Lady Eternity, Dear Lady Death.
Letters that bear witness to a single life,
Scribbles that dance like raindrops
Drizzling over the squares,
Lanes that scatter about in disguise,
The lines of the letter being marked by death.
I keep on walking.
      I am home, at last:
Khreshchatyk, number fifty.
I come to halt. An unfamiliar figure
Shadows me into the vestibule.

The stairs smell of mold and piss,
Darkness is rotting in the corner.
Full of smoky heavy thoughts
I drag my head on sloped, tired shoulders.
Heart like ground meat, body wasted.
Arching over me
The building lifts like a maddening hearse.
The floors, immobile and silent coffins,
Are stacked on top of one another,
And silence shatters into tiny shards,
Its fragile stream rushes by my ears.
Doors are locked and curtains are drawn.
A chest stuffed with wretched silence and peace.
A bubble filled with liquid light
Dangling on a cord.

Someone has climbed the stairs:
Convulsive breath and the rustle of soles,
The sound of clothes rubbing the wall.

Якийсь підпилий шалапут,
Бо для відвідин пізно доста!
І раптом зворухнувсь,
           ожив холодний кут,
І вийшла звідти темна постать.
І бачу я туманний обрис тільця,
Що з закутка ступило наперед,
І через тільце—чорні бильця,
Іржавий сходів парапет.

II

Стоїть, зіпершися на трость,
В старенькім синім віцмундирі …
—Чого вам треба, ваша мосць,
В моїй неприбраній квартирі?
І поповзли дві п'явки брів,
І два шматки м'якого м'яса
Проплямкали пробачливу гримасу,
Нужденну посмішку й привітних пару слів.
І то ж: не сни химерні сняться,—
Вони відснилися сливе,—
І вир яких галюцинацій
Сухі клітинки мозку рве?
Я запитав:
          —Ви хто такий,
Що стурбували супокій?
Чи то не вас на вулиці я стрів?
Чому ви не спите,
              і хто вас пробудив?
—Ночі сухі. Сни сухі.
В петлях вулиць заплутався крок,
За які гріхи,
         за чиї гріхи
Мені серця дано шматок?
Воно задихнулось,
            воно звиса,
І слина тече з язика.
Так кров'яна дешева ковбаса
Шкварчить на блюді кабака.
Великий,

A wasted brat I bet, since
It's too late for house calls!
The freezing corner comes to life,
The shadow steps to the fore,
Murky silhouette of a phantom
Steps from the dusty corner.
The body leans against the railing,
The rusty balustrade of stairs.

II

He leans on a cane in his old blue
Frock coat—How can I help you sir,
In my untidy home?
Two brows like leeches rise,
Two pieces of soft flesh
Grimace back apologies,
Friendly words forced through a smile.
These aren't odd dreams or whimsies,
They have dissipated one by one.
A vortex of hallucinations seems
To make my brain cells explode. I asked,
         —Who are you, in fact?
And why disturb my quiet night?
Didn't I just meet you on the street?
Why aren't you asleep?
Who woke you up?
—Dry nights, my dreams are dry.
My steps get lost in a maze of streets.
What sins, whose sins am I paying for
With a morsel of my heart?
It is limp
         And hanging.
Saliva drips from a tongue.
Cheap blood sausage is sizzling
On a pub's hot plate.
A giant,

величний,
                    російський кабак
І розжоване серце моє!
Синя габа, від петлі габа
На серці у кожного є.
Кожен серце кричуще своє розіп'яв
На столах кабаків,
                    на хрестах перехресть,
І ніхто не закрив,
                         і ніхто не сховав
Язви велику честь.
Язва віків,
            язва століть,
Благословенна язва та
На тому ж небі процвіта,
Де й п'ятикутний знак горить ...
—Ти брешеш, тінь,
                    ти брешеш, тінь!
І гниль із слів твоїх тече!
Наш день, що знявсь у височінь,
Не на твоє зіперсь плече.
І язв твоїх беркі герби
З сердець здирали ми.
Віддали кабаків доми
На самосуд юрби.
Ішла юрба, моя юрба,
Не бруком—по серцях!
Розбито впень, ущент, упрах
Великий твій кабак.
І марно намагався ти
Ховать свої герби.

Ламали людям ми горби,
Щоб вирівнять хребти.
Коли ж зламався, то впади
І серце з рук роняй.
Ми звикли з'єднувать ряди,
Бійців лічить щодня,
І нести серце, як трофей,

majestic,
        Russian pub,
And my chewed-up heart!
Blue trace of a noose
Adorns the edge of every heart.
All screaming hearts
Are crucified on the tables of a pub.
And nobody hides or heals
Sores of honor.
Sores of centuries,
        Sores of epochs.
Blessed be the sores
That flower in the sky,
The sky that holds
A blazing, five-pointed star …
—Shadow, you are lying,
        Shadow, you are lying,
The rot drips from your words!
Our sun stands high, it does not lean
On shadow's shoulder.
Eager signs of sores we tore
From our hearts.
We gave the corner pubs
To crowds. And then those crowds
Walked on our hearts, instead of cobbles!
Your giant pub is utterly smashed,
And your attempt to hide the signs
Was useless. Instead, we broke
the humpbacks of our comrades
To straighten out their vertebrae.
Once you are broken, take a fall,
And drop that heart.
We take apart and close
The rows with fallen soldiers. All
Of us carry the trophy of the heart

Порубаний в боях,
Як славний стяг, почесний стяг,
Цей знак живих людей,
Знак вітру, бурі й зненавид,
Вогню й заліза гордий слід ...

III

—Б'єте в громохкий барабан,
У барабан із людських шкір!
В людей замало в серці ран,
Зате багато дір.
І то не вітер—протяг то
В грудях людей свистить.
Не змиє і не змив ніхто
Клейна з людських лахміть ...
—Клену і рву твоє клейно!
—Не рви, бо я—то ти,
Бо ти і я—
            завжди одно,
І нам у парі йти.
І тінь моя країною бреде,
Столика тінь оця,
І не зустріла ще ніде
Зачинені серця ...
Я на банкет безумства й глупства
Несу в кишені серце й карт
Колоду повну.
                Милий жарт,
Дотепніший за самогубство!
І в кабаках землі веду одчайну гру,
Як божевільно п'яний банкомет.
І трьох партнерів я собі беру:
То вбивця, шлюха і поет.
І карти кидаю з руки
На лишаї процвілі столика,
І ніч розлазиться в боки,
Мов чорні вени в серці алкоголіка.

A banner crushed in combat.
Sign of the human race, banner
Of wind, of storm, of hatred,
Of iron and fire, a proud trace …

III

—You strike a thundering drum,
Made of human skin!
Humans have fewer wounds,
But plenty of ugly tears.
A draft, not wind
Whistles inside a chest.
None will, or have erased
The trademark from filthy rags.
—I curse and tear your filthy trademark!
—Don't curse, since I am you.
Since you and I are always one,
We walk as a couple, too.
My shadow drags itself from pole
To pole like a cunning explorer.
It never met, not once,
A heart that was closed …
To the feast of madness and stupid acts,
I brought my heart and a deck of cards.
                              What a lovely joke,
Wittier than a suicide!
In the pubs of the world I desperately gamble
As if a mad and drunken croupier.
I take three partners for myself:
A murderer, a poet, and a hooker.
I shoot the cards on the moldy surface,
The night spreads out to the sides,
Like black veins in a drunkard's heart.

І вбивця перший робить знак,—
Стиснув у руку похололу,
Мов круглу рану, мідяний п'ятак,
І ми згинаємось до столу.
Повія в банк для гри дарунок,
Мов перстень, здерши з губ, дає—
Дання невитворне своє:
Смердючий шлюхи поцілунок.
Поет блідий сидить між нами,
За столиком, на самому краю,
І частку сплачує свою
Дешевими й фальшивими словами.
Зім'явши серце в довгих пальцях,
Найбагатіший я між них ...
О, серце,
            серце,
                    не печалься;
На ешафот столів брудних
Кладу тебе, нічну офіру,
Серед вселюдського трактиру,
І граю партію свою,
І програю,
            і завше програю ...
Лишаю серце на столі,
Нехай лежить у бруді плазма.
Усі вітри землі,
                всі подихи землі,
Немов натхнень надлюдських спазма,
Стискають горло, в груди б'ють,
І ніч кінчається,
                й мені лисніє путь ...
Але не знаю я, куди тепер іти,
Коли у грудях цупко—тиша,
І бідне серце—бідна миша
Не прогриза тупі кути ...
Й не треба знати!
        Я пройшов
Багато кабаків,

The murderer sends a signal first
By squeezing the round wound of a penny.
We fold ourselves over the table.
The hooker bets with the gift of a kiss,
A stinky ring she rips off her mouth.
The poet, pale, sits on the edge
Of a table, and pays his part
With a cheap deck of phony words.
My crumbled heart
Is squeezed between long fingers,
And I am the richest one in this gang …
Oh heart,
  My heart,
    Don't be sad;
On the gallows of dirty tables
I place you, nocturnal sacrifice,
In the midst of the human farce.
I play a round,
    And I always lose …
My heart is sitting on a table—
I let the plasma lie in the dirt.
All winds on the surface of the earth,
Spasms of superhuman inspirations,
Hold my throat in a convulsive twist,
And beat my chest.
The night is almost over,
    And my path is glistening …
But where will I go?
My chest is tight and silent,
My poor heart—a poor mouse,
Cannot gnaw through an obtuse angle …
No need to know!
    I passed through
Many pubs,

і більше ще церков
І цвинтарів країн.
Ніде нічого не знайшов,
Крім серць пощерблених, і звихнутих голов,
І зігнутих колін.
А я шукав (чи то верзеться?)
І слів, і женщин, і уяв,
Лише одного не шукав:
—загубленого серця.
І під сльоту нічних хвилинок,
Серед брудного кабака,
Не простягав, як руку жебрака,
Незграбний серця втинок.
Благословенна кішл імла
І сухоребрих стін осуга!
Худа печаль і довга туга,
Мов потопельник, пропливла.
Але приходять рівні ранки,
Часи уважності, години самоти,
І потрясаєш тіло ти,
Машинко лихоманки!
І подаєш до герцю знак ти,
І марширують по мені
Упевнені, нахабні і нудні,
Твої прокляті такти.
І я тебе не переможу
Ніяк, ніколи і ніде ...
І серце в путь мене веде,
І я не йти—не можу ...

IV

Він замовчав,
і губи труться білі,
І очі розкрива, мов вікна зачапілі,
І чоловічок, наче чоловік,
Зіперся на лутки запалених повік,
Як гострий орден в грудь худу,
Вчепилась лампа в тьму.

churches, markets,
And graveyards of countries.
I found nothing,
Apart from ruined hearts, twisted
                              Conversations,
And folded knees.
I searched for (am I blabbering?)
Words, *femmes*, and dreams,
But not my lost heart, it seems.
Under the slush of nighttime minutes,
In the filthy pub,
Unlike a lonely beggar,
I have not stretched my hand,
Clumsily holding onto my torn heart.
Let the fuzzy haze be blessed,
The dry bones of walls be tainted!
Emaciated sadness and prolonged anguish
Float by, like a drowned body.
When even mornings come along,
Those focused lonely hours—
The fevered engine shakes the body!
Your signal calls me out to fight,
Your arrogant, dull,
And confident measures
March over me ... damnation!
I won't prevail,
Not here, not now, no way ...
My heart leads me down a path,
I can't refuse ...

IV

Silent he has become,
His white lips mumbling,
His eyes open, like chilly windows.
The pupil, as if a human being,
Is leaning over the closed shutters of eyelids.
The lamp's light pierces the darkness,
Like a sharp medal—through a meagre chest.

Я в очі зазирну йому
І одійду.
І зникне час, і буде тиша
Шукати, де лягти …
—То тінь твоя
                        за тінь хреста святіша?
А що нам хрест,
                i що нам ти?
На смітниках чужих
                твоя сконала Русь
Собакою голодною й худою.
Юродивий твій пристав—Іісус
В вінку з шипшин
                        не стане наді мною.
Святий городовик
                i пристав нищих душ,
Цей лицемірний бог
                        Распутіна й Малюти,
Мене не подола,
                за ним я не піду
В його нудний участок для покути.
І я знущаюся, глузую і сміюсь
Із цього сторожа смиренності й моралі,
З наглядача тюрми, що ви її назвали
Струнким і ясним словом—Русь.
Мені не храм—
                бордель твій і трактир,
Запльовані столи—
                мені не сповідальні,
Ненавистні мені
                акафісти печальні,
Насадні молитви
                твоїх холопських вір.
Тримай же серця випнуту ґилу
Безсилими і хтивими руками,
Як синій жмут кишок,

I'll look into his eyes and walk away.
Time evaporates, and silence
Is looking for a place to rest …
—So your shadow is holier
               Than the shadow of a cross?
And what's the point in a cross
Or in your distress?
In foreign dumps, like a starving dog,
Your Rus' expired.
Your bailiff, holy fool Jesus
Won't hover over me in a wreath of dog-roses.
Holy policeman
And the bailiff of miserable souls,
The angry lord of Malyuta[1] and Rasputin,[2]
Won't prevail over me.
I won't follow him
Into a dull penitential jail.
I mock, ridicule, and laugh
At the custodian of humility and ethics.
The prison guard christened with the neat
Transparent word—Rus'.
Your brothel and your pub—
          For me are not a temple;
The filthy tables—
          Not my confessionals.
How I abhor
          Your sad akathist hymns,[3]
Fake prayers
          Of your laymen's faith.
Hold your heart's protruding form
In your powerless and lustful hands!
You drag your ugly, rotten shadow,
          beneath your feet,

---

1 Malyuta Skuratov (d. 1573) was one of the notorious leaders of *oprichnina*, a state policy implemented during the reign of Ivan the Terrible between 1565 and 1572. The policy included mass repression of the *boyars* (the Russian aristocracy), public executions, and confiscation of property.
2 Grigorii Rasputin (1869–1916) was a Russian mystic and self-proclaimed healer, who gained considerable, yet controversial, influence on the family of Tsar Nicolas II.
3 *Akathist* (from Greek "not seated") is a type of hymn recited by Eastern Orthodox Christians. It is dedicated to the holy event or Holy Trinity and is an important part of Easter services.

тягай попід ногами
Потворну тінь свою,
потворну і гнилу.
І всі слова твої—
то шорох тих інерцій,
Що зсовують серця людей набік,
Тому влютовуєм ми в ребра кожне серце,—
Так цвях вганя в будівлю будівник.
Ти кажеш, що я твій, а я клянусь—
готовий
Дволике серце розламать навпіл
І дати псам напитися із жил,
Коли є крапля там
твоєї злої крови.
Я знаю—ти живий,
я знаю—ти не здох;
Кричу,
кричу тобі я:
доки
Ще шкутильгатимуть лякливо кривобокі
Серця людські по трьох сажнях підлог,
В тинькованій труні, в коробочці труни,
Ковтаючи слова горлянками вузькими?
І дикі, як одчай, припадки тишини,
Ці діри в вічність, ломляться, під ними.
І клоччям котиться із уст і піт, і слизь,
Із уст, що випнулись глибоким, чорним колом ...
І зашморгом шляхи всі заплелись
Оцим христосикам, хлистам і богомолам.
Столоначальники, убивці, сутенерики,
Раби раба і служники слуги,
Сини російської великої істерики
І всеросійської великої нудьги,
Всесвітнє падло і вселюдська гнусь,
Здихайте у своїй зачиненій конурі!
Повстала у вогні, в пожежі, герці й бурі
Вкраїна інша й інша Русь ...
І що,
і що тепер мені
Твій зойк, твій біль і зненавида?

Like a bunch of blue bloodless guts.
All your words are but a rustle of inertia
Displacing people's hearts.
Every heart squashed into the ribs—
Like a nail hammered in a house.
You claim that I am yours, and swear to god—I am ready
To break your traitor's heart in two, and throw it
To the dogs, to drink the evil blood,
If there is a drop
               Of your evil blood in there.
I know—you are alive,
               I know—that you did not bite the dust,
I scream and scream at you:
               How long
Will the hunched hearts be limping, terrified,
On three-foot floors,
Pitiful coffin of a home,
Cramming words down narrow throats?
The wild, desperate, and convulsive silence,
a black hole into eternity, will break under their feet.
Sweat and mucus gush from their mouths,
Bulging like deep black circles …
All roads tied like a noose
For those little jesuses, *khlysty*,[4] and preachers.
Placemen, murderers, and pimps,
Slaves of a slave and servants of a servant,
Sons of Russian grand hysteria,
Of pan-Russian worldwide *ennui.*
You—universal, all-human hyena,
Expire in a closed kennel!
She raises up in a fire and storm, challenged,
A different Ukraine and a different Rus′ …
What on earth is the use
Of all your screams, pain, and hatred?
The lamp's radiance walks by in silence,

---

4   *Khlysty* (Russian; singular, *khlyst*) was an underground sect that split from the Russian
     Orthodox Church in the mid-seventeenth century and whose representatives were known
     for ascetic and ecstatic rituals.

І мево лампи, як сновида,
Пройшло повз мене в тишині.
І було чути, як парує вільгість,
І випар тьми, мов тінь густа, застиг,
Тлетворна тінь, де сіпається тільки
Скажений живчик на кістках сухих.
Не заховає хижа тьма
Відблиска глухої муки,
І Достоєвський сухорукий
Горбатий лоб, як брилу, підійма.
І мружаться, мов ласі звірі, вилиці
І рот слова несказані жує ...
Серце,
        тихе серце моє,—
Той помививсь, хто не милиться.
Тож хай сьогодні швидше буде вчора,
І в двері хай твої не стука гість нічний ...
Як штопор, в горло коридора
Вкрутився протяг довгий і в'юнкий.
Шарпнувшись, тіні стали строго
В чіткі і правильні ряди,
І темний круг ...
                Вдивившися туди,
Я не побачив там нікого,
Лиш пліснява полізла по стіні,
Де звикла з року в рік тулитись.
Спинялись,—не могли спинитись
Дрібненькі хвилі маячні.
Але все стало просте й звичне:
Пошарпана підлога і стіна,
І лампа на стіні, й простора тишина,
І водогону стукання ритмічне.
І кожен стук—життя міцного знак,
Життя земного, простого, як подих.
І серце так мені сказало: «Так»,
І вітер шелестів по сходах ...

Like a somnambular.
One can hear the moisture of the steam
And how the vapor of darkness
Congeals into a shadow.
The awakened shadow dances
On the bones.
Hideous darkness
Cannot conceal the glow of dull anguish.
And Dostoyevsky with his withered arms,
Lifts his humped forehead like a boulder.
His temples wink like ardent animals,
His mouth chews unspoken words ...
Heart,
    My quiet heart,—
The one who thinks himself infallible,
Has fallen.
So let today turn into yesterday,
And let no night guests come knocking at your door ...
The long and crawling draft
Is stuck in the corridor's throat, like a corkscrew.
The jolted shadows organize themselves
Into neat and proper lines,
And staring
    At the dark corner,
I saw no one,
Only mold creeping up the wall,
Where it gathers year after year.
The minute waves of delirium
Were about to cease but never did.
Yet everything became so habitually simple:
A battered floor, a lamp
On the wall, and spacious silence,
The rhythmic gurgle of the water pipe.
Every beat is a sign of life's enduring cares,
It's down to earth and simple, like a breath.
My heart said to itself, "O yes."
The wind kept whispering on the stairs ...

Translated by Oksana Rosenblum and Jon Frankel

Short Poems (1923–1927)

Translators' Essay

Just a Trick, Just a Flip

OSTAP KIN, AINSLEY MORSE, AND MYKYTA TYSHCHENKO

L ike most Futurists early in their career, Mykola Bazhan wanted to impress right away—his pen name Nik Bazhan is an immediate testimony to this ambition. The traditional Ukrainian name Mykola converts into the snappy, Western-style pen name Nik—superfluous letters are dropped, and a brand-new sound acquired. This kind of energetic play with the sound and appearance of words—and of the poem on the page more broadly—is characteristic of the following selection of five early poems, which Bazhan wrote between the ages of nineteen and twenty-three.

Thematically, these poems cover the gamut from somewhat Brutalist agit-prop commentary on current events, to fantastical, cavorting "beyonsense,"[1] and even—surprisingly—melancholy lyricism ("Elegy for Circus Attractions"). This trajectory seems entirely in step with the times. The earliest, most youthful poems come on the heels of the recent civil war and the ongoing struggle to establish Bolshevik rule in Russia and neighboring countries and assert the new state's interests abroad. They are full of swashbuckling bravado and the heady haze of bold military action:

---

1 This is Paul Schmidt's translation of *zaum*, the Futurist neologism that refers to invented language that reaches "beyond the mind" (*za um*). See Schmidt, *The King of Time. Selected Writings of the Russian Futurian*, ed. Charlotte Douglas and trans. Paul Schmidt (Cambridge, MA: Harvard University Press, 1985), 3.

THE HEART IS A BROWNING

loose

    from its holster!

Closer your ranks,

ranks closer!

Stinnes:

    y'hear?

It's breathing

this mass of barricades.

Can't stop 'em,

step—not shriek

into this chain of chests.

        Clang go the swords of

        October.

Bazhan mobilizes violent military imagery in three poems that are, unlike similarly phrased Civil War poetry, not actually about wartime battlefields. Rather, he uses martial rhetoric to express support for the German people's passive resistance to the French occupation of the Ruhr/Rhine territories, on the one hand, and more generally to promote the struggle to build socialism and fend off its enemies.[2] The (military) march was the music of the age, and it drives poems like the above-cited "Zurma Swarm" (a reference to a trumpet-like Ukrainian folk instrument), "Ruhr-March" and "Aero-March." Indeed, "Aero-March" combines stirring military rhythms with a direct call for contributions in its last lines: "did you contribute/to the cause of the Red Fleet?"

    Some of the more overtly Futurist poems that we translated for this selection demonstrate Bazhan's eccentric and radical ideas about composition and ideas, while exposing the influence of senior contemporary poets. The included, of course, Vladimir Mayakovsky, the self-appointed loudspeaker of revolutionary poetry.[3] It is important, however, to note the significance of Bazhan working with both this brash Futurist aesthetic and the bold, warlike rhetoric in Ukrainian. While Mayakovsky's poems were known all over the

---

2   The background for the references to the Ruhr in Bazhan's poems was the 1923 French occupation of the German coal- and steel-production region based in the Rhine/Ruhr river valleys (southwest Germany), in response to Germany's failure to pay the reparations to France that were stipulated in the Treaty of Versailles.

3   See, in this volume, Lavochkina's note and Babak's introduction for a more detailed account of the Ukrainian Futurist scene Bazhan was a part of during this time.

vast Soviet Union in Russian, Bazhan had a necessarily more intimate relationship with his readership. One imagines that the Donbas coal basins and Ukraine's general proximity to Europe made Bazhan's fiery support of the German miners' resistance more sincerely than the same sentiment in the hands of the Moscow-based poet.

Bazhan's virtuosic play with the sounds and shapes of his native tongue is particularly evident in this selection's wackiest poem "Circus." Dated to just a year after the agit-prop poems of 1924, it bears no trace of the "Red October" rhetoric, instead diving headlong into a faintly absurdist tour de force that magnificently embodies the topsy-turvy acrobatics of a high-wire act:

I will grunt like a checkered racer
at the crumpled balls of newspaper.
                    JUST A TRICK.
                    JUST A FLIP.

        a hiccup
                    coocoos
                                    drop by drop
                    into a firework
        dusk.
                    full stop
                                    like a painful torment
        further
                    DEATH.
                    HIP.

As evident even in this short excerpt, this complicated poem has a dark undercurrent running alongside the maniacally cheerful contortions of bodies and syntax: the "painful torment" and "DEATH" that will reemerge at the end, after the bright, bold "hip-hip-hoorays!" have faded into the background. Perhaps this is where we can see a tenuous connection between the struggling, bloodlashed rhetoric of Bazhan's agitational poems and the manic play of typically NEP-themed pieces like "Circus."[4]

---

4   NEP, the New Economic Policy, was a modified form of state capitalism introduced in 1921 as a means of restoring the economy following the devastations of the Civil War. Culturally, the NEP period was a sort of Soviet "roaring twenties," a time of carnivalesque, youthful aesthetics.

The final poem in our selection, "Elegy for Circus Attractions" is the latest (1927) and best-known of the five—children still read it in Ukrainian schools. While it does continue the circus theme, the poem is radically different in terms of form and overall tone. As we might expect, given its title, we are given a poem deeply mired in an elegiac mode. Mournful, regretful, even bitter, it is, however, elevated by the stark beauty of the vivid and intricate images: "the fluttery fuss of a flute/in the gutter of voices flowing"; "a gallop as dry as a drumroll." The greater formal regularity of the poem, with its neat stanzas and regular rhymes, also acknowledges a kinship with prerevolutionary Symbolist and Romantic poetry. However, there are strong Expressionist elements here (consider the equally elegant, but grislier "dried-out joints of the heart/go on creaking midst ribs that are rusting"), and the neat stanzas of the poem's beginning only serve to emphasize the shocking collapse of stanzaic regularity around the middle of the poem. Even when the stanzas reemerge, the potential for the circus's unhinged madness to shade into something sinister (hinted at in "Circus") is fully realized here:

> The throat will warp into a hump,
> the scream will halt in place,
> when it hangs, like a flag, from the trapeze—
> the black tongue of human speech.

The hanging tongues of speech are given even further grisly development by the poem's last line, with the voices that started out flowing (albeit in a gutter) now "swinging like corpses on threads." From the perspective of a person looking back from a distant future, it's hard not to read this poem as an elegy for the antic, anarchic aesthetic freedom of the Soviet 1920s, which would shortly be reined in by the "cultural revolution" introduced (along with the collectivization of agriculture that would particularly devastate Ukraine), in 1928.

* * *

One of the many tricky aspects of this translation project was textological. As it turns out, a few of the poems were published only once (in a journal or literary supplement to a newspaper) during the poet's lifetime, or even after his death. And although Bazhan's body of work enjoyed attention from state-run publishers during the Soviet era, and his works appeared in various multivolume editions, the poems composed during his Futurist years were typically excluded from those collections. They therefore have long remained underread, if not wholly undiscovered, for a broader readership. Relatedly, we faced some of the typical problems of onetime newspaper publications: mysterious words or phrases that, in an inventive Futurist poet, might have been wildly creative neologisms, but actually turned out to just be typos.

Finally, a word about our translation process. Our team consisted of two native Ukrainian speakers with excellent English and one native English speaker with excellent Russian but zero Ukrainian. We thus literally triangulated our way through Bazhan's originals, which sometimes—given his inventive streak with language—kept all three of us guessing. In such cases we resorted to consulting the hive mind of Ukrainian-speaking Facebook users, with much-appreciated results.

Translator's Essay

The Elegance of Bazhan's Obscurity

SEÁN MONAGLE

Poetry is what is lost in translation; poetry is what survives translation: opposing views that can never, as matters of taste, be resolved. As a translator and one who loves poetry and reads it in translation, I can easily understand and sympathize with both views. As a translator, I recognize the elements of an original work that cannot be borne across the chasm between two languages. As a poet, however—as paradoxical as this may sound—I fully embrace the view that poetry is what survives translation. I acknowledge the impossible standards implied by the former view even as I begin my task with the hope, passion, excitement, and apparently inextinguishable naivety of one who gives credence to the latter one.

Anzhelika Khyzhnya, my cotranslator, and I began our work with the assumption that, for all its obscurity and difficulty, "Mene zelenykh nih" "means": it is not a verbal object in which sounds and hermetic images accumulate to form or "be" even partially a poem without regard for semantics. It is not "zaum." Our shared concern was to suggest, if we could not convey fully, the aural and visual richness of Mykola Bazhan's language and imagery, its musicality and vividness, sometimes making semantic accuracy a secondary value to do so, but only when absolutely necessary. On the one hand, we sought to make our version "mean" what the original meant; on the other, to endow it with the music, playfulness, darkness, and charm of the original.

Bilingual in Russian and Ukrainian, Anzhelika is also fluent in English; I am a native speaker of English and have some Russian, but no Ukrainian. To go from Ukrainian to English and back again, Russian thus served as our lingua franca on questions such as grammar or case, syntax or part of speech. The historical and cultural allusions and nuances of the original, of course, are of the Ukrainian of Bazhan's era; those of our translation must be in and of a contemporary American English.

Let me descend from this lofty level of generalization to offer an example of our work in the trenches. In the last two lines of the second stanza, the alliteration of the letter "l" in "Lie on the kilim,/lad of longing, ..." matches exactly that of the original. (The syntax, however, is not reproduced.) We were able to convey (as opposed to simply suggest) much of the semantic and aural qualities of the two lines. Yet in the two lines in their entirety a difficulty appears: the phrase "groves of the lagoons" (the elision of which above is marked by ellipses), which appears in apposition—but to what? It bears no grammatical connection to the preceding lines. It stands discrete, unconnected, as neither a metaphor nor a simile. It can only be a metonym—but of or to what? Which word or phrase? "Longing"? "Lad"? Or, most improbably, "kilim"? We were at a translator's crossroads, the signs there posing questions that would have to be answered: have we missed something? Do we interpolate a word or phrase here for an implied meaning? Do we allow the lacuna, apparently a deliberate one, as it appeared to us in the moment and consistently thereafter, to stand? We let it stand. Our decision was a leap, our best guess. Bazhan, we surmised, left the ambiguity in place in order to suggest manifold associations applicable possibly to both "longing" and "lad." Once seen, this deft and subtle device showed itself elsewhere. We were not imagining things. Readers of these lines in the original, we also reasonably surmised, would have been faced with the same conundrum.

Why the obscurity? I ask this question more as a poet than translator. (I am inveterately interested in questions of other poets' strategies and technique.) I speculate that Bazhan's obscurity counterbalances a certain patent bluntness, a bawdiness of treatment, yet lends to his theme of desire a certain gravitas. "[S]himmering shingles of waves," "groves of the lagoons" and "a ground coiling around a circle of pools" appear proximately in a poetic landscape of legs, lying down, dancers, moss, moans, hints of intoxication, and a skirt—even horror. Bazhan offers, to use T. S. Eliot's phrase, "objective correlatives" of desire, some explicit and undeniable, some remote yet unmistakably sensuous. They and the associations that they invoke are reinforced stylistically by the music and cadence of the lines, by alliteration and assonance, by the density of diction and the range of allusion.

I love the force and music, the panache and rigor of "Mene zelenykh nih." I love its demands on my attention and on that of any reader who senses a deep and broad understanding of the power of the erotic, one that is borne in on us forcefully, whose mystery remains.

СУРМА ЮРМ[1]

До травня
від октября
заряди Рейн
        Рур,
вибухом заради!
Серце—бравнінг
тра
            з кобур!
Міцніш ряди,
ряди міцніше!
Стінес:
            чуєш?
Дише
груда барикад
Не спиниш,
Крок—не крик
В грудей гряд.
        Брязка штин
            октября.
Коли шахт б'є серце на алярм,
коли серця чавунами розіллються,
        буде Німеччина—плацдарм
        всеєвропейських революцій.
        І щодня пульсує Роста
            про вибух, глиби бурь,
бо жде на аванпостах
            Майн, Рейн, Рур.
            Сотні, ваш крок, як гарт.
            З'єднуй ряд,
                Брат!
Перед Всесвітом наш парад
            вперед, вперед парад!
В криса кулю,
на бій набий мій.
Ні Штреземан, ні Мюллер

---

1   First published in *Zhovtnevyi zbirnyk panfuturystiv* (Kyiv: Golfstrom, 1923)—*Editors' note.*

ZURMA SWARM

Till May
from October
load the Rhine
    the Ruhr,
load it with **a blast**!
The heart is a Browning
loose
      from its holster!
Closer your ranks,
ranks closer!
Stinnes:
    y'hear?
It's breathing
this mass of barricades.
Can't stop 'em,
Step—not shriek
into this chain of chests.
       Clang go the swords of
       October.
When the hearts of the mines hark alarm,
when hearts flow like cast-iron oceans,
    all Germany will be the platform
    of all-European revolutions.
    And every day ROSTA is pulsing
    with explosions, the depths of drill bores,
for waiting there on the outposts
    are the Main, the Rhine, the Ruhr.
    O hundreds, your steps are like tempering.
    Brother,
    hold the line!
Our parade in the face of the Universe
    forward, forward, goes the line!
Load your bullets,
magazines ready for the melee.
Neither Stresemann nor Mueller

не видере скрегіт зубів.
Гриви пряде заграва,
в край грає Рейн.
СРСР—наша гавань,
Жовтень—наш рейд.
      Гасло
      гати
в мільйони голов ти—
      не згас
всесвітній Жовтень.
Революцій вгрузив вже
багряний на плечі німб
й не в сльозастій заклякнути жіжі
тобі, робітник Німеччини.
Залпом з трибуни
В шерег наруг:
Рур—
Комуна,
      Комуна—Рур!
Уст роз'ятрений кратер
гуркотом, гаком гук.
В дротах, димарях заграти
впряжем плавку югу.
І ніччю, коли домни сплять,
Шахти попече рев.
Похмура сурма юрм
ударить в броню черев.
До крови скроні здер це
крок криць Бессемера.
У вас в руді, під серцем
вібрує СРСР.
      СРСР:
      з ангара
      смерть.
      Вдар
      в дах,
лий в шахти сталеву ропу.
      Шахтар,

can bear the rasping of these teeth.
Manes winding in the glow.
The Rhine plays out to the end!
The USSR is our harbor,
October is our anchor.
    You hammered
    your motto
in a million heads—
    nothing could dampen
our universal October.
Heaved upon your shoulders
the revolution's bloody halo
to keep you, German workers,
out of this tearful mire.
A volley from the tribune
into the jeering ranks:
Ruhr—
is a Commune,
    the Commune is Ruhr!
The wounded crater of the mouth
The hook of its roaring and cries.
In the wires and the pipes of the blaze
we'll harness smelting to the mist.
And at night, when blast furnaces sleep,
our roar will scorch up the mines.
Zurma swarm, fully bleak
will hit hard on the armor of paunches
these steps of Bessemer steel
scratch your temples to the quick.
In the ore beneath your hearts
vibrates the USSR.
    The USSR:
    death
    from the hangar.
    Hit
    the roof,
fill the mineshafts with steel brine.
    Hey miners

руцокоп

з шахт!

Бути Руру новим Перекопом.

В пуп шлаку хмар

язик лез кинь.

Сталевий буде ангар

на Рейні й Шлезку.

Берліна морфій,

гарем, кабаре

захлнеться в Рейні

і встане

не

Людендорф і Пуанкаре—

ЛЕНІН.

1923

РУРА-МАРШ[2]

Селянин, червоноармієць і пролетар

Радянської землі.

Чи зустрінете ви цей удар

Знову напруженим: плі?

Так

Гарматами по бруку

Серця рев.

—Ради—не Рур,

—Пуанкаре!

Назад ні кроку!

Крис в руку.

Стій!

Б'є барабан тривогу,

Б'є барабан бій.

В ногу, арміє, в ногу,

Чи зойків злякаємось чиїх?

За нашого одного

— тисячу їх.

---

2   First published in the newspaper *Bil'shovyk*, May 17, 1923—*Editors' note.*

and diggers
        out of the mines!
The Ruhr will be a new Perekop.
        Toss your tongue blades deep
        into the dusty slag belly.
A steel hangar will rise
        on the Rhine and Śląsk.
        All Berlin's morphine,
        its cabarets and harems
        will fall into the Rhine
        while rising comes
            not
LUDENDORFF OR POINCARÉ—
                    LENIN.

Translated by Ostap Kin, Ainsley Morse, and Mykyta Tyshchenko

RUHR-MARCH

A peasant, a Red Army soldier and a proletarian
                of the Soviet land.
Would you meet this blow
                again at the ready: fire?
Yes.
    Like cannon fire against cobblestones
Is the heart's roar.
—The Reds are no Ruhr,
—Poincaré!
Don't give an inch!
Take up your rifles.
            Freeze!
Drums sound the alarm,
Drums tap a battle beat.
Move like one, army, like one,
Whose screams do we fear?
For each of ours
                —a thousand of their shrieks.

З робітничих рук
Не видерти кермо.
Ради—не Рур,
Керзон.
В наших руках—не бравнінг,
      —в наших руках молот,
Але силою з вами рівні,
Аж нас не збороли.
Наша відповідь: мавзери з кобур,
      Порох тримать сухим.
Ради—не Рур,
Слухайте—глухі!
Нас не злякають ноти
      Керзонів, Пуанкаре,
Червона Армія й Флота
      в карре!
Перед мільйоном червоних Рур
      фашизму язви замусляні.
      Ради—не Рур,
      Муссоліні.
Ми в чеканні,
      Хоч прагнемо помсти ми,
Бо постріл в Лозанні
Буде першим за фашистами.
      Ми напоготові.
      В бій—тортури
      Всі в одному слові.
Геть капіталізму мур.
      Ради—не Рур,
      Нас не руш.
Хоч в руках не меч—рало,
      Ради—не Рур,
      Генерал Фош!

1923

Our workers' hands
Won't give up the wheel.
The Reds are no Ruhr,
Curzon.
Our hands hold no Browning,
     —our hands hold a hammer,
Though your strength may equal ours,
We've never been overpowered.
In response we yank Mausers from holsters,
  We keep our powder dry.
The Reds are no Ruhr,
Listen up, hard of hearing!
We're not afraid of notes from
   the Curzons, Poincarés,
The Red Army and the Fleet
   are in formation!

In the face of millions of red Ruhrs
   the ulcers of fascism are still oozing.
   The Reds are no Ruhr,
   Mussolini.
We are waiting,
  Though we long for revenge,
for the fascists in Lausanne
will be first to shoot.
  We're ready.
  To go into battle—
  All tortures lie in that word.
Down with the wall of capitalism.
  The Reds are no Ruhr,
  Hands off us.
Though we may hold hoes in place of swords,
  The Reds are no Ruhr,
  General Foch!

Translated by Ostap Kin, Ainsley Morse, and Mykyta Tyshchenko

АЕРО-МАРШ[3]

Струнами
в кобзу хмар
ескадрільї Комуни.
На аероплан-пролетар!
Не в іграшки гратись:
капіталізму останній час настав
і з пожарища Федерацій
по небу скачки заграв.

Ні слова—роз'ятрений кратер
вріжте в єдиний лозунг
—брате,
з неба загроза нам
в небі
зграї ворожих птиць
і треба, всім треба, треба
спільним бажанням злитись.

Перепони на землі збороли—
лишився один бар'єр.
Хіба не викує наш молот
Мільярди ескадр ССРР?

Буде
Європа в огні,
коли червоних орлів принесе
східний вітер.

Ні.
Зі сходу революція гряде,
капітал у порох зітрем,
в майбутнє одчинимо браму.

Буде
Диктатура пролетарів в повітрі
Повітря—нам.

Загуде

---

3   We are not keeping the original orthography of this poem, which is slightly different from the orthographical rules of contemporary Ukrainian. For instance, "игрaшки" in the original becomes "іграшки." The layout of the Ukrainian printed text is preserved here. First published in the newspaper *Bil'shovyk*, July 21, 1923—*Editors' note*.

AERO-MARCH

Like strings
into the *kobza* of clouds
come the Commune squadrons.
Proletarians—to the aeroplanes!
We're not playing games here
the final hour of capitalism has come
and from the sputtering Federations
gallop horse races into the sky.
    Not mere words—our slogan's
    carved in like a rankling crater
                          —brother,
    this danger, it comes from the sky
the sky is full
of flocks of enemy birds
and we must, we all must, we must now
merge in our common desire.
    We overcame obstacles on earth—
    Only a single barrier remains.
    Won't we forge with our hammer
    billions of Soviet squadrons?
        Europe
    will lie in flames,
when red eagles swoop in on
                          an Eastern wind.
    No.
Revolution is rising in the East,
We will blow capital to bits,
will open a gate to the future.
    The air will
breathe the proletarian dictatorship
        this air—is for us.
            Hear

залізокутим рокотом
червоних ескадр поломеніючий
                               міст
і рознесуть багрові Фоккери
революцій сталеву вість.
А зараз з неба нам
повітроплави ворожі
не принесуть манни молебенів
божих.
Сталевою зливою бомб
затремтить земля.
Назустріч розпеченому грому
     пролетар—на аероплан.
     Стяг революцій триматимем
доки сурма повстань не заграє
     і в одповідь на ультиматума
ультиматумів зграя.
     На мільони миль
пропелерів побідний спів—
          це
червоні ескадрильї
селян і робітпків.
     Всі-одни.
Слова—мов оскард
          Де
Шерег аеро-ескадр?
     серце голоти
     єдиний лозунг стис—
          ти вніс
на користь Червоної Флоти?

1923

                    ✳✳✳4

Мене зелених ніг
Тіл тюль люля хміль.

---

4   First published in *Chervonyi shliakh* 1–2 (1924): 51—*Editors' note.*

the iron-edged roar
of the blazing bridge of red squadrons
    and crimson Fokkers will spread
the steely news of the revolution.
And now from the sky
the enemy airships
won't bring us manna and heavenly prayers.
A steely downpour of bombs
will set the earth shuddering.
Moving towards fiery thunder
    Proletarians—to the aero-planes.
    We will hold firm the revolution's flag
until the zurma of uprising blows
    and our answer to your ultimatum
    will be a flock of ultimatums.
    For millions of miles:
the victorious singing of propellers—
    these are
the red squadrons of
peasants and workers.
    All—are one.
  Words are like a pickaxe.
  Where's
the column of aero-squadrons?
    The poor masses' heart
      fit to burst from our slogan—
    did you contribute
to the cause of the Red Fleet?

Translated by Ostap Kin, Ainsley Morse, and Mykyta Tyshchenko

HOPS OF GREEN LEGS

The hops of green legs lull me,
of bodies, tulle.

О, хто зазирає ввечері на зорі
В хвиль сльотну толь?

Маг гамм втом—
Гілля хили чоло.
Лягай, гаї лагун
На килим, легінь лон.

О коло, локон лих
У голих ніг і мхів твоїх.
    Не келих хилить літо то—
        А плахту,
    не конопель стон—
        Жах туг—
      Тінь туг.
    Коло плеса оплетене тло
       Навкруг.
    Плахта там.

1924

ЦИРК[5]

СКОК
СКОК   ЕКСЦЕНТРИКИ
    перекувирк
    все-таки
    геть трико
НОГИ ВИЩЕ ГОЛОВИ.

 всякі секи тюкань
Карком втру.
 викли**К**аю тільки гру
 ТІЛ**ь**ки трюк.

---

5   First published in *Nova generatsiia* 3 (1927): 23–26—*Editors' note.*

O, one who eyes in the evening
the shimmering shingles of waves.

Magus of the gamuts and languor,
Bow your branches.
Lie on the kilim,
lad of longing,
groves of the lagoons.

O, circle, locks of sorrows,
There you are on bare legs,
on bare mosses.
It's not the goblet that summer tilts
but the skirt.
It's not the moans in the hemps—
there's horror of yearnings—
shade of yearnings.

A ground coiling around
a circle of pools.
There—a skirt.

Translated by Seán Monagle and Anzhelika Khyzhnya

CIRCUS

jump
      ACROBATS
jump
        upside down
        and anyway
        to hell with our tights
    HEELS ABOVE OUR HEADS.

        any milli-billi boo-rah
  My neck'll handle it.
        I declare it's just a game
        Just a trick.

з смерковим какаду
в трик-трак
прийду

без брюк
а так
ЦЕ ГРА
ЦЕ ТРЮК
не тік аттак.
вибрик,
карабкається вибрик
по линві на дах сердець.
теліпається душ колібрі
далеко десь.

ВИБРИК.

тільки вибрик
тільки ляльки ки - ки - мор.
пікантна весна, мов сир брі
і диктові жмихи з блох.

підтюпцем:

гоп - са - са
серце
лицаря
дзенькоти ляпаса
скоками
шпіцами
гикати, окати.
ЦЕ ШКІЦ?
ТАК.
в пики голих фей
блощицею брика матюк.
розкручений очкур галіфе.
сальто-мортале.
ТРЮК.

with a pitch-black cockatoo
    playing trictrac
here I come
no pants
        just like that
A GAME

A TRICK
        not a track-attack.

      a prank,
    a prank a clambering
take the tightrope to the hearts' roof
hummingbird of the soul dangling
far off.

   A PRANK.

    just a prank.
   just a raggle-taggle dolly.
the spring is piquant like brie cheese
with a plywood flatbread of fleas.

    at a jot trot
        hop—tsa—tsa
     heart
       of a knight
clatter of slaps
    through jumps
        over spires

hiccuping, oh-and-ah-ing.
        IS THIS A SKETCH?
YES.

into the muzzles of naked fairies
the swearing flings like a bedbug.
undid belt of peg-top trousers.
    flip flap.
        TRICK.

картатим скакуном захрюкаю
на скумливі шпальти.
ТІЛЬКИ ТРЮК.
ТІЛЬКИ САЛЬТО.
гикавка
капкою
кука
в фейєрверк
смерк.
крапка
як дика мука
Далі
СМЕРТЬ.

ГІП.
ляк
мук
душ
стек
цвях
в сміх
пик
джаз
зойк
спраг
кульш.
ніч
блідь
блим
зик.

ГІП.
СТОРЧ
канкан душ
випнутих душ кікапу
смерч
сій сміх
на лошачий скуйовджений круп.

I will grunt like a checkered racer
at the crumpled balls of newspaper.
        JUST A TRICK.
        JUST A FLIP.

    a hiccup
        coocoos
                drop by drop
  into a firework
dusk.
    full stop
             like a painful torment
further
    DEATH.
    HIP.
        fear
            tormented
                souls
     whip's
         nails
            to laughing
                mugs
   jazz
      squeal
         thirsty
             thighs.
   night's
      pale
        blink
            squeak.
  HIP.
  HEADLONG
souls' cancan
   a whirlwind
  of beaked Kikapu souls
  sow laughter
on the horse's disheveled mane.

сонця
      цяцьки цькуй
в гору втік хвіст
            я
ЦИБАТИЙ ЦВІРКУН
сонячноі кувиркноі гри.
         зойк
   стій пропелер
   махаон дум
            ОЙ
пне крізь пельку
лякливий какаду.
душу шкереберть
серце нічичирк.
            ЦЕ
               ЦИРК
                  ТАМ

СМЕРТЬ.
1924

      mock
    the sun's tchotchkes
  the tail takes off up
       I
A LONG-LEGGED LOCUST
in this sunny somersaulting game.
      squeal
    stop propeller
     thoughts' butterfly
      OH!
a timid cockatoo
presses an upside-down
soul through the throat
heart's silent.
      THIS
          CIRCUS
            THERE'S
DEATH.

Translated by Ostap Kin, Ainsley Morse, and Mykyta Tyshchenko

Long Poems (1929)

ГОФМАНОВА НІЧ

По рубаних щаблях—
    в провалля, в яму, в тьму,
По рубаних щаблях, по сходах обважнілих
І по обвислих, висклизаних схилах—
В брухатий льох, в забрьохану корчму.
В корчму без вивіски, без назви і наймення,
В корчму скажених бюргерів, голодних волоцюг,
В корчму фантастів, візників і шлюх,
В корчму огидного й ганебного натхнення.
Роззявилась вона, закопана в землі,
Мов кислий рот п'яниць, де, наче зуби трухлі,
Стирчать свічки, ллючи жовтавий лій
На стіл дубовий і дебелі кухлі.
Мов кулаки бубняві й круглі,
Мов яблука важкі, плоди добра і зла,
Лежать на випнутих на кремезних столах
Наллятi оливом, вином і лоєм кухлі.
Скриплять, вискрипують, вилискують столи,
Вином закаляні і пальцями залапані.
Смердючий лій шкварчить в окапинах,
Що зі свічок поволі попливли.
Поважно правиться затаєний обряд
Бенкетів виспреніх, замислених пиятик,
Де кожен із п'яниць—філософ і фанатик,
Сновида й брат, Серапіонів брат.

Тут тисячі годин, тут тисячг ночей
Регоче й п'є єхидний Амадей,
Поет злих слів і вигадок свавільних,
Король нічних, врочисто божевільних
І похоронних асамблей.
Ось він сидить, цей куций Мефістофель,
Недобрих учт похмурий бенкетар.
Ах, що йому до жінчинин пантофель,
Врядовницьких чинів, і ордерів, і чвар!
Ковтає мовчки дим, вино слизьке і слину,

HOFFMANN'S NIGHT

Down the steps,
Into the abyss, pitch-dark pit,
Down the hewn steps of a heavy staircase,
On slippery, bedraggled railing,
Into the teeming larder of a filthy tavern
Without a sign or name.
Into the inn of city madmen, hungry hobos,
Of coachmen, fantasists and whores
Of sickening, repulsive inspiration.

It's gaping open, dug into the ground,
It's like a drunkard's rancid mouth, where, like decaying teeth,
Candles stick out, and yellow tallow pours
Upon an oaken table and buxom beer mugs.

Like round bloated fists,
Like heavy apples, fruit of good and evil,
The massive tables bulge, overcharged
With brimful jars of oil, wine and suet.
The tables squeak and screech and gloss,
Stained by the wine and grubby fingers.
The stinking tallow sizzles,
And oozes down from the candle stems.

A secret rite is being meticulously carried out—
A pompous banquet, wistful spree,
And each of those drunks, a sage, a devotee,
Soothsayer, monk, Serapion's brother.

It's here that for thousands of hours and thousands of nights
The spiteful Amadeus drinks and guffaws,
The poet of impish words and wayward pranks,
The king of solemn, brazen
Funereal confabs.

And here he sits, the petty Mephistopheles,
The gloomy master of malicious feasts.
What does he care for domestic life,
For squabbles, titles, ranks, intrigues!
He swallows smoke and spit and oily wine,

Мовчить, і дивиться, і гне свою живу,
Загострену, мов голий нерв, брову,
Неначе сласний кіт худу і хтиву спину.
То ж він—гігантський кіт, улесливо солодкий,
То ж він—замучений уявою маньяк,
В гурті розпутників, поетів і кривляк
Сидить з лицем диявола й девотки.
То ж він—гігантський кіт, добрячий котик Мур
То ж він гне спину й випускае кігті
І тут, в сліпій корчмі й в нуднім камергерихті,
У веремгі кішл, у млі магістратур.
Театр потвор, театр п'яниць-калік,
Він одкривається для мрійника й фантаста,
Й презирливо брова згинається зубчаста,
І в ясна б'є розбещений язик:
—Не п'яний я! Мов смертник той, я щедрий !
Хазяїне, свічок! Хазяїне, вогню!
Хазяїне, вина! Нам цукру, спирту й цедри ...
Віват, поезіє! Так випиймо ж за ню!
Підпалюй спирт! Святе аутодафе,
Де спирт пала, мов християнські душі ...
Кричіть, захоплені кликуші,
В берлінському блюзнірському кафе!

Шумує грайний пунш, і майорять огні
Блакитні язички підплигують угору
В лункім, як черево, блискучім казані
—Панове, пуншу Теодору!
Натхнення й істина в вині ...—
І наче ватра тайних інквизицій—
Холодна заграва гарячого вина.
—Так що ж, черпаймо з казана,
З товстого казана пекельної водиці!

Парують і шумлять отруйні пугарі,
І вогники стоять, як пальці сяйні й сині,
А над людьми кружляють угорі
І діри в тьмі, і дим, і тіні.

His eyebrow sharpened, a raw nerve,
Like a lascivious cat, his thin voluptuous spine.
He is a giant cat, palaver-treacly,
He is a maniac weighed down by his dream,
Surrounded by lechers, poets, clowns,
He sits there, Janus-faced: a devil and a nun.

He is a giant cat, a well-fed Tomcat Murr,
He arches his back and draws his talons out
Here, in this blind tavern, in boring chambers,
And in the anthills of the magistrate courts,
The theater of freaks and drunken cripples—
The curtain rises here for dreamers, fantasists,
The rigged eyebrow arches in derision,
The gums are cudgeled by the shameless tongue.
"But I'm not drunk! My heart is big, like a death row inmate's!
Host, fetch more candles! Give me fire!
Pour us more wine! Bring sugar, spirit, lemon zest …
All-hail to poetry! Let's drink to Her!
Set booze on fire! The sacred act of faith,
Where spirit burns like Christian souls …
Yell, holler, zealous firebrands
In this blasphemous Berlin tavern!"

The punch bowl fizzes, fire flickers,
Blue tongues of flame leap up—
The shiny echo of the cauldron.
"Hey gentlemen, more punch for Theodor!
In vino veritas, in vino inspiration …"

Like bonfires of secret Inquisition—
The cold flare of the boiling wine.
"Let's ladle from the bowl,
The thick-walled cauldron of infernal water!"

The toxic glasses steam and jangle,
The fire spreads like shining bluish thumbs,
Over the people, high above
Holes whirl in darkness, smoke and shadows.

Розплившися, пливуть в його уяві хворій
Червоні ліхтарі зашарених облич;
Підносяться шляхетні шпаги свіч;
Рушає карнавал нічних фантасмагорій.
Лютують блискавки страшної тишини,
Роти провалюють, розтявши губи лезом
І котячи слова по кручах фрази в безум,
Неначе в прірву круглі валуни.
Встає огонь, як стовп, встає, як стовп, гармидер,
Як стовп і сгогін,—над старим столом.
—Я в смерті ще раз хитро видер
Кипучу ніч з натхненням і вином.
Кладу на плечі ніч кипучу,
Як хрест ганьби, як чорний слуп.
І труп, свій власний, бідний труп,
Мов некрофіл, ґвалтую й мучу.
В ганьбі, огиді, шалі й трясці
Наказую я привидам-словам:
Із прірв свідомості, з найглибших людських ям
Ви павуками тихими вилазьте!
Мов павуки пухкі й ослизлі,
У тільці несучи отрут скупий пухир,
Повзіть з шпарин проламаної мислі,
Щоб я, поет, святоха і блюзнір,
Поклав вас трупами на зляканий папір,
Щоб череп репнув й звідти, з чорних дір,
Потворні мрії вистромляли ссальця.
Тоді перо, як крик, накидується в пальцях
На плеканий, заплаканий папір ...
Так хорони ж, скрипучий манускрипте,
Пекучу порохню з сандалів сатани! . .
Брати! Вина! Вина мені насипте!
Нехай киплять ізнов бурхливі казани!
Хай гугонять ключе напружено і густо,
Прозóристі бурштинові ключі ...
Приходь! Чекаю уночі
На тебе, творча зганьблена розпусто!

His inflamed fancy blurs
Red lanterns of the blushing cheeks;
The noble swords of candles taken up;
The phantasm carnival is marching,
The raging bolts of scary hush,
Mouths gape, black holes, and lips are slashed by razors,
And words roll on the slopes of phrases into madness,
Like round slabs, tumble down the abyss.

The fire rises like a mast, the tumult rockets,
Above the shabby table, groaning pillars soar.
"Yet once again, I tore from the Reaper's talons
A boiling night of wine and muses.

I load the boiling night upon my back,
Like a disgraceful cross, a pitch-black beam.
And in a necromaniac bout,
I rape and torture my own corpse.

Disgrace, repulsion, madness, fever:
I order the word-ghosts
To creep out from the deepest manholes of the mind,
Like quiet spiders of the hidden soul!

The downy slimy spiders, carrying
A tiny bleb of venom in their paunch,
Crawl out of cracks of broken thought,
So that I, poet, bigot, heretic,
Pile up your corpses on the terror-stricken page,
May my skull crack, and from its pitch-black caverns
Disgusting dreams would stick out their tentacles.

The quill will squiggle, holler in my fingers
Onto the pampered tear-stained page …
So, squeaking manuscript, do bury
The singeing ashes from the Satan's sandals!
Pour me more wine, my brethren!
May the scalding cauldrons boil again!

May fountains bubble with massive power,
Transparent amber streams …
Do come! I'm waiting for you in the short hours,
Ignominious creative lechery!

Сердите серце рве на ланцюгу,—
На ланцюгу проклятий волоцюга!..
І келиха бере із рук старого друга,
Щоб загасить суху свою жагу.
Кричать розмовники. А він стоїть і слуха,
Стоїть і давиться скажений Амадей.
Мов краб, чіпляється ущиплива ядуха
У голе горло втомлених людей.
Наважившись бенкету край покласти,
Знесилівши від слів і від вина,
Просмолений, тягучий, чорний кнастер
Уважно в жмені мокрій розмина.
Ще в казані хвилюється заграва,
Та тиха тьма росте й шепоче круг стола.
Служниця заспана недбало принесла
У картузах тютюн масний і кучерявий.
Пливе вихлястий дим з фаянсових люльок,
І довгі цибухи гарчать, уже захрипши.
Хвилини мовчазні, найлюбші і найліпші
Хвилини млявих мрій, поплутаних думок!
Приклавши до ротів люльки, немов кларнети,
Струю із цибухів висмоктують смачну
Утихомирені, замислені поети.
О музико люльок, кантати тютюну,
Злетілих вгору струй блакитні піруети!
—Ах, ах! Доволі слів, натхнень, верзінь і смерті!
Він не страшний—німецький добрий чорт.
Де ноти, Гофмане? Де Гайднові концерти?
Музикусе, на вас чекає клавікорд ...
Акорд би стиснути оцим рукам блідим,
Щоб наливався звук й стенався композитор!
І він підводиться, і стеле вірний вітер
Йому під ноги, наче стяги, дим.
Кладе свою правицю волохату
На білі щелепи приборканих клавіш.

The angry heart is rattling on its chain—
Be chained, confounded vagrant!
He takes the mug from his old crony's friend
To quench the drought in his rough throat.

They blather loudly, and he just stands and listens,
He stands and stares, the crazy Amadeus.

Like an octopus, the bristly wheeze
Tears tired people's bare throats.

He dares to put an end to this carousal,
He languishes from words and wine,
He kneads a sooty, viscous bundle
Despondently in his wet palm.

The glow still stirring in the cauldron,
A quiet dusk grows, hums around the table.
The sleepy, absent-minded maid has brought
Tobacco in cartouches—greasy, crumpled.

The curly smoke sails from the faience pipes,
Long stems are hoarsely snarling.
The cherished minutes of charmed silence,
The spells of languid dreams and tangled thoughts.

With pipes in their lips like clarinets,
The tranquil, pensive poets
Suck in the luscious streams of smoke.
O music of the pipes, tobacco cantata,
The soaring pirouettes of light blue gusts!

"Please no more words! Enough of death, of hazy inspiration!
The German devil is not frightening at all!
Where is the score, friend Hoffmann? Where are Haydn's concertos?
Musician, the clavichord is waiting …"

These sallow fingers yearn to clutch the chord
To make the sound swell, to make the tunesmith shudder!
He rises, and flags of smoke are laid
Under his feet by loyal wind.

He puts his hairy hand
On the white jaws of docile keys.

Та б'є дванадцять раз. Стискаються щільніш
Два чорні пальці циферблату,
Мов діючи нічну посвяту
Серапіоновому брату,
Вмочивши пучки в час, в свячений час і тиш.
—Панове, час іти. Подайте-но плащі!
Не будьмо, друзі, надто романтичні ...
—Надворі дощ ...—
        Скриплять ізнов дощі,
Мов над папером пера педантичні.
Старий Берлін розписують дощі
Готичним почерком, рясою крапель гострих ...
І крізь колючий дощ, мов крізь густі кущі,
Хто продереться, подолавши острах?
То радник Гофман по калюжах човга,
Підплигуючи, йде і марить у півсні,
А вулиця за ним, як гама рівна й довга,
Пливе, кружляючи, і тихие вдалині.
Плескаті площі заросли дощем,
Стрімким кущем дощів глухих і нерухомих,
І над п'яницею, безумцем та митцем
Хитається, як звук, їх виміряний помах.
Ах, колонади тонкостеблих струй,
Ах, дощ химерний—в прорізах і стрілках,
Хитайся і злітай, хитайся і лютуй,
Трощи в трикутничок знайомого причілка!
Знайомий дім, де жінка й тепла грілка,
Знайомий дім, з шухлядами кімнат,
Ковпак нічний, бавовняний халат,
Огрядна пічка і приємний чад
Із мідного прокислого кадилка ...
—Амеліє, ти спиш? Амеліє, та де ж ти?
Йди двері відчини, бо тричі стукав хтось! . .
—Це ти, Амадею, ти? Приплентався нарешті?
Скидай-но туфлі, бруду не нанось ...—

He strikes twelve times.
Two pitch-black clockface fingers
Clench closer together,
As if performing midnight blessing
For a Serapion brother,
Dipping their fingertips into the mass of time,
Into the holy time of stillness.

"It's time to go, gentlemen. Please help us into our cloaks!
Let's not be oversentimental …"
"It's raining outside …"
The rains are squeaking yet again—
Pedantic quills on paper.

Calligraphy of rains in old Berlin,
In gothic hand, in sharp drop spikes …
Through prickly rain, like through a copse,
Whoever would blunder, scorning fear?
It's Councilor Hoffmann squelching through the mud,
He dodders, raving, half asleep,
The street behind him, long and even scales,
It floats, winds and falls silent in the distance.

Flat squares are overgrown with rain,
A rapid bush of deaf and static rains,
Above the drunken madman of an artist,
Their measured noisy gusts are wobbling.

Oh thin-stalked torrent colonnades,
Delusive rain in slits and arrows,
Shake, wobble, fly and rage,
Slash the triangle of a familiar gable!

Familiar home, his wife, and his hot-water bottle,
Familiar house with little troves of rooms,
A nightcap and a cotton dressing gown,
A sturdy stove, a pleasant sour tang
Exuding from a copper censer …

"Are you asleep, Amelia? Where are you?
Open the door, I've knocked already thrice …"
"Amadeus, is that you? Turned up at last?
Take off your shoes, don't make the floorboards dirty …"

І, туфлі кладучи до груби, щоб протряхли,
Сміється Амадей замислено собі,
І посміхаються з полив'яної кахлі
Рожеволиці лицарі й дівиці голубі,
І черевань, розцвічений у блейвас та цинобру
(Полив'яна ідилія голландських мулярів),
До себе пригортаючи свою коханку добру,
Теж посміхнувся ввічливо й замріяно зомлів.
Фламандська піч, розпарена, в квітках,
                                    пташках та бантах,
Мов дівка угодована, паруючи, стоїть,
Полива жирна топиться, гладкі блищать драбанти,
Червець на них вилискує, зелінка і блакить.
Рипить підлога повагом, скриплять кульгаві двері,
І Гофман—у притулкові своїх буденних чар,
Де на пузатому старому секретері—
Перо крилате й ситий каламар …

1929

ГЕТТО В УМАНІ

Жахтить земля, жахтить іржа і пил,
Як жар фурункулу чи виразка трахоми,
І сонце над усім—як вибух плям і стріл,
Як вибух мовчазний і тяжко нерухомий,
Цей маньякальний круг, що виплива в зеніт,
Це коло, зроджене в огні галюцинацій,
І семисвічники розлючених акацій—
Підносять перед ним свічки убогих віт.
При корені дерев вирує й пломеніє
Плескатих одблисків рябий калейдоскоп,
І вкручуються так маленькі чорторії
У монотонний сонячний потоп.

Самум небесного страшного Ханаану,
Безодні жару, хлані мовчазні,
То перекинулись, мов мідні казани,

He casts his shoes to dry them at the stove,
Accompanying his thoughts by quiet laugh,
Blue maidens, pink-cheeked cavaliers
Smile from glazed tiles;
A fatso painted in vermilion and white lead
(a glazed Dutch idyll);
He snuggles up to his kind lover,
Smiles politely—and goes out like light.

The sultry Flemish stove bestrewn with flowers, birds and ribbons,
Stands like a fattened steaming maid.
The oily glaze is melting, trabants glisten
With scarlet, cyan and sap green.

The floor creaks gently, lame doors squeak,
And Hoffmann takes refuge in his quotidian charms:
His old pot-bellied bureau
A sated inkwell and a flying quill.

Translated by Svetlana Lavochkina and Pavel Gitin

GETTO IN UMAN'

The earth is burning, along with the rust and dust,
With the fire of furuncles and ulcerous trachomas,
While the sun, a maniacal orb,
Silent, heavy and motionless,
Sails up to its zenith
In an explosion of stains and arrows.
That orb is born in the fire of hallucinations.
Menorahs of inflamed locust-trees
Raise toward it their candle branches.
Around tree roots a reddish kaleidoscope
Of fragmented reflections spins and glows,
And little eddies work their way
Into the monotonous flood of sunlight.

The Samum of a terrible, heavenly Canaan
From brass cauldrons
Has poured seas of fire and silent abysses

На землю спалену, розпадену та пряну.
І в пил проллято, втоптано й прибито
Мозаїку з движких червоножовтих кіл
Плямистий тиф розпачливого літа.
То жовч живу калюжками у пил
Проллято витворно.
              І звівся над землею,
Як вихор, ореол палаючих корон,
Що коронують ветху Іудею,
Цей одногорбий, цей старий Сіон.

Сіон у полум'ї,—і так стоїть віки
Над ним огонь без трепоту й пощади,
Чи то огонь кривого Торквемади,
Чи райнських огнищ гострі язики,
Чи віхола пожеж, розхристана й крута,
Залізнякової порвистої ватаги ...
О, пагорбе жалю, і розпачу, і згаги,
Голгото нації, з огнем замість хреста!
Жорстоким полум'ям Сіон себе вінча—
В'язниця й царство,
              ватра і химера
Оскаженілого у мандрах Агасфера,
Безумця, мрійника, раба і шукача.

На лобі пагорба, як віра прирекла,
Вчепивсь обшарпаний, обсмалений і строгий
Ковчег квадратної рудої синагоги,—
Ковчежець з Торою, прип'ятий до чола.
Зачумлений мокрець—огидний сірий мох,
Що дхне гниллям і склизею на трупах,
Повзе по каменях, по ребрах і по слупах
Худих і лютих синагог.

Стовп сонця вковано чи вкопано стовма
У жовтий щовб плюндрованого гетто ...
Не спи, Ізраїлю!
              О, шма Ісроель, шма!

Onto the scorched, cracked, and lacerated earth.
A mosaic of mobile, red-yellow circles
Has formed and been stamped into the dust and become fixed.
It is the spotted typhus of a despairing summer,
The living gall intricately
Poured into dust.
                    Like a storm, there appeared above the earth
An aureole of flaming crowns,
The crowns of ancient Judea,
Hump-backed, old Zion.
Zion is burning—above it an unwavering and unmerciful flame
Has arisen for centuries,
Whether the fire of twisted Torquemada,
Or the sharp tongues of the Rhine's bonfires,
Or the sweeping, unkempt, and treacherous storms
Of Zalizniak's desperate gang …
Oh, mount of pity, despair and thirst,
A nation's Golgotha
On top of which a fire instead of a cross!
Zion has wreathed itself in a pitiless fire—
A prison house and kingdom,
                         the campfire and chimera
Of madman, dreamer, slave and seeker Agasuerus
Enraged by wandering.

On the brow of a hill, as faith decreed,
Clings ragged, scorched, and austere
The ark of a boxy, ruddy synagogue—
An ostensorium and Torah fastened to its front.
Over the stones, ribs and posts
Of thin, furious synagogues
Crawls a scabby plague, a disgusting grey moss
Stinking of rot and slimy corpses.

The sun's pillar stands upright, securely planted
Into the yellow rock of the plundered ghetto.
Do not sleep, Israel!
        Oh, Shema, Yisrael, Shema!

Ізраїль твердо спить,—і серць, і сонця летарг
Сліпучий свій туман над гетто підійма.
Не спи, Ізраїлю!
                    Не спи і проклинай
Туман огню і погар синагоги!
Твої, Ізраїлю, не всі ідуть дороги
На зганьблений Сіон, на страту і одчай!
Не спи, Ізраїлю!
                    Не спи і проклени,
Як чорну неміч, молитов судому,
Тих молитов хасидського Содому,
Що спалюють роти, що рвуть серця і сни!
В ротах розпечених, шершавих і кривих,
Горить язик безумного хасида.
О, рот роззявлений—благань глухий барліг,
Де віра—як ганьба,
                    де плач—як зненавида!
Діра розбещена,—
                    і бовтається в ній
Та шарудить язик, скрегочуть чорні зуби.
Правець релігії, трясущий та жахний,
Хижацтво віри,
                    радість самозгуби,
Оргазм безумства,
                    апогей і шал,
Шал тріумфальної надсади
Гримить, немов органні колонади,
Що з циклопічних нот споруджують хорал.
О, темні сховища на людському шляху—
Святебні урвища, судоми пишні ями!
Всіх рас і натовпів розкриті навстіж храми
Ревуть тим голосом хітливості й жаху.
О, душе людська, зморена й жива!
Ще не закрилася, мов язва, під тобою
Оргазму віри яма трупова,
Смердюче й пишне лігво супокою.
Прадавні молитви, знесилені жалі,
Тисячолітні привиди одчаю—
Вас, лементуючи, ще часто зустрічають,

But Israel sleeps soundly. A lethargy, both of the heart and the sun,
Spreads its blinding glare over the ghetto.
Do not sleep, Israel!
                    Do not sleep, but curse
The fire's glare and the charred synagogue!
Not all your paths, Israel,
Lead to defamed Zion, to execution and despair!
Do not sleep, Israel!
                    Do not sleep but curse,
Like a black sickness, the convulsive prayers,
The prayers of the Hassidic Sodom
That turn mouths to ashes, that tear hearts and dreams!
The mad Hassid's tongue burns
In hot, rough, twisted mouths.
Oh, gaping mouth, dull pleading in lairs,
Where faith resembles shame,
                    and tears resemble contempt!
This is a pit of dissolution,
                    in which tongues bob
And lisp, and black teeth grind.
A religious stupor, trembling and combustible,
A ruthlessness of faith, a joy of self-destruction,
Create an orgasm of madness,
          an apogee of frenzy.
Frenzy's triumphant excess
Roars, like an organ's colonnades
Building chorales from cyclopean notes.
Oh, dark hiding places along human pathways,
Precipices for devotees,
                    luxurious convulsive pits!
Thrown wide open, the temples of all races and crowds
Roar with the same lustful and terrible voice.
Oh, tired, vital human spirit!
Beneath you the burial pit of faith's orgasm,
That stinking, magnificent bed of tranquility,
That pestilence, has still not closed.

Ancient prayers, fatiguing sorrows,
Thousand-year-old ghosts of despair—
Can still be met, lamenting,

Немов володарів недужої землі.
І, впавши ниць, з печер порожніх душ
Виводять, як мерця, зламавши кустодії,
Сповиту у сувій,
        завжди одну і ту ж
Молитву-плач сліпого Єремії.
Її ведуть, як речника скорбот,
Її ведуть, як воїна й пророка,—
Кричить юрба сторота і стоока,
Немов один епілептичний рот.
На згарищах Каббал і на руїнах Біблій,
Між трощених колон,
           повержених метоп
Своїй могилі й вірі вже загиблій
Вклоняється скажений гробокоп.
І, щоб в останній раз покласти в землю сів,
Рука сгареча, хижа й ненажерна,
Збирає слів тверді і чорні зерна
З рядків талмудових, як з лущених стручків.
На землю ятрену,
        на рани і на близни
Впаде зерно зловіщої сівби,
І родять висохлі Сіонові горби
Іржаві трави розпачу й гнилизни.
Та жнець уважний нивами не ходе,—
Проклятий урожай на корені згниє.
На інших нивах родиться твоє
Прийдешнє,
     змучений, знеславлений народе!
Сіон у полум'ї—
        огню важкі корони.
Сіон у полум'ї—
        огонь, і тлін, і твань.
Сіон у полум'ї—
        нехай горять Сіони,
Катівні нації і плахи мордувань!

1929

Like rulers of a sick land.
Falling prostrate before you, from the caves of empty spirits
They summon like a dead man, having broken his custodians,
Still wrapped in a shroud,
                the one and same
Prayer-lament of blind Jeremiah.
It expresses their suffering.
It is their warrior and prophet.
The crowd of a hundred mouths and eyes
Utters a single epileptic cry.
On the ruins of Kabbalahs on the ashes of Bibles,
Among shattered columns
                and fallen metopes
A furious gravedigger bows
To his grave and his already dead faith.
In order to plant seeds in the earth one last time,
He gathers words from the lines of the Talmud,
Like hard, black seeds from opened pods.
The inauspicious seed falls
Onto the fervent earth,
                its wounds and scars,
And the dry mounds of Zion
Give birth to rusted grasses of despair and rot.
But the careful harvester does not walk these fields,
Where the cursed harvest is decaying at its root.
Your future is born on other fields,
        exhausted, defamed people!
Zion is in flames,
                heavy crowns on fire.
Zion is in flames,
                fire, decay and mire.
Zion is in flames,
                let them burn—all those Zions,
Torture chambers of nations and scaffolds of suffering.

Translated by Myroslav Shkandrij

Bazhan's "Blind Bards"

Translator's Essay

GEORGE G. GRABOWICZ

To the memory of Bohdan Krawciw

A SPECTRAL TEXT

Mykola Bazhan's poem "Blind Bards" (Ukr.: "Sliptsi," "Сліпці") was first published in the Kyiv "thick journal" *Life and Revolution* in two installments in late 1930 and early 1931.[1] It appeared on the eve of the Stalinist repressions that were soon to follow: the genocidal famine (the Holodomor of 1932–1933); the massive purges of Ukrainian intellectuals, writers and artists that had already begun in the late 1920s and lasted through the 30s and beyond; and the radical realignment, more correctly, perhaps lobotomy, of Ukrainian literature and culture as its Modernist, broadly experimental, and multifaceted profile of the 1920s was turned into a pale Socialist Realist shadow of itself in the following decades. Not surprisingly, in the sliver of time between 1930–1931 and the full repressions that soon followed, the poem had no reception other than the several predictable ideological denunciations that appeared in the early 1930s.[2] More surprisingly, given the fact that Bazhan survived the Stalinist period and lived to old age, attaining various honors and distinctions (Academician, Hero of Socialist Labor, chief editor of the *Soviet Ukrainian Encyclopedia*, etc.), "Blind Bards" was not only never reprinted (even in part) in the various later editions of his works, but until virtually the end of his life, was never even mentioned in the various official histories of literature. For all practical purposes, the poem did not exist; in Ukraine, it remained taboo and basically unknown until independence in 1991.

There was, however, a second birth. In late 1969, exactly a half century ago, the Ukrainian émigré journal *Suchasnist'* (*Сучасність*)—*The Contemporary Times*—republished the poem in two issues and then in a separate publication, along with an assiduously reconstructed history of its reception by the

---

1 Cf. *Zhyttia i revoliutsiia* 7, 8, and 9 (1930), as well as 4 (April 1931).
2 See Bohdan Krawciw, introduction to "Sliptsi" by Mykola Bazhan, *Suchasnist'* 10 (1969): 20–29.

Ukrainian émigré poet, bibliographer, and world-class map collector Bohdan Krawciw (1904–1975).[3] This can now be seen as part of a larger effort begun a decade or so earlier to reclaim and restore to memory large swaths of Ukrainian culture destroyed and banned during the Soviet experiment.[4] Importantly, too, in his introduction Krawciw voices the hope that the third part of the poem, promised by the author somewhat obliquely in a footnote, would come to light.[5]

This proved to be illusory. The missing third part, let alone any subsequent fourth part of the poem, was never found. The initial critical reception of the poem in fact presaged for Bazhan almost a decade of fear and uncertainty as he was hounded for "Ukrainian nationalism." Despite his general adherence to the party line in his poetry written after "Blind Bards," in keeping with the general paranoia of the Stalinist 1930s the secret police (NKVD) was apparently prepared to arrest Bazhan at any time; what seems to have saved him was his highly prized translation (published in 1937) of the Medieval Georgian national poet Shota Rustaveli's poem *Knight in a Panther's Skin* for which he received a Lenin prize in early 1939 after Stalin's express intervention.[6] In light of this, and his ever more prominent official stature after 1940, continuing with "Blind Bards," whether in the early 1930s or all the more so later, must have seemed a futile and exceedingly dangerous tack. As bold as Bazhan was in various poetic initiatives and formulations, he was also a survivor, albeit ever the intellectual and prepared to test various strictures (especially after his official recognition).[7] But what could hardly have been predicted in 1969 when Krawciw and *Suchasnist'* were republishing the poem, was how little critical attention "Blind Bards" would generate,

3   See George G. Grabowicz, "The Passions of Bohdan Krawciw," in *Ukraine Under Western Eyes. The Bohdan and Neonila Krawciw Ucrainica Map Collection*, ed. Steven Seegel (Cambridge, MA: Harvard University Press for the Harvard Ukrainian Research Institute, 2011), ix–xxxii.
4   A central landmark here is the large anthology: Iurii Lavrinenko, ed., *Rozstriliane vidrodzhennia* (*The Executed Renaissance*) (Paris: Kultura, 1959). This was one of several such efforts which continued well into the 1980s and beyond.
5   See Krawciw's quotation of Bazhan's footnote 35 in part II of the original 1931 edition. That is, "Kapnist, Poletyka, Kochubei, Rzewuski (Revukha)—were magnates of Ukrainian background and the tsar's subjects (except for Rzewuski—who was a Pole; about whom there will be more in the third part)" (Mykola Bazhan, *Sliptsi*, with an introduction by Bohdan Krawciw [Munich: Vydavnytstvo "Suchasnist'," 1969], 59). The *Suchasnist'* edition of "Sliptsi" was given to the Ukrainian poet (then the young quasi-dissident) Vitalii Korotych sometime after its publication to be hand delivered to Bazhan in Kyiv. Whether it reached its destination, and what impact it had on Bazhan, is unknown. It did reflect, however, the broader interest in the Ukrainian emigration in Bazhan's person and fate; see below.
6   See Aheieva, *Vizerunok na kameni*, 182–184.
7   Aheieva seems to be suggesting, beginning with the somewhat passé "(non)Soviet" in her subtitle, that the two hypostases were so interwoven as to be inextricable.

or, perhaps more correctly, allow. A sea change was occurring in Ukrainian litera-
ture after independence, with a general, albeit highly chaotic melding of the three
de facto subcanons of Ukrainian literature in the late 1980s and early 1990s—
that is, the Soviet, the émigré, and the dissident, and incorporating on top of that
various pockets of unofficial, "maverick," or "samizdat," and even highly eccentric
or "crazy" literature. But with literally dozens of major writers and works being
rediscovered and scores, if not hundreds, of lesser writers and works reentering
the canon, "Blind Bards" was still conspicuously, and somehow inexplicably,
absent. A major work, generally considered a chef d'oeuvre of a poet of the high-
est rank, remained, as before, obscured and largely ignored.

… AND SOME OTHER APORIAS

The long absence of "Blind Bards" from the canon of Ukrainian literature is not
the only aporia projected by this work. There are other core features that continue
to constrict and impede the poem's reception. Most immediately difficult is the
very fabric of the text: its heavy and recherché language (described as "Baroque"
by some critics) with locutions going back to the Polish-influenced early mod-
ern Ukrainian idiom seldom found even in academic dictionaries (Bazhan him-
self felt obliged to provide some footnotes explaining his language); its many
arcane allusions; its frequently opaque narrative; and the rapid shifts of scene
and voice. The poem, then, is forbidding for both the specialist and "common"
reader alike. It is hard to believe that it was written when it was, as the man in
the street is clearly not the poem's ideal reader.[8] One almost wonders whether
there was an implicit dispensation from the ultimate censor—the *Khoziain*, Sta-
lin himself—as if anticipating the case of Mikhail Bulgakov who seemed to have
a special relationship with the prototype of the *Master and Margarita*'s Woland,
that is, the hyper-magician in the Kremlin. (In real life, to be sure, the dictator
did give Bazhan his dispensation, but somewhat later, and for a different work.)

As if part of this pact with the devil, "Blind Bards" also rather unambig-
uously expresses an ideological fealty towards Stalin's regime that, to this day,
the reader may find unpalatable: beyond the baroque and vertiginous shifts of
tone and narrative, one is also confronted on the level of ideas with scenes and
arguments that seem nothing short of the new and obligatory Soviet verities,
particularly as they relate to the most ideologically fraught topic of all—the

---

8   In Ukrainian poetry of that time this evocation of the language and mind-set of "the man in
the street" was done with great experimental flair (and with striking parodic effects) in Pavlo
Tychyna's small but fraught collection *Chernihiv*, 1931.

question of Ukrainian national consciousness, of Ukrainian identity as such. In the few short years before the writing of "Blind Bards" an examination of profoundly vexed issues was more the rule than the exception and in the writing of the various key figures of the time. The prose writer and essayist Mykola Khvyl'ovyi, the poet Pavlo Tychyna, the playwright Mykola Kulish, to mention only the most prominent actors, frequently broached controversial ideas, both during and after the so called "Literary Discussion" of 1925–1927, and especially in publications, discussions, and disputes energized by the short-lived "Free Academy of Proletarian Literature" (VAPLITE) which Khvyl'ovyi organized, and to which the above mentioned writers and Bazhan belonged. There was still the short-lived "Literary Fair" (Literaturnyi iarmarok), December 1928 to February 1930, by all indications the high point of Ukrainian Modernism and free albeit masked discussion under the Soviets, but night was falling fast. When "Blind Bards" appeared in late 1930 and early 1931, it must have seemed (and still does now) as though an unbridgeable chasm had opened between two different epochs. But what is particularly striking is how despite the gathering clouds, and, as we explicitly see at the end of the poem, fully conscious of the magnitude of the approaching storm, Bazhan finds it in himself to address crucial and universal issues with a force that is still palpable.

In short, "Blind Bards," a work that appears to be a ruthless attack on traditional values, is also an implicit rethinking of the collective itself, its past and its prospects. Paradoxically, the fact that it is unfinished is arguably part of the poet's victory, not his defeat. To see this, one has to contextualize the scene, however, and briefly take a few steps back in time.

THE KOBZARS AND THE LIRNYKS—AND THE QUESTION OF IDENTITY

In Ukrainian culture in the modern period, and before that in the early modern, folklore, oral literature, song, and various musical other forms of music, occupied a highly privileged place—and for two basic and interconnected reasons. One is that these traditions were ancient, reaching back a thousand years to pre-Christian times, regionally varied, and particularly rich, standing out not only in the narrower Slavic context, but on the larger European and even world stage. The other was that when Ukrainian high culture, reflecting the vagaries of political developments, had moments of both flowering and decline, folklore, oral literature, and the realm of the ethnomusical provided a constant and ever-growing repertoire of self-expression and self-assertion, establishing a powerful and symbolically varied form of collective identity—one that implicitly included, or at least affected and nurtured *every* stratum of society. As in many other European countries, the Ukrainian national revival of the nineteenth century—often identified with the Romantic period, although in various ways anticipating it by several decades, and then extending well beyond it—as articulated particularly in literature, but in various other art forms as well, is intrinsically focused on, and draws its inspiration from, the life of the common people, the *narod*, the rural collective. Within that collective the mostly blind itinerant singers (primarily men, but occasionally women as well) had a remarkably privileged place as carriers of tradition. They were living, ambient witnesses to the life of the collective, narrators of various traditional, epic, balladic, and often heroic narratives. Most importantly, they were enablers of the numinous, fundamental dramatic performers who could take the universal human experience, and human predicament—most basically their own benighted status as itinerant beggars, sufferers from the awful affliction of blindness—and turn it into a moment of self-knowledge, self-revelation, compassion, and renewal. Theirs was a universal social, artistic, and existential task of rediscovering the dramatic in everyday life—without the theater and its institutional and commercial accretions, through spare and naked performance as such.[9]

In the Ukrainian literary tradition, and the national revival that it animated, the role of the itinerant blind singers was given special prominence by the Ukrainian national poet Taras Shevchenko (1814–1861), who named his first slim collection of poetry *The Kobzar* (also known as *The Minstrel; Kobzar;* "Кобзар," 1840) and implicitly put the oral, itinerant, and even "underground" native tradition at the heart of his poetic self-projection. In time (still during his lifetime, but especially in his posthumous life as a national icon) Shevchenko came to be known simply as the *kobzar*—an iconic name that is unmistakably and uniquely his to this day. Throughout the nineteenth century, especially in the latter half, collecting the repertoire of the *kobzars* and *lirnyks* became a major field of Ukrainian ethnographic studies, especially as related to the epic songs, the *dumy*, that dated back to the seventeenth century and earlier and depicted in part the battles with the Turks and Tatars of those centuries and set a pattern of heroic national self-identification in which both the past and keeping the past alive were central collective values. Within the Romantic frame the apotheosis of the *kobzar*

---

9   See Oksana Grabowicz, "*Dumy* as Performance," in ЖНИВА, *Essays Presented in Honor of George G. Grabowicz on His Seventieth Birthday*, ed. Roman Koropeckyj, Taras Koznarsky, and Maxim Tarnawsky, special issue, *Harvard Ukrainian Studies* 32–33 (2011–2014): part 1, 291–313.

is again provided by Shevchenko, in various incarnations in the course of his poetry, but especially in an early poem "Perebendia" (1839), which appeared in the original *Kobzar*, where the eponymous singer is heroized in two different but paradoxically complimentary keys. On the one hand, he is the collective voice of the people. His repertoire of songs conveys the variety, experiences, and topoi of the life of the rural people—songs of love and for weddings, comical songs, ballads, songs of religious injunction or *memento mori*, and not least a range of historical songs about the heroic or tragic past;[10] he is, in short, a living *lieu de memoire*, a conduit to collective consciousness and collective memory. At the same time, as vital as he is to the life of the collective, as much as people think they know him ("Perebendia, old and blind—/ Everybody knows him!") he is definitely not one of the people, and in an essential way he is not understood by them, indeed is unknowable to them. Shevchenko's poem focuses precisely on this aporia. Poetic individuality and the power of the imagination stem from the natural order itself; but in keeping with Romantic convention this also separates the poet from the people. On a deeper level it comes from the transcendent power of poetry conceived as the Word of God, ultimately as prophecy—a model that Shevchenko is already formulating in his earliest poetry and which was rooted in the quasi-religious role of the *kobzars* as myth-carriers.

The blind singers that were first noticed by the early collectors of folklore, and then so powerfully depicted by Shevchenko, were initially seen as inspired folk artists who at the same time were carriers of national memory; that feature has always been a component of their reception. An awareness of their social circumstances and functions, their sociological setting was to come considerably later—in the latter nineteenth century and at the beginning of the twentieth.[11] It was then that the institutional life of the blind singers came more fully into focus—and this is what also constitutes the uniquely problematic and fraught focus of Bazhan's poem, of the *kobzars* and *lirnyks* as an institution, as a guild with multiform rules and conventions, rituals and modes of behavior—and, purportedly, an *ideology* as well. Characteristically, Bazhan's view of the blind bards encompasses the various instruments, modes, and implicit repertoires of the singers, focusing especially on the players of the *bandura* (also known in its

---

10 Shevchenko specifically names about ten songs or clusters of songs. Their implied number is considerably larger; see the comments to the scholarly edition—Taras Shevchenko, *Tvory v 5 tomakh* (Kyiv: Dnipro, 1984–1985), vol. 1, 617–619; see also http://litopys.org.ua/shevchenko/shev111.htm.

11 See Natalia Kononenko, *Ukrainian Minstrels: And the Blind Shall Sing* (New York: M. E. Sharpe, 1998).

earlier variant as the *kobza*, and also related to the *torban*, or *theorbo*, that in the eighteenth century was popular among the Ukrainian gentry). The earlier and more widespread *bandura* was related to the lute that stemmed from the late Middle Ages and was also used in Western Europe; it was most often used for performing the high "epic" mode of the *dumy*—and in the late eighteenth and early nineteenth century came into favor with the wealthier classes. The *lira*, much like the Western hurdy-gurdy, with the player turning the wheel that produced the plaintive drone of the instrument, and which in its performance by the *lirnyk* was much more directly focused on laments and begging songs, was uniquely suited for evoking their melancholy and contemplative repertoires. Despite the specialization, both modes and repertoires were explicitly focused on begging.

The structured, professional nature of the calling of the blind bards is highlighted in Bazhan's poem by its initial focus—in fact, it is the only focus through all of part I of the poem—on the ritual of *odklynshchyna*, of "release" or "manumission" (as if echoing a release from serfdom). In this ritual, the new adept, having served his three years and three months as a novice with his *kobzar* master or instructor is examined on his knowledge of the music and lore of the singers before a conclave of his soon-to-be peers. If he passes the test he becomes one of them, with full rights to ply his trade, his imagination, and his wit, and to make his way in the outside world of constant begging and—as the poem puts it—of constant humiliation. Even a cursory reading of the poem will show that this is but the mildest and most euphemistic of renditions of the ordeal that is in store for the newly minted *kobzar*. The reality—signaled through all the senses from the very outset of the poem, when the novice who comes to be examined, released, and then inducted into the brotherhood of the blind singers first smells the first, still-fragrant grasses that hang in clusters around the house or are strewn on the floor of the anteroom—will appear darker and darker, until it reaches the full darkness that comes with incurable, irredeemable blindness. If there is anything about this poem that stands out, it is that it does not flinch from the truth; there is nothing in it that is euphemistic, saccharine, or squeamish—even if, or precisely because, these are the very qualities, the defensive mechanisms, that have so consistently accreted to the popular rendering of the blind singers and their fate and role and in so doing have prevented or skewed a deeper understanding. But the subject demands it. In terms of the narrative itself, the setting and experiential reality of the poem is totally centered on the utterly liminal, marginal, and benighted predicament of blindness and mendicancy of its protagonists, but it also unswervingly confronts their fundamental moral or spiritual raison d'être—the task of bearing the collective's memory and identity, of instilling in their audience, "the crowds that are blinder than you," a sense of vision that will lead the collective through the trials that await it. This also, of course, addresses a universal topic: the role of the poet in society, particularly those who consciously and programmatically articulate their role. In effect, the so-called "national poets."

THE STALINIST PERIOD

The Stalinist assault on Ukrainian culture and cultural institutions as seedbeds of "bourgeois nationalism" began in earnest with collectivization and the first five year plan (1928–1932). Starting with a radical reorientation of the Academy of Sciences of Ukraine that basically implied the elimination of the humanities, culture as such, and all things western and liberal, it continued with an evisceration of other institutions in the humanities, literature, and the arts and with broad attacks on the intelligentsia and all forms of tradition and implicit or suspected resistance to the Soviet order.[12] A prominent component of this was a multipronged campaign to delegitimize and demonize as "reactionary" and quintessentially "bourgeois nationalist" the blind singers themselves; and specifically to condemn their instruments—the *bandura, kobza,* and *lira*—and their repertoires as weapons of class enmity directed against the revolution. In a society ever more controlled by police and totalitarian strictures, such designations, along with various police and administrative measures preventing free travel and, of course, begging, especially in the countryside, sounded the death knell for the world of the blind singers; for all practical purposes they disappeared for the next six decades or so—reappearing only after independence in 1991. The broadly accepted popular legend of a special congress or convention of the blind singers called by the NKVD (the date when this was to have happened varies widely, but is generally placed in the 1930s) to gather them in one spot, snare them in one dragnet, and then exterminate them, articulated the common perception of a ruthless campaign to eradicate them as a phenomenon. While there is no documentary evidence that the congress took place, its work, in fact, was done by other, less dramatic, but no less effective means. On the other hand, various official governmental attacks on the *kobzars,*

---

12 See my "The Soviet and Post-Soviet Discourses of Contemporary Ukraine: Literary Scholarship, the Humanities and the Russian-Ukrainian Interface," in *From Sovietology to Postcoloniality: Poland and Ukraine from a Postcolonial Perspective,* ed. Janusz Korek (Huddinge: Södertörns högskola, 2007), 61–81.

their repertoire, instruments, and overall reactionary essence in the course of the late 1920s and 1930s, as well as NKVD protocols of execution verdicts and other repressions against the *kobzars* are amply documented.[13] The mass media was conspicuously involved, trumpeting that "We can confidently say that the *kobza* has died along with its epoch, because our economic and cultural state demands new songs and new music";[14] or, as the critic Andrii Khvylia put it, "we should never allow that our musical front be limited only to the *bandura* and *kobza*, that our musical front be limited only by '*dumas* about the Cossack Baida,' that our musical front orient itself to the time of the Hetmans. As to the question of what to utilize from our past, we need to approach it in a Bolshevik, in a proletarian manner. ..."[15] Along with paving the way for the physical destruction of the traditional singers this campaign also led to a fundamental realignment of how *kobzars* and *bandurysts* could perform: forced to perform in groups and ensembles on stage, they were turned into regimented entertainers—essentially changing their individual and implicitly symbolic role and vitiating the dramatic content and spiritual bond of the performance.[16]

The violence done to Ukrainian culture in the Stalinist period has never been fully and systematically studied; and this lacuna is a particularly malign consequence of the fact that since independence the Ukrainian state (with some exceptions in the Yushchenko and Poroshenko administrations—but still without any programmatic thought or follow-up) has had no clear cultural policy relating to the Soviet period, on how to see it and analyze it, and what lessons to draw from its toxic legacy. In large measure this coincides with the seamless *institutional* continuity between the Ukrainian Soviet and the post-Soviet periods where some key institutions, most notably the Ukrainian Academy of Sciences, remained unreformed, in essence as Stalinist in administration, structure and scholarly priorities now as in the 1930s. The resultant vacuum was particularly noxious for historical reassessments of the Stalinist period, as amateur historiography and a propensity to conspiracy theory, and

---

13 See Kost' Cherems'kyi, *Povernennia tradytsiï* (Kharkiv: Tsentr Lesia Kurbasa, 1999). See also the 2014 Ukrainian film "The Guide" (*Povodyr*), which brought the story of the Stalinist repressions against the *kobzars* to a wide audience.

14 M. Korliakiv, "The mass character [*masovist'*] of the kobza," *Komsomolets Ukrainy*, May 3, 1927, cited in Cherems'kyi, *Povernennia tradytsiï*, 113.

15 Ibid., 119. For all his efforts in fighting "Ukrainian bourgeois nationalism," Khvylia himself was "liquidated" in the terror in 1938.

16 For an overview of Stalinist efforts to install this "parallel culture" in the musical realm in Ukraine, see William Noll, "Paralel'na kultura v Ukraïni u period stalinizmu," *Rodovid* 5 (1993): 37–41.

beyond it an understandable resentment of official nihilism and tolerance of Sovietism stepped into the breach. In a climate of official laissez faire on the one hand and amateur historiography on the other, various positions, works, or stances expressed during the literary discussion of the mid-1920s and beyond were adduced as evidence of collusion with the emerging Stalinist assault on Ukrainian culture. One instance of such guilt by hearsay is the tarring of Mykola Khvyl'ovyi for his purported contribution to this assault on the *kob-zars* and their ethos. Special rancor and condemnation, however, is reserved for Mykola Bazhan whose "Blind Bards"—illustrated by several quotes taken almost at random (sharper ones could more easily be found)—is seen as par-ticularly enabling the anti-*kobzarist* assault.[17] As "confused and half-baked" (to use a locution from Bazhan's own poem) as this charge of collusion may be, this is the place to start because it so clearly highlights the crux of the poem: what is his understanding of the blind bards? Or, more directly: why the negativity of their portrayal and is it only (or primarily) an ideological attack in the spirit of the unfolding anti-*kobzar* campaign? And further still: how does it work in Bazhan's poem? What does it ultimately mean?

THE POEM: OPACITY AND ALLEGORY

While a full examination of the poem is still a task for the future, one should begin with what is both general (true of poetry as such) and particular to this work: what does the poem's structure, here especially its recursive and often opaque narrative, its general denseness and difficulty, tell us about the work? Because in its original Ukrainian version—and presumably any native speaker could confirm this—the poem is denser, more compact, and more difficult than it is in translation—this or (in all probability) any other. The translation is always but an approximation of the poem—and also an interpretation, a reading, which may give it "greater clarity," but which hardly improves on it. In this poem, difficulty—as density and opacity, as misdirection and ambiguity—is the very essence of things; it is the poem's being or tone, its purpose. It is a core that is projected and adumbrated by all the poetic means in this poet's formidable arsenal. An immediate inference one can draw is that this opacity reflects the world of the blind, the world of darkness, misdirection, and uncer-tainty, of ambient anxiety—and of fear. And all of these moments also point

17 See Hennadii Makhorin, Serhii Cherevko, and Halyna Shubina, *Narysy z istoriï kobzarstva v Ukraïni* (Zhytomyr: Vydavnytstvo FOP Ievenok O. O., 2012), 21; the charge is also dissem-inated on the internet.

to the real, outside world of the poem as-it-is-being-written, particularly the encroaching darkness of Stalinism. This is manifest, for example, in the final sections of part II where ambient fear is directly thematized ("Fear! Fear of this world! How can one not see you not hear you ..."; cf. lines II.594–595) and would thus seem to refer both to the poem's heightened political (and historical) self-awareness (which is confirmed by many other references) but also to its creative, psychological, and ontological core (which is particularly evident in the also highly thematized disquisition on doubt—e.g., II.346–375).

The conflation of the "inner" and "outer," or the thematically given world of the blind bards in the poem and the historical world in which the poem is written suggests an allegorical cast to the work where any number of moments, scenes, or themes evoke this double frame. One can imagine, for example, that the grotesque and gross feast that concludes part I may also reflect an egregiously hyperbolic or demonic depiction of an official party banquet. The Expressionist poetics at work here can easily be directed at various targets—although the rhetorical, not to say ideological strictures clearly rein things in. Not every moment is implicated, of course, and the work itself does not inhere in a period poetics that is attuned to and governed by the allegorical (as in medieval literature, paradigmatically in *The Divine Comedy*)—but it is markedly present and various key moments are defined by it. Most fundamentally this projects the basic self-reflective thrust of the poem as blindness becomes a metaphor for the human condition—signaled by the key apothegm defining the blind bards' calling:

> Go through the villages,
>   orchards
>   and fields
> In your all-seeing blindness and silence.
> O, blind guide
>   look sharply and lead
> The crowds that are blinder than you! ...
>   (I.231–237).

The final, impassioned and powerful monologue of the young bard in part II, beginning with "Standing over us is an age like a black palisade ..." (i.e., lines 548–615) may be applicable to the early nineteenth century where the action of the poem seems to be set; but its true and eerily accurate resonance is with the Stalinist period, both through the sense of an impending, cataclysmic storm and the speaker's sense of himself (with his voice now clearly merging with that of the author) cast as nothing but a plaything of ominous, inhuman forces.

VOICE AND IDEA

Somewhat deceptively (or with the kind of misdirection that one encounters in musical works) the poem begins with a slow and seemingly methodical description of the setting, and even a short meditation on silence itself. Only after some two pages (or exactly seventy-six lines) does it introduce the human voice. From there on, however, voice seems to become all-important as the poem reveals itself as a series of dialogues loosely positioned around or within some narrated action. This applies to both of its parts, although the interplay of dialogue, the weight put on the logical exposition of argument, and so on, is clearly more intense in the second part than in the first. At the same time, if the dialogues suggest a dramatic work they do so very loosely: characters and their positions or situations (background, role, motivation, etc.) are not drawn at all—at most just implied. If it is a dramatic work it is one where ideas and not actual people are the players. But these are not abstract ideas; on the contrary, they are not so much ideas as ways of voicing and experiencing them. They all circle around one central idea which is the collective Ukrainian experience and the right to address it—and what to see and remember.

As a result, despite the dramatic tension that is constantly just under the surface of the poem, the portrayal of characters, let alone the development or transformation of character is minimal. Apart from Perebendia, the leader of the "beggarly bunch" who is presented at the outset, no one else is even named. Thus, too, the young man with whose entrance the poem begins is first described as timid or diffident; and then by the end of part I he is a fiery incarnation of the poem's indictment of the blind bards, a bold, hard-edged spokesman for rejecting a bardhood cast as corrupt and moribund: "Your fires are guttering you lying kobzar/And those shouting by the roadsides are corpses! … (cf. I.340–353). As such, of course, he appears as the author's *porte-parole*, his voice is implicitly that of the author. Or is it? For as we see from the transition to part II, where the young bard of that part is by all indications the one who was inducted into the brotherhood/community in part I, his position, his ideas, while given with undiminished fervor—and his lines clearly have an edge over those of any other speaker—do not necessarily carry more weight. At the very least the movement of the poem decenters them and makes them into one position among others. The very dialogic principle that has been established throughout the poem robs him of the presumption of final authority—his is only one side of the debate.

THE HISTORICAL MOMENT

As much as the dialogic or, indeed, the dialectical seem to be safe topics underlying as they do the then hegemonic Marxian discourse, the issues they are being applied to are fraught in the extreme: the nature of collective memory and its transmission—specifically the manner in which it is to be done and the very right to do so, and ultimately the most fraught issue of all, the nature of Ukrainian identity and who can speak to it and nurture it. That Bazhan is still addressing this as late as 1930–1931 suggests a certain boldness shading off into recklessness. Perhaps his key formal device for justifying the topic, for neutralizing in some way its explosive potential, is the convention or, more likely the mere pretense, of historicity. By calling his work a "historical poem," or, as I have rendered it in my translation, as "a poem about history," he seems to be "cloaking" it or "packaging" it in a less-than-offensive genre, like a period piece that can be forgiven its outworn eccentricities, buffering at least in some measure his discourse from the relentless requirements of orthodoxy. That this may well be a defensive, rhetorical tactic, or dodge, is suggested in part by the paucity of historical detail that he provides. Part I is almost entirely lacking in historical specificity or context—other than the name of Perebendia, which of course refers to a fictional character and in so doing seems to be mocking the convention, as if calling attention to Bazhan's manipulation of convention, his very pretense of historicity. In part II, the historical material is adduced in considerable detail, ranging from the time of Mazepa and the fall and massacre of his capital Baturyn in 1708 to the *hajdamak* uprising of 1768, and the destruction of the Zaporozhian Sich in 1775. With references to such historical characters as (Vasyl') Kapnist, (Hryhorii) Poletyka and (Wacław) Rzewuski the chronology is brought into the late eighteenth and early nineteenth century. But as much as these figures and the causes they stood for are genuinely historical, their presence in the poem is unabashedly nominal, essentially on the surface. They may evoke history, as do the various songs or legends or narratives in which they may figure, but this does not of itself make the poem historical. The time of the poem remains indefinite, suspended between that nineteenth century past and the early twentieth century, specifically the Stalinist present. Its historicity remains somehow putative, unsubstantiated (perhaps purposefully so) by other historicizing narrative detail; and it certainly does not alter or hedge on the allegorical thrust.

Curiously, too, the notion of the poem's historicity is undercut by its openly expressed and clearly nonhistorical but contemporary or trans-temporal meditation on the past and the future, on the impossibility of a "final future" (cf. II.590–591). This seems to implicitly challenge the Soviet dogma of a culminating or final stage of mankind's development, couched in the notion of a final revolution. It is given with passion—and clearly issues from the voice of the author—but it also implicitly refers to the present, not the past.

In the polysemous way the poem works, the notion of historicity may also project a different and unexpected nuance, which would particularly correlate with the long final monologue of the young bard at the end of part II and its examination of the way history turns on itself. Nightmarish questions—"Or maybe, you devil, the future's in the past?/Or maybe, God damn you—for now it's forever—/ (All ears being deaf, all hearing now lost)/It's the scream of the future that's entombed in the graves?" (II.604–607)—meld time past and time future into a kind of metaphysics or indeed nightmare of history. If that is the case, the notion of the poem's historicity would need to be expanded to see it as also commenting on, indeed specifically highlighting, its focus on the Stalinist period—in effect, suggesting something that could be read as "Blind Bards: A Historical Poem (of the Stalinist Period)." That of course is putting it literally, and Bazhan is protected by convention and rhetoric (and not all possible readings are read); but the opening to this reading is there in the text, which also says only a few lines later, "Strange specters are roaming around the bazaar ..." (II.644).

On the other hand, and not least of all, the pronounced psychological and ontological cast of the poem would seem to argue against its historicity—especially when it is used as a device of mediation, buffering, and self-protection. In its self-reflective mode—which is also defining—the poem is above all about feeling and about experiencing in the here and now. It is, among other things: a meditation on becoming a poet and entering a less-than-edifying guild (to put it mildly); being a brother to various unsavory types; suffering the pangs of creation; wandering blindly; stumbling, falling, and getting up again, only to fall once more. That may very well trump the late eighteenth and early nineteenth century taken together.

DEPICTING THE BLIND BARDS

The core (if not the entirety) of the poem is the depiction of the blind bards (сліпці)—both in their collective form as seen in the ritual of *odklynshchyna* in part I and then out earning their living individually in the bazaar in part II. What should we see here and how do we parse it? In several ways, of course—and by considering even some of the options we see that the picture that emerges is murky not clear. On the most obvious level, anyone from the original implied Ukrainian audience who is basically literate cannot but see its origins in the literary canon and an implicit polemic with Shevchenko: Bazhan's Pereben-dia would seem to be the very opposite of Shevchenko's. But that simple fact is problematic too, because, as is often the case, the polemic here is also an homage, a constant celebration of the spirit and inventiveness of the national poet. To begin with, "Blind Bards" is written in the form (such are the rules of poetic polemics) dictated by Shevchenko's "Perebendia," that is, amphibrachic tetrameter (veering off at times into amphibrachic trimeter). Since this meter and rhythm also mark out Shevchenko's epic verse, particularly in *Haidamaky* (1841), there is a temptation for critics to also see in "Blind Bards" an epic strain or principle—which is basically unpersuasive, although here and there, in part II especially, such moments are echoed in some "historical" reminis-cences. However, the tenor of the whole is not epic. If anything, it is "philo-sophical"—but as the term has been so bastardized in the Ukrainian critical idiom, and basically shunned in the English, it is best to avoid it.

The crux of Bazhan's "polemic" with Shevchenko is that he presents the blind bards without a trace of idealization—although for Shevchenko the issue is not idealization as such but a principled and systemic reading of the blind folk singers as emblematic of *communitas*. They represent the power of the down-trodden, as carriers of the numinous: they are certainly not just entertainers, let alone conmen. Shevchenko's *parrhesia*, speaking, as Foucault defines the notion, not just truth to power but risking dire consequences for such truth, is also in the background for Bazhan, although his room to articulate it is rapidly shrinking and in a few months after writing the poem will be gone altogether. Concretely, textually, Bazhan's Perebendia emerges in the poem not as a soli-tary blind singer communing with nature and God and often shunned by his own people, but as a hulking and ominous "carouser." He is characterized by a seemingly unconstrained cynicism ("What we want here is flesh—women and beef"; "Who waits on the spirit—can ask for meat/lots of meat,/loads of meat" [I.324 and I.374–376]), reminding us that the world of these bards is also the world of the marginal, the down-and-out, "vagabonds," "rascals," and all but thieves ("felons" [II.285]; in the original, *zdraitsi* [p. 31, Krawciw edition]).

The main issue of the poem, of course, is that the original Shevchenkian and later generally populist (*narodnyk*) frame, created not so much as an apologia for, but as a vision drawing on the numinous and salvational word (implicitly carried by the *narod* but expanded into a millenarian vision in Shevchenko's poetry), is now merged by Bazhan with his vision of full, unsparing physicality—which is so powerful and total as to seem almost equally metaphysical. Typically for Bazhan, however, he does not at all dispense with the spiritual and intellectual.

By all indications his is not just a radical physicalist (or materialist) vision, often identified simply with naturalism. Much of part II is devoted to extensive meditations on, and elaborations, of conceptual, even quasi-theoretical, takes on the past and present, and on the nature of man, society, and reality. But for Bazhan the physical is at the heart of things and determines them. Much as in his "The Blood of Captive Maidens" (Krov polonianok, 1926)—essentially a meditation on national character, on defining the features of collective Ukrainian ways of feeling and experiencing—takes the etiology of that national character back by putting it into a poem containing a scene of the collective rape of Ukrainian captive girls by Mongol invaders in the mid-thirteenth century (i.e., before their descendants became simply "Tatars"). This mixing of genes—and the physical act of violence that engendered it—shapes, so the poem seems to show, the contemporary Ukrainian national character. An intellectually and politically bolder gesture—even if concealed in a twenty-five-line poem—is hard to imagine. It is also hard to fathom how Bazhan got away in print with this anti-Marxism.

In "Blind Bards" the primacy of the physical is on full display, especially in the gross and grotesque banquet with which the *odklynshchyna* of part I culminates. The colossal gluttony of this anti-Eucharist (particularly stressed with the mock prayers that usher it in) is also accompanied by ample rhetorical flourishes—all of them implicitly in the authorial voice—dilating on the disgust this elicits and is explicitly *meant* to elicit. The device of the latter, this leading of the reader by various cues and "editorial" comments, the evident manipulation of rhetorical effect for ostensibly ideological satire, deserves further analysis. (At the very least to consider how the poem-as-narrative and the poem-as-rhetorical instructions-on-how-to-read-it begin to diverge in part I and then are reintegrated—or not—in part II.) What also deserves to be noted is that the focus on physicality is not of a piece; that, in fact, it is quite nuanced. One such moment is that the run-up to the feast, the introduction of the massive variety of food that is brought in and eaten clearly echoes analogous feasts in the Ukrainian canon, particularly in Kotliarevs'kyi's *Eneïda*, and is presented as both good-humored and iconic. The episode is hardly satiric. The benign aspects of the physical, and the pure physicality of the Ukrainian countryside and the Ukrainian way of life, is particularly stressed in part II—as is the way that the old Ukraine of Cossack ways, and constant strife, is changing into a new, commercial, and universal order.

What is particularly notable in both parts, indeed presented from the outset and periodically emphasized, like a recurring leitmotif, are depictions of the *kobzars'* diseases, their scrofular and suppurating eyes—an anatomically detailed and insistent reminder that their blindness is not abstract, that it is real, painful, and permanent, or about to become permanent; that it is an awful curse and affliction that defines them. To merely note this disease—which is precisely what the earlier tradition beginning with, and implicitly including, Shevchenko had done—is not to do justice to it. It is a curse that underlies a *kobzar*'s very being—and explains, even when not excusing, his many flaws and sins. In short, the fundamental issue of the bards' blindness is presented insistently and unsparingly—and nothing in that presentation has even a hint that it lacks sympathy, let alone that it is tinged with scorn.

Another moment that is central to the depiction of the bards, even as it is confined only to the poem's first part, is the argument that they and their songs are an organic part of nature *and* of the Ukrainian land, countryside, past and present, and indeed part of all things Ukrainian. It is a sweeping and awe-inspiring claim of a chthonic bond with the land couched in a huge epic simile (cf. I.172–222) unmatched in any Ukrainian poetry of the twentieth century, save perhaps for Tychyna. The bards' songs are seen as an elemental dark water, a great underground river, an underground Dnipro; they emerge in countless wells and through the troughs and sound holes of countless *banduras* and *kobzas*; they connect everything in a huge network of rivulets, channels, and viaducts of images and emotions, not only throughout the country but throughout time and history; they affect and mold the untold number of those countrymen who are all somehow part of it. Told by one of the *kobzars* as a kind of collective article of faith, this image of dark water is a remarkable acknowledgement of the power of the collective unconscious and its hold on that very collective national character that Bazhan implicitly and explicitly addresses both in "Blind Bards" and various other works. Most extraordinary, perhaps, is the fact that as much as the position of the bards may be addressed or attacked from various perspectives, including that most ideologically trite and shopworn—that is, that they are articulating Ukrainian "bourgeois nationalist" positions "to avoid sowing fear among those who have power,/The nobles, the gentry, the lords and the squires" (I.488–489)—their chthonic presence in the collective unconscious is not challenged at all. They may be attacked for gluttony and other vices; they may be mocked for their decrepitude, though emphatically not for their affliction; their "political" loyalty may be indicted through a bizarre permutation of Marxian logic, despite their being the lowest of the low, the poorest of the poor. Yet their (chthonic, trans-rational) authority remains basically unchallenged.

The above "charges" or "indictments" are made by the implied authorial voice and in the first part of the poem. That voice is no longer there in the second part, as the young bard no longer carries any authorial prerogative. Even more, he now explicitly thematizes his doubt and in the process becomes altogether human—and his predicament both engrossing and universal. His implied rhetorical authority is undercut and he departs, stumbling in the aura of his own doubt. He is still clearly endowed, however—as a true poet should be—with powerful honesty and prescience, particularly as to the poem's central topoi of the coming storm and the demonic nightmare of history.

Two more tropes in the depiction of the bards should be mentioned here. One is the broad issue, developed at length in the second part of the poem, of the fundamental transformations occurring in Ukraine as in the course of the eighteenth century it changes from the Cossack days to the Ukraine of the nineteenth century, trading in its heroic character for one of (presumably) greater public good and, of course, peace; a Ukraine that is modern—that is, part of the world of commerce and universal economic laws, to which the bards, one assumes, remain oblivious and in which, seemingly, they are superfluous. The changes that are occurring, as the debate makes clear, are all largely for the worse as commerce and markets dehumanize and demean the traditions and basic assumptions of the bards—particularly the imperative of knowing and respecting the past. To the extent that they remain true to their calling the bards end up appearing as cogs, tools, and finally buffoons in the new market machine—as the young bard insists on needling his old comrade in their long dialogue at the end of a market day,

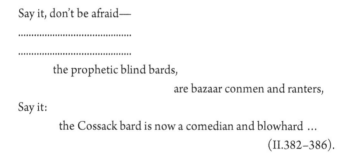

Say it, don't be afraid—
....
....
        the prophetic blind bards,
                are bazaar conmen and ranters,
Say it:
        the Cossack bard is now a comedian and blowhard ...
                        (II.382–386).

How is this charge, made with irrefutable economic and also Marxian logic, meant to be answered? The answer is: it is not. It is not answered because both protagonists have different positions and the logic of the one does not engage the other—although their answers are real and dialectical (even if the young bard, who leaves, whether as winner or loser is not clear, has the stronger lines). But in this impasse a special truth, or indeed strength, of the poem emerges as it refuses to take sides and allows each protagonist to tell his own truth—thereby dispensing with the authorial rhetorical thumb on the scales that supposedly decided the debate (such as it was) in part I. Ultimately, ideological duty is left in the lurch as the poem concludes with its own more persuasive logic.

The second concerns the nature of deviousness and deception in the picture of the blind bards—but that should be left for a longer discussion.

THE TRAP OF COMPLETION

The final issue concerns the unwritten but promised third and fourth parts of the poem and how they might reflect on the whole. Other than the footnote promising a continuation, the poem does not provide any answers and arguing from absence is notoriously unrewarding. But Bazhan's writings may provide some clues. One such clue is a triptych he wrote two years earlier, the programmatic poem "Edifices" (Budivli, 1929), of which all three parts appeared—"Sobor," "Brama," and "Budynok." The result is telling and cautionary: the first two are excellent and problematic; the second, dealing with a walled up Baroque gate obliges the poet to polemicize, in effect with the whole Baroque period and excoriate its main Ukrainian political representative, Mazepa (it is 1929, after all). However, dynamism, complexity, and even ambiguity characterize both parts. The third and last part describes a modern building in the process of being built. Not a Stalinist wedding-cake skyscraper (those would come later) but perhaps a modern Bauhaus or Art Deco building; or simply one that is modern— and, of course, Soviet and revolutionary. It is also, as any objective reading would say, the least persuasive of the three—if not a failure (as compared to the earlier two), then clearly weaker. Because the only role left to the poet is to apotheosize the revolutionary effort: problematization is superfluous. Is this enough to illuminate "Blind Bards?" Probably not. But the precedent is worth noting.

And then there is the indubitable—indubitable, that is, in the here and now, according to what we now have. New facts may upend it. Bazhan may have indeed written a continuation, that is, the third part. We know that in the 1930s, in fear for his life, he gave the whole manuscript of his poem, presumably with that third part, to his then friend, the writer Iurii Ianovs'kyi for safe keeping (Ianovs'kyi being presumably less vulnerable); at some point Ianovs'kyi also felt threatened and presumably burned the incriminating manuscript.[18] What was in it we do not know. What we do know is that in the 1970s, when the

---

18   Aheieva, *Vizerunok na kameni*, 150–151. Tellingly, Aheieva argues that Bazhan was being evasive when he suggested that it was the only copy of the (complete?) poem.

pressure was most likely off, when Bazhan was proposed for the Nobel prize in 1970 and a year earlier his work (the first two parts) appeared in the West, he probably could have made efforts to complete the poem. The prospect of the great master being raked over the coals may have been small (although one never knows). He did not—for reasons we also do not know.

But it is also likely that as a great poet he must have seen that the conclusion of "Blind Bards" that we have is as strong as any continuation or completion he later wrote—that the powerful and ambivalent ending it had was enough, that any attempt to burden the poem with the requisite orthodoxy and pathos would only suffocate it. Its "unfinished" status—he may have realized—would allow his work to keep breathing until freer times arrive.

EPILOGUE

My involvement with Bazhan's "Sliptsi" began in late 1969 when it was republished in the Ukrainian émigré journal *Suchasnist'* and reentered a canon that was again on the cusp of reviving a nation. I was then a graduate student at Harvard, and along with my coursework in Slavic, comparative literature, and literary theory I was immersing myself in Ukrainian literature, which (although I did not know it at the time) was to become the centerpiece of my future academic career. I remember very distinctly the impact "Sliptsi" had on me then—a sense that I was reading a poem of breathtaking complexity and quality, a work that marked not only a new standard for Ukrainian poetry but for poetry in general. In the years that followed, beginning in 1970 when I started teaching my first course in twentieth-century Ukrainian poetry—formally the course was offered by my mentor Omeljan Pritsak, but in practice, though just a teaching fellow, it was I who actually designed it and taught it—Bazhan and the poem could not but figure prominently in it. In the many iterations of that course that followed over the next fifty years, Bazhan and his poem remained at the very center of things.

But something else stands out from that time, something which still tantalizes me, or in truth, gnaws at me with regret for memory's blurred detail and for missing textual evidence. Because it was then, sometime between when "Sliptsi" came out in November–December of 1969, and before the end of term in 1970 when I was teaching my first course, that Omeljan Pritsak, who was already well into establishing Ukrainian Studies at Harvard and who was to play so central a role in my life, asked me which living Ukrainian writer I would propose for the Nobel Prize. The question was not idle chitchat: he wanted a name and some reasoned arguments because he had been asked to submit a nomination. For me this was not a dilemma, especially since the impact of "Sliptsi" was still so fresh in my mind. The next step—Pritsak never shied from delegating what could be delegated, especially if he detected competence and enthusiasm—was to write up a succinct argument, which I did. I do not now have a copy or notes from that statement in front of me; perhaps I never did leave a copy for myself. But write it I did, with reference to Bazhan's extraordinary synthesis of classical national traditions and avant-garde experimentation; and, not least of all, to the fact, which I still hold to be true, that here he stands as an equal to his great forerunner Shevchenko. I was gratified to hear earlier this year at a conference dedicated to Omeljan Pritsak's one hundredth anniversary that he wrote to Mykola Bazhan to inform him of the Nobel Prize nomination and mentioned the "assistant" who helped him in this process. In Pritsak's archive now housed in Kyiv there is also, reportedly, a reply from Bazhan—which is appreciative and, not unexpectedly, modest and noncommittal (Soviet Ukrainian writers were not supposed to encourage such things).

In 1970, the Nobel Prize for literature went to Solzhenitsyn, and understandably so: he exemplified the profound change occurring not only in Soviet but in world literature. And he was widely translated. For me the 1970s marked, perhaps, the period of my greatest growth, but "Sliptsi," as much as I continued to be fascinated by the poem, remained a task deferred. I kept addressing it anew it in my lectures, however, and over the years two of my students published essays on it—no doubt, steps in the right direction.

In 2011, with the general intent of making at least a preliminary reading of the poem available to students who could not approach it in the original, I began translating it—almost as a dare, as an experiment to see whether a poem of such reputed and evident difficulty could even be translated. To be sure, some five or more years earlier I had started to translate Ukrainian poetry into English, focusing primarily on Shevchenko, but later also turning to contemporary poets—so some initial, anticipatory steps had been made. They hardly prepared me for "Sliptsi," however. By 2016 a draught version of part I and some sections of part II were ready for students and in a year or so the whole began to emerge. Nothing so empowers an understanding of a poem as translating it—not only every line and every image, but every word, every intonation, every pause or swerve should ideally be factored in. My original enthusiasm for it remains strong, but I also feel that my understanding of it, and of Bazhan, has grown immeasurably—and in unanticipated ways. I see the present reading as a first step; hopefully, a fuller examination will soon follow.

СЛІПЦІ

поема історична

Розділ Перший

Як бранка, до ніг припадає,
Як тіло солодке,
ляга
І зілля татарськеє—аєр,
Й холодна, скрипуча куга.

Хрумтить на долівці вертепу,
Як гість чобітьми розімне,
Цей поріст татарського степу—
Клечання запашне.

Шумить над лавками, над піччю,
І, раптом гойднувшись, майне
Странному гостю в обличчя
Клечання маю майне.

Гість стрепенеться і стане,
Буде прислухатися мить,
Як клечання дзвонить духмяне,
Як муха на шибці дзижчить ...
Приглушених звуків висока ігра,
Піднесшися, б'ється об сволок,
Де в'ється ритмічно різьба тесляра,
Оздоба хрищата, карбівка стара
З різьбленого листя та голок.

Суворої хати похмурий узор—
Ця бинда дубова, ця камка,
Вмурована в плечі рогатих підпор,
У в'язи стовбатого вламка,
Що, лігши на нього, підпершися ним,
Мов скриню яку найдорожчу,

BLIND BARDS

A Poem About History

Part I

Like a slave girl embracing your feet
Like a sweet body clinging
The gentle aroma of sea sedge
And the cold crackling reeds
That crunch on the floor of the cottage   5
When the boots of the guest
Release a bouquet of the Tatar steppe
That drifts over the table,
        and the massive tile stove
And suddenly caresses the face   10
Of the guest with the lush breath of May.
He shudders and stops in the doorway
And listens intently again
As the fragrant spray tingles
As a fly does its buzz on the pane ...   15
A sublime minuet of half-muted sounds
Then whirls and ascends to the roof beams
Where the carpenters' rhythmical carvings
Compose ancient runes of needles and leaves.
The sash made of oak and the trussing   20
Impose a design on the house that's severe—
[21]¹⁹
Mortised in muscular shoulders of buttresses
Powerful stanchions
        embrace and enfold,
Like a rare and invaluable treasure chest,   25
With crossbeams and thick bulky ropes
That knit up the dry-rotting rafters.

---

19 Numbers in square brackets—for example, "[21]"—refer to the page numbers of the 1969
Ukrainian edition: Mykola Bazhan, *Sliptsi*, with introduction by Bohdan Krawciw (Munich:
Vydavnytstvo "Suchasnist'," 1969), which is a reprint of the poem that appeared in *Suchasnist'*
10–11 (1969) some forty years after its first publication in the Kyivan journal *Zhyttia i revoliutsiia*
(1930–1931). See the accompanying translator's essay. A PDF of the 1969 Ukrainian edition of
the poem is available at http://diasporiana.org.ua/poeziya/1116-bazhan-m-sliptsi/.

Зав'язує сволок мотуззям міцним
Увесь перехнябений ощеп.
Розпарену скриню сопух розіпхав,
Випар цвілі,
              вологого шмаття,
Сморід жирних ротів,
                  ще жирніших страв
І пах солощавий латаття.
Здається,
           от-от, закипівши у ключ,
Проллється, за келих повніша,
Прилюдних бенкетів, розбещених учт,
Як чара, піднесена тиша.
Та владно уз гостя, побіля чола
Тишина зупиняється строга.
Навколо всіх звуків, замкнувшись, лягла
Мовчазна, нерухома облога.
Пальцями ловлячи тишину,
Тишу хвилясту й налляту,
Рукою обмацуючи стіну,
Як в слово, вслухаючись в хату,
Йде гість під стіною, де вбито гака
І вчеплено кобзу знехаяну,
І торбу,
          й лахміття кобеняка
Старого гуляки-хазяїна.
Хазяїн недбалий—гуляка старий,
З розважністю можновладця,
Сидить за столом у господі своїй
І гостей поруч нього—двадцять.
Хазяїн і двадцять голодних сіром,
Неборак та гуляк пропащих,
Схилились понуро над голим столом,
Над полем розваг непутящих.
Мовчать і готуються, сівши уряд,
До лютих своїх колобродин,
І, навіть рипіння учувши, назад
Не обернувся жоден.

A chest bloated by fumes, full of mold,
Effusions of mildew,
    and musty old clothes,   30
The smell of greasy mouths
      and still greasier meals,
And the cloying sweetness of lilies.
Any moment it will roil and boil up
The silence of weighty and portentous rites,   35
A chalice of silence poured out by the bushel.
Circling the table,
    stalking the guest,
The ominous silence
      commands him to stop.   40
Securing things tight, surrounding all sound,
A silent and motionless siege hunkers down.
Catching silence with his fingers,
Its rolling and pulsating stillness,
Feeling the wall with his hand,   45
Absorbing the house like a word
The guest skirts the wall,
    and its hook,
On which there's a sack,
     and the threadbare garb   50
And beat-up bandura[20]
      of the master-carouser.

[22]

With the air of a lord the old rascal sits
At the table with his twenty carousers.
The master and twenty of his hungry knaves,   55
Scoundrels, lost souls and ruffians all,
Hunched and morose round a slippery table,
Their arena of senseless diversions.
In silence, just waiting, all in a row,
Biding their time for their furious show,   60
And even when hearing the creaking behind them
Not one turns around.

---

20 *Bandura*—the best known of the traditional folk instruments, similar to the lute; see transla-
  tor's essay (TE).

Та нагло бандура на стінці дзвенить
Голосом мідним і простим.
Здригнувшись, озвалась приструнена мідь.
Зачеплена зляканим гостем.
І обертаються
                кобзарі,
І ока жовтавого
                жовна
Здимається,
                пухне в глибокій дірі,
Гидка,
          зацікавлена
                      й повна.
Бухтить, наливаючись соком в мокві,
Гнилим набираючись соком,
На двадцять одній голубій голові
Сорок одне око:
—Гей, хто там?!
                    —Гей, гостю, озвися!
—Який несподіваний гість?
—Який навіжений гульвіса
З яких розпроклятих обійсть?
—Напутники добрі, учителі!
Братіє перехожа!
Бандурники, лірники, скрипалі,
Пісенности пильна сторожа!
Я—
      учень сліпої громади,
                        слуга
Вчителя, майстра і пана,
Одного із тих, хто іще зберіга
Занедбані тайни торбана.
Прийшов одклонитись громаді, узять
Заслужчину рівнюсти й дружби—
Тяжку, невідрадну оту благодать
Сліпецької блудної служби.
За давнім звичаєм старих сліпаків
Мені вже кінчилися строки:

But when the bandura that hangs on the wall
Rings out its coppery and simple sound,
As the shuddering brass abruptly resounds   65
To the touch of the terrified guest—
The kobzars
        turn around,
And their yellowish orbs
           distend   70
And swell in their craters of wrinkles.
Suffused with a mute curiosity
Engorging and throbbing in their hollows,
Dilating with sickly secretions
In twenty-and-one graying heads   75
Stare the forty-and-one eyes:
[23]

—Who goes there?
          —Hey you, you better respond!
—A gatecrasher with gall!
—Who's this vagabond   80
            from some damn hole in the wall . .?
—Good mentors, kind teachers,
Peripatetic brothers—
Bandurists, lyrists, and fiddlers
Vigilant guardians of song!   85
—I'm
     but a pupil of the blind community,
               a servant
Of my teacher, and master and lord
One of those who nurtures the lore   90
And abandoned arcana of the torban.[21]
I've come to obtain my release,[22]
To earn my good name as an equal and friend,
To become one of you and embrace
This heavy, unforgiving grace   95
Of blind and devious service.
In keeping with custom of the ancient blind bards

---

21 *Torban*—alternative name for the bandura.
22 Release or manumission (as from serfdom); *odklynshchyna* (одклинщина) in Ukrainian:
    ritual for testing an adept's knowledge of the craft and, if approved, affirming his membership
    in the guild; see TE.

За майстром, як джура покірний, ходив
Три місяці і три роки ...

Поволі підвівся із тесаних лав
Хазяїн похмурий жебрацького кішла.
—Юначе збентежений, душе недішла!—
До зайди принишклого слово сказав.
—Хочеш кобзарські одклинщини справить?
Прийшов, щоб узяти тут визвілок наш?
Та, може, прийшов, не подумавши навіть?
Юначе, скажи мені!
         Слухай і зваж!
Береш бо бандуру—
            не панциря й тарча,
Не на двобої—
         на жебри ідеш! . .
І мовив юнак:
        —Я наважився, старче.
Наживсь на все ... І на зганьблення теж ...

Старий Перебендя—хазяїн завзятий
Вперед нахилився всім тілом своїм:
—А, може, ти брешеш, як зрадник проклятий?
А, може, ти—зрадник, а не побратим?
Юначе!
     Скажи мені правду попросту:
Чи не втомлює рук,
           чи не муля плеча
Співоцький риштунок, добро лірача—
І торба,
    і кобза,
        і костур?
—Вірте, громадо, мені
           і узять
Дозвольте торбана у руки несмілі!
Сиділи діди, хай онуки сидять
На Савурі,
       на славній могилі!

My tutelage is now at an end:
I have followed my master as a humble attendant
For all of three months and three years ...   100
[24]

Slowly the master gets up from his bench,
A menacing master of a beggarly bunch.
—Young man, you are clearly confused and half-baked!—
So to the diffident novice he starts to address,
—You want to begin the kobzar's release?   105
You've come to receive manumission?
But maybe you've come with hardly a thought?
Young man—you just tell me,
                just listen and ponder!
You're taking the bandura—   110
                not a shield and some armor
You're out there to beg,
                not to duel!
And the youth merely said:
                —Old man, I am ready   115
I'm ready for anything ... including the shame ...
Old Perebendia—the fanatical master
Leans forward with all of his frame
—But maybe you're lying, you cursed intruder?
Perhaps you're a traitor, or just playing a game?   120
Young man!
                tell the truth and say it straight out
Is your arm not all numb,
                is your shoulder not sore
From the singer's equipment, the lyrist's store   125
The sack,
        the staff,
                and the kobza?
—Believe me, my brethren, and permit me to hold
The torban in my tentative hands!   130
[25]

Let the grandsons now sit like the grandfathers sat
On Savur, the grave mound of old.[23]

---

23 *Savur* or *Savur mohyla;* see TE.

—Починаймо одклинщини, друзі святі,
Середульші,
   і старші,
     й молодші!
Питатиму я.
    На запитання ті
Відповідай нам, пан-отче! . .

І от Перебенді стає на одвіт
Найстарший з лебіїв дорослих.
—Запам'ятай же,—
     промовив цей дід,—
Ми києм караємо ослух.
Киями карається ослух у нас
Чи вдаром гінджала улучним ...
Ти щось ворохобився, бувши ввесь час
Невірним й непевним учнем.
Та хай!
   Але тута наважся лишень,
Спробуй лишень—
     зворохобся!
Незрушних законів і вірних пісень
Від посвячених требує кобза! . .

—Братчику чесний козацьких сліпців!
Чи слухняного й вірного джуру
В три лади настроювать кобзу навчив,
І ліру, й торбана, й бандуру.
В три лади, в три строї, на три голоси,
Що кожен із них—
     стоголосий,
В три лади, що названі в давні часи
Бандуристський, скрипошний та косий.
—Як відав, як знав, як умів, так учив
Ремества потайного лебіїв.
Три роки учив, і три роки ходив
З Почаєва з ним аж на Київ ...
—Чи навчився

—So let's start the release, my holy companions,
All of you, young,
                    middle aged   135
                              and old.
I will ask, and you old man will answer for him.
In response to Perebendia's dictum
The oldest of the company now rises to speak.
—Remember this well, says the elder,   140
                    we strike with the staff
We punish each fault with the stick
Or if need be a jab of the dagger ...
You must have done wrong in a passel of ways
You false and duplicitous pupil ...   145
But we'll let that pass ...
                              but if you try it today ...
If you even think of defiance ...
From its champions the kobza demands full observance
Of immutable laws and dependable songs.   150
—Venerable brother of the blind Cossack seed
Have you taught this devoted and obedient servant
To tune the kobza's three keys,
As well as the lira,[24] the torban and bandura.
[26]

Three keys and three modes and three voices   155
With inflections of each in the hundreds,
The three keys that are known from the oldest of times
As the bandura, the hybrid, and fiddle?
—As I knew, as I felt, as I could so I taught
The Lebians' secretive artwork.[25]   160
Three years I've instructed him
                    and three years I've walked with him
From Pochaiv all the way to Kyiv ...[26]

---

24 *Lira*—another basic instrument, analogous to the hurdy-gurdy; developed at length in part II of
    the poem; see TE. The player of the lira was generally known as a *lyrist* (Ukr.: *lirnyk* [лірник]).
25 *Lebian, lebii* (лебії) in Ukrainian is a general term for the peripatetic singers, beggars, and blind
    men (occasionally women)—performers and carriers of traditional Ukrainian folk music.
26 Pochaiv in western Ukraine (Volhynia) and Kyiv (in north-central Ukraine), the capital,
    were seats of the two major Orthodox (the former also briefly Uniate or Greek-Catholic)
    lavry, that is, monasteries and centers of religious learning and cult.

від нас тобі даний юнак,
Як майстер струни і приструнку,
Набирать в деревляний священний коряк
Тяжкого пісенного трунку,
Де зварено добре,
на троє ключів
Троїстого ладу тройзілля,
Щоб напувати німих слухачів
Для розмислу, стуми й весілля?
Проклята отрута,
проклята вода,
В струну, як в броню, закута!
Невже завмирає,
невже пропада
Пісенна підземна Славута?! .
Нестерпну вагу притамованих вод
Співці схороняють одлюдні
В співучому тілі торбанних колод
Немов у мурованій студні.
Вгинаючи цямру,
ламаючи кліть,
По кліті з чорного дуба
Вода, як руда, цебенить і гримить,
Водиця землиста й груба.
Гримить,
припадає,
влипає на спід
І світиться потаємцем,
Неначе лицарства розбитого щит,
Шаблями й вітрами шліхований щит,
Відкинутий спадкоємцем.
І наші криниці, як сурми, ростуть
В землі гайдамацької пущі.

—This youth we entrusted you did he then learn
How to master the strings and the keys,   165
How to gather in the holy and resonant trough
The burdensome potion of song
Which steeps and which simmers
                in three modes and three rhymes
A threefold and magical mixture of herbs   170
To slake the thirst of mute listeners
For reflection, for grief and for joy.
Anathemized poison,
              anathemized water
Encased in the strings as in armor!   175
Can this ancient and underground river run dry?
Can the underground songs ever vanish?
The reclusive old bards preserve for all time
In the resonant shells of the torban
The unbearable weight of waters pent-up   180
In the deepest stonework of wells.
[27]

Buckling the rim,
             deforming the facing,
Water gurgles and thunders, heavy as ore,
In a stream that is earthy and thick.   185
It pools and secretly fills the well floor
And shines
      like the shield
              of a knighthood destroyed,
Polished by winds and by swords it's a shield   190
Which the heirs then discarded.
And our wells grow like trumpets
In a land of haidamak[27] thickets.
In the pipes of the trumpets the cursed waters

---

27 *Haidamak* (Ukr.: гайдамак/гайдамаки) was a general name for bloody peasant uprisings
(with some Cossack participation), and their participants, in Right-Bank (west-central)
Ukraine in the course of the eighteenth century; particularly the Koliïvshchyna (коліївщина)
of 1768; see TE.

В колодязях трубних гримлять і ревуть
Води Славути клятущі.
В міцній облямівці,
         в лункім джерелі,
До дна прикипівши зненацька,
Розкривається око глухої землі—
Мертва вода вовкулацька.
І світяться зорі,
         і тліють жалі,
Стенаються грози,
         схиляються люди
Над оком уважним і мертвим землі,
Однаково й рівно усі віддалі
Відбившись на плівці полуди.
І відблиски гроз, і людей, і подій,
Переламлені та розпухлі,
Лежать, як осуга, в безодні сліпій,
В земному, бездомному кухлі.
Всі води країни,
         всі тіні віків
Ховає в безодню неситу
Око роззявлене сліпаків,
Всевбирущий колодязь світу ...
Дві краплі страшної тієї води—
Прикраса сліпецтва двоїста,
Ознака,
    і велич,
        і карб сліпоти,
Тяжкий талісман бандуриста.
Вмуруй же, жахнувшись,
         між лобних кісток
Дві грудки заклятого змроку,
Щоб тік,
    щоб спливав
         аж до мозку із скла
Смертельний його холодок!

Thunder and roar as an underground Dnipro.[28]
In conduits of stone, in resonant wells   195
They suddenly pool at the bottom
And stare like the eye of primordial land,
Like the lifeless water of werewolves.
The stars shine on, embers of suffering glow
And storms come and go and the people bow low   200
Over the morbid and vigilant eye of the earth
Over the occluded lens that sees all.
Reflections of storms, and of men and their deeds
Are refracted, and bloated
And spread like a mist over unsighted depths   205
Of the earth's bottomless beaker.
[28]

All the country's waters
                    all the shadows of ages
Are contained in the insatiable depths
Of the staring eye of the blind—   210
The all-encompassing well of the world …
Two drops of this terrible water
Are the twofold distinction of blindness
The mark,
            and the grandeur   215
                    and stigma of blindness,
The bandurist's dread symbol.
So shudder and affix in the sockets of your skull
Two drops of this damnable darkness and pain,
So its death-dealing chill   220
Can leak,
        and flow into,
                    and fuse with your brain.
Don't envy the prince's luxurious ways

---

28 The Dnipro river, flowing generally north to south and emptying into the Black Sea bisects
    Ukraine into the Right-Bank (the western) and Left-Bank (the eastern) parts; the Dnipro
    Delta (the "Great Meadow," *Velykyi luh* [Великий луг] in Ukrainian) also had special signifi-
    cance; see below.

Не князівської пишної прагни тропи.
Вищий над князі підніжок!
Гидуй пишнотою, й достойно ступи
На сліпецький лукавий обніжок.
На людських дорогах і тропах сиди,
Прийнявши посвяченість чорну.
І кобзу прохожим під ноги клади,
Як голову мудру й покорну.
Проходь же крізь села,

                  поля

                        і сади

В всевидящій сліпості й тиші.
Незрячий водію,

       вдивляйсь і веди
Юрби, за тебе сліпіші! . .
—Я чую вас, юрби сліпі й навісні,
Я чую вас,

             герці і учти!
Пісні,

          о, стороті прокляті пісні!
Вас мучу я,

           й ви мене мучте!
—Хтось мучить тебе,

               а ти мучиш всіх нас ...
—Тягти теревені ці доки?! . .
—Чекатимеш знову, як згавиш цей час
Три місяці і три роки ...

Над кодлом замовклим висить тишина—
Дзвону чоло без'язике,
Перекинута вінцями вниз глибина,
Велике,

       нестерпно велике
Піднесення звуків, і рухів, і душ ...
Так бий же в бездонного дзвона,
Дзвонарю поглухлий!

               Хитаючи, зруш
Тишини громової колону! . .

You, his footstool—who's so much higher than he.   225
Have disdain for his luxury, and with dignity
Go forth on the guileful path of the bards.
Sit on men's byways and highways
Embracing a calling that's utterly dark.
Place your kobza at the feet of the passersby   230
Along with your wise and respectful head.
Go through the villages,
                    orchards
                        and fields
In your all-seeing blindness and silence.   235
O, blind guide
            look sharply and lead
The crowds that are blinder than you! ...
[29]

—I hear the blind and maddening crowds swell,
I hear the banquets and duels,   240
And the songs—hundred-mouthed and accursed!
I torment you and you should torment me as well.

....

—Someone's tormenting you,
                    and you're tormenting us all ...
—How long will we suffer this drivel?!   245
—You'll wait again,
            if you fumble this ball
                        another three months and three years ...
Above the still lair the silence is dense
The tongueless brow of the bell   250
An immeasurable inverted depth
An unbearably huge,
                and intense
Elevation of sounds, of movements and souls ...
So strike then this bottomless bell   255
You deafened bell-ringer.
                Pendulate, knell,
And stir this column of thunderous silence! ...

Бий же, дзвонарю,
                    бий же наодліг
Не в дзвони,
              а в морди й серця!
В замовклім, засмердженім кодлі
Роззявилась тиша—
                    рот мерця.
Рот—
      зашкалубина хмура,
Сурма товста живота,
Волога й липуча рура,
Що блює, ремига і ковта.
Волоцюгам сліпим, крім рота,
Нічого не треба.
                  І от
Розкривсь, як діра ешафота,
Двадцять один рот:
—Віками йшли ми
Дорогами злими,
Землями злими, роками злоби.
Мов на катівні, на площі й майдани,
Як голови, клали сакви і торбани,
Мов бунчуки, простеляли чуби.
В баюрі, у куряві, в тузі і лжі,
Карка зломивши, мовчки лежи
І в землю, як в жертву, вгризайся!

Землю і руки свої гризучи,
На всіх перехрестях лежать стогначі,
Лірники—жальники й здрайці!
Здобич розпачлива—пил й пироги,
Зелені сирітські нужденні шаги
І вдовині чорні окрайці!
На всіх перехрестях сліпа голова,
Як пастку смертельну, своє розкрива
Піднебіння страшне трупоїдства.
Склепіння облудних жалів і скорбот,
Огидою й порохом напханий рот,

Lash out, you bell-ringer, in every direction
Not at bells,   260
        but at mugs and at hearts!
In the now speechless and stench-filled lair
Silence yawns like the mouth of a corpse.
The mouth—
        a grisly protrusion   265
The thick trumpet of the stomach
[30]

A moist and sticky pipe,
That vomits, and chews and swallows.
Blind vagabonds
        need only a mouth.   270
           And lo—
Springing open like the trap of a gallows
Are twenty-and-one gaping mouths:
—We've been trudging for ages
Over roads that are anguished   275
Through lands that are anguished, through years filled with malice.
As if at beheadings, in squares and maidans[29]
We would place our sacks and torbans
Like heads on the chopping block
And spread out our hair like pennants   280
In puddles, and dust, and in grief and in lies
Breaking our necks we would silently lie
Gnawing the dirt like we do our alms.
Gnawing the earth and their arms
On every crossroads lie the moaners,   285
The lyrists, complainers and felons.
Their sickening booty—some crumbs and some dust,
Miserable green pennies from orphans
And a widow's black crusts!
On every crossroads a blind head   290
Gapes with its trap for prostrated souls—
Necrophagia's terrible maw,
A cavern of fraudulent grievance and woe,
A mouth stuffed with dust and disgust,

---

29 *Maidan* (Ukr. майдан, from the Turkic languages) is a town or village square; also as in
    Kyiv's Maidan (of 2013–2014)—the city center itself.

Зморхлий капшук безстидства.

Капшука не зашморгуй—

всихає нехай!

Хай!

Дай, Боже, дай

За ганьбу,

За злобу

Твоєму рабу,

Щоб смиренні були і мудрі.

Во ім'я Отця

Трішки м'ясця,

Трішки винця,

Й кожному—хоч по лахудрі!..

Споїли,

крехтіли,

гарчали,

ревли,

Смерділи,

змокрілі та голі.

Над черевом мокрим бундючно трясли

Бородою на в'ялому волі.

І воло трусилось,

спадаючи з ший

Схвильованими обручами.

І сказав Перебендя:

—Брате мій!

Ти побратався із нами!

Слухай, кобзарю,

жахайсь і мовчи,

І тайни почуєш многі:

На всіх перехрестах лежать лірачі,

А зводяться тут лиш на ноги!

То ж м'ясо жіноче й волов'яче—

нам!

Голод і пісня—

для бидла!

Нарід наготує своїм співакам

A shrunken and shameless pouch of gall.   295
—Don't shut that pouch
                    —let it shrivel away!
[31]

So hey!
Give us this day, o Lord,
For the shame,   300
For the rancor,
Give us, your humble servants,
To make us pious and wise
In the name of the Father,
A little fodder,   305
A little flesh and a little wine,
And a whore for each one of us …
They wheezed,
            they groaned,
                        they growled   310
                                and they roared
They stank
        wet and naked.
Over bellies that glistened they proudly displayed
Their chins on shriveled up goiters   315
That billowed in circles on wobbly necks.
Perebendia then spoke:—My brother!
—Since now you're our brother, you're now one of us—…
Listen, kobzar,
            be shocked if you want,   320
                        but bear with me,
And many a mystery you'll hear:
On every crossroads the lyrists lie prone
But here they get up on their feet!
What we want here is flesh—women and beef.   325
Hunger and song
            —that's for cattle.
For their bards our people will gladly supply
[32]

Гори жінок та їдла.
Братія лірницька,
                                  віщий нарід,
По усюдах блукаючи,
                                  швендя,
І скільки пісень—
                                  стільки мсти й зненавид!—
Так сказав Перебендя.
—Збираючи сльози, серця й п'ятаки,
Втулища й душі, як жертви,
Блукають, мов блудні огні, сліпаки,
Огні невмирущі і мертві …
—Вогні ваші гаснуть,
                                  брехливий кобзарю
І трупи кричать по дорогах уже!
Так бити ж по трунах!
                                  Я перший ударю!
Ударю?
            Невже не ударю?
                                  Невже?! .
Я знаю, як страшно—
                                  цей ляпас—
                                  як страшно!
Кричить по дорогах юродливий мрець!
Смердять ваші тризни,
                                  гниють ваші брашна,
Гниє огонь ваших сердець! . .
Скиглію, замовкни!
            Слухай!
                        Мовчи:
Великий звитяг ошуканства …
—Звитяг?—на підлозі, в блювоті, в мочі?
В гарчанні любіння й п'янства?
Музика козацька—
                                  в сакваx кавдуна?
Свячений—
            в свинячій печені?

Piles of women and food.
The lyrist brotherhood,   330
                the folks who do prophecy,
Wander
      and loiter wherever they will
And in all of their songs
            —there is vengeance and hate!   335
Thus spake Perebendia.
—Collecting tears, hearts, and pennies,
Offerings of souls and pudenda
Like will-o'-the-wisps the blind bards wander
Like fires both deathless and dead …   340
—Your fires are guttering you lying kobzar
And those shouting by the roadsides are corpses!
So we'll hit back at the corpses!
             and I'll be the first!
You don't think I'll do it?   345
        You doubt it?
          Do you?
I know how it scares you—
        this blow—
           how it scares you!   350
Quaking cadavers shout by the roadsides.
Your wakes give off stench
        and your flour is rotten
The fires of your hearts are corrupt …
—Shut up you whiner!   355
      Be silent!
        Don't say it!
The sacred victory of deception …
—Victory?—in gorging, in vomit, with lice?
[33]

In groans of mating and boozing?   360
Cossack music—
        in a stomach's rumblings,
A knife that was blessed now stuck in a roast?[30]

---

30 Blessed knife: alluding to the "blessing of the knives" that allegedly took place just before—
    and gave religious validation to—the peasant uprising known as the Koliïvshchyna of

Не перший кобзар я, що тут проклина
Музику таку й ці свячені!
—Годі!—
        кричить Перебендя.
                  —Послухай!
Розум пропий, а сумління лиши
Там,
      де шумує сивезна сивуха—
У міддю окутім, дубовім ковші.
М'ясо й сивуха—причастій окраса.
Таїна причастій відома для нас:
Хто служить духу—той просить м'яса,
Багато м'яса,
        досхочу м'яс!
Христимся ж розп'ятим жовтим маслаччям
І плоттю свою причащаймо же плоть!
Сором видющим лишає Господь;
Сліпі,—
      отже й сраму не бачим!
—Що ж бачите,
        люті й сліпі водії?
Що в піснях зберігаєте
         й в серці?
Несуть животи, наче кобзи свої,
Розбещені страстотерпці!..
Хоч людськеє слово почути!
           Не чуть!..
—Жерти давай Перебенді!..
—Добре тим жерти, у кого, мабуть,
Кендюх—
    за серце,
        й за кендюх
Серце,
      де істина, розум і суть ...
—Несуть, вже несуть

I'm not the first kobzar to curse
Such music and such blessings!   365
—Enough!—
                    cries Perebendia.
                          —Listen!
Drink away your mind, but leave your conscience in place
There   370
          where the silver vodka shimmers—
In its oaken and copper-clad vessel
Meat and vodka bespeak our communion
For the Eucharist's mystery is known to us all:
Who waits on the spirit—can ask for meat   375
Lots of meat,
              loads of meat!
We'll make a cross with yellow thigh bones
And link our flesh with the flesh of the Lord.
God leaves shame for the sighted: 380
But we're blind and we don't see the shame!
—What do you see then,
                  you blind and ferocious guides?
What's preserved in your songs
                  and what's in your hearts?   385
For these desperate lechers
              just carry their stomachs like kobzas?
A kind word would help!
                    But when did you hear it? ...
[34]

—Chow for Perebendia! ...   390
—Gorging's the thing when you've got
A stomach for a heart
                  and heart only for stomachs
A heart
Where reason and truth and becoming ...   395
—It's coming, it's coming,

1768—a central moment in popular memory and in Taras Shevchenko's poem *Haidamaky*
(St. Petersburg: A. Sychev, 1841–1842); see TE.

Манашки нам кашки
І борщику в горщику ...
Доброго, Боже, пошли борщу!
Грудей у кошулі,
Сала й цибулі
На серце тще й на душу тщу!
І на полумисках, в макітрах, на тарелях,
Де опухами жир позастигав,
Несуть, в руках тримаючи дебелих,
Врочисті кучугури страв.
Воно розпарилось, розбухло і розквітло
І пишні випари, як стяги, простеля
Оце гливке й волокнувате їдло,
Тяжке, немов земля, і владне, як земля.
Пливуть на плеса нерухомі столу
У пахноті плавкій, як в голубій імлі,
Ковбаси згорнуті, немов кадні кодоли,
І часником напахчені драглі,
Міцні шари просоленого сала,
Сметани холодок у глечиках дзвінких,
Шльопки вареників, що плямами на них
Прозоро-жовте масло поспливало,
Засмоктане в трясовину підлив
Качаче гузно, гуся гола шийка,
Міцний, немов з кори дубової настілка,
Узвар із груш рудих і глянсуватих слив,
Борщу густі, зелено-темні верстви
В мисках мальованих, ясних, немов бурштин ...
О, він поглине все,
                        він змиє все,—цей плин
Бучного й лютого, як розпач, ненажерства!
—Сала накришено, м'яса нарубано,
Всипано в миску по вінце борщу!
Ковтаю, вминаю, жеру і трощу,
Щоб кавдуни задзвеніли, як бубони,
Щоб ...—
І замовкли ураз сліпаки,
Мову ввірваній одверту й нехитру.

Stews made by nuns
And some borshch with buns.
Yes, send us, O Lord, some good borshch,
And breasts in chemises   400
Some bacon and onions
For a heart that is hungry and a soul that is famished.
And on platters and plates and in bowls
With congealed gobs of fat they bestow
With gargantuan arms a sublime hoard of dishes   405
That steam and swell and bloom
And waft their voluptuous pennants.
Heavy as the earth and imperious like the earth,
Victuals clotted and massive,
Float up to the surface of the placid table.   410
With liquiform smells and in a bluish haze
Come sausages tiered like smoky logs,
Gelatinous meats stuffed with garlic,
Voluminous layers of rashers,
Cool portions of sour cream in resonant pitchers,   415
Huge piles of dumplings with yellowish globules of butter,
And all but concealed in the bottomless depths,
A tail of a duck and the neck of a goose.
[35]

Thick compotes of pears and shiny blue plums
Dark like the extract of oak bark,   420
Dense layers of borshch now black and once green
In painted and shining amber tureens …,
Insatiate juices as proud and as fierce as despair
Will liquefy all,
                will digest it all.   425
—The bacon's apportioned, the meat's all cut up
The borshch has been ladled to the brim!
They swallow and devour, they gobble and chomp
So their bellies can throb like a drum
So that …   430
                suddenly the blind bards fall silent
And break off their open and guileless palaver.

І поповзли по столі п'ястуки,
Наче раки слизькі, обчепивши макітру.
І чує сліпець—
                        в шарудінні, в імлі
Череватою сунуть горою
Двоногі потвори по вгнутім столі,
Трясучи над столом бородою.
Обсмоктують лодви,
                        облизують стіл
Голодні розкошелюби,
Звісивши клапоті слини і жил—
Прищуваті й ослизлі губи.
Губатого м'яса зчорнілий шмат—
Розплатана мертво корогва
Сліпецьких утіх, насолод і розрад
Кобзарського тайного логва.
Слина бучавіє на губах
Із салом розтопленим вкупі.
Плямкає стяг,
                        недочавлений стяг
Учти пророків і трупів.

Кинувсь кобзар, щоб не чуть, щоб втекти,
Кинувсь наосліп праворуч—
Репають рти, гугонять животи,
Глухо блює хтось поруч.
Ліворуч метнувся,
                        крутнувся навкруг—
Глуха, нездоланна задуха огиди!
Черево репає в твого сусіди,
З насолоди конаючи, стогне смердюх.
Стогни, захлинайся,
                        страшна салотопне,
Ротами людей і ротами бандур!
Як опух зчорнілий,
                        роздувшися, лопне
Серця розбовтаного міхур!

Fists crawl onto the boards of the table
With slimy crab claws they envelop the bowls
And the blind man hears   435
                in the dusk and the clatter
A mountain of paunches advancing
As the table's invaded by two-legged monsters
Shaking their chins,
             slavering over the trays,   440
                      licking the boards
The famished lechers press on
Dribbling their drool over their flabby skin
And their slimy and cankerous lips.
Blackened slabs of squamous flesh   445
Hang limply like a drooping banner
Of blind men's joys and sport and jests,
Of the kobzars secret coven.
Spittle bubbles on lips
Melding with glistening lard.   450
[36]

The banner still flutters,
                  the banner's still rampant,
Of this banquet of prophets and corpses.
The kobzar starts up—not to hear, just to flee
Blindly he turns to the right—   455
Mouths chomping, stomachs resounding
Someone vomiting dully beside him.
He turns to the left, he turns around,
And all around him—total, choking disgust.
Your neighbor's stomach ready to burst,   460
The stinker just moans as he's dying of delight.
So moan, and engorge
              you factory of lard
Through the mouths of men and the mouths of banduras,
Until like a blister   465
             your churning black heart
Will distend and explode. ...

Реве Перебендя, підспівують інші,
І звуки приглушує смороду повсть.
Зайшлись, збожеволівши, співи одклинщин
І одклонений надсадно зайшовсь.
Тіла посудомила чорна хороба,
Потрясає ротами падуча бола,
І піт прилипає до чорного лоба,
До чорного лоба, тяжкого чола.
Голови людські—болючі, як чирій,
Що вгвинчений довгим і впертим нуртом.
Поволі підноситься млілий трикирій
Трьох пальців старечих над мокрим чолом.
Старий Перебендя перехристився:
—Ну, що ж, одклонений юначе,
                                        у путь!
Одклинщини справили. Ти помолився,
Та й кожен із нас помолився, мабуть ...
—Годі, святобливі!
                  Я зрозумів
Із пишних літаній,
                    з напучувань кожних
Службу лукаву сліпих кобзарів—
Щоб не тривожити ясновельможних,
Шляхти, підшляхти, панів, підпанів,
В холодну колоду навіки закута
Ваша прокисла, проклята Славута,
Баюра глухих і сліпих хуторів!
Ваших колодязів заспані води—
Принада й загибіль у ніч глуху!
Revіте, народи,
                  конайте, народи!
Із піснею легше вмирать на шляху!
А я умирати не можу,
                      не хочу,
Смерду й рабу не зламаєте карк!

Perebendia roars on, the others sing along,
But the sounds are muted by a thick layer of stench.
The songs of release reach a frenzy of madness   470
And the released kobzar is enveloped as well.
Bodies contorted as with the black ague,
Mouths quaking with epileptic shakes,
Sweat sticking to black foreheads,
To deep furrowed foreheads, to the heavy brows;   475
Human heads, aching like boils
Deeply implanted with itching and pain.
[37]

Slowly the frail triple candlestick[31]
Of the old man's fingers is raised to his forehead
As old Perebendia crosses himself: 480
—Well, then, you're released young man—time to set out!
The manumission's complete. You've prayed,
And each of us has prayed no doubt …
—Enough, my worthies!
       I now understand   485
From your orotund litanies,
         From each of your homilies
The mendacious profession of the blind kobzars—
It's to avoid sowing fear among those who have power,
The nobles, the gentry, the lords and the squires.   490
Your sour and accursed underground river
Is chained for all time in a channel of ice;
Your backwater ponds and blind homesteads,
Your wellsprings' somnolent waters,
Are only a trap and a nighttime temptation.   495
Nations may roar,
       peoples may perish,
With a song it is easier to die on the road.
But I cannot die
       or rather I will not,   500
This is one slave and commoner whose back you won't break.

---

31 *Trykyrii* (трикирій in Ukr.) is a ritual Orthodox (also Greek Catholic) triform candlestick;
   see TE.

Вам не фортеця—

                   ваш хутір,

                            фільварок,

Вам не сховатись за пісню пророчу!

У ваші пророцтва й дороги не вірую!

Убийте! Розіпніть!

Не вірую я в «Отче наш» і «Вірую,»

В рабську покору століть!

Вірую—

               не кобзою,

                        вірую—

                                  не лірою,

Вірую—

               полум'я серця і гнів

Моєю непишною буде офірою

Для смердів,

               для хлопів,

                              для храпаків!

Малою офірою,

                        нікчемною жертвою.

Бо десь аж на всохлому, бідному дні

Водою сліпою,

                    водою мертвою

Забризкано очі і серце мені!

Бунти і народи!

               Пожежі і воля!

Як зранений пес, по дорогах повзу!

Голодні роти серед голого поля

Кричать про повстання, ревуть про грозу

Ноги зламаю,

               серце розчавлю,

Таки дожену вас,

               таки дожену,

Юрмища мужні!

               Конаючи, славлю

Бунти і бої,

               пожарища й війну!..

Manor house
     and estate
          are hardly a fortress,
And you cannot hide behind prophecy's song.   505
I don't believe in your path and your prophecies!
So kill me! Crucify me!
I don't believe in your "Our Father" or "Symbol of Faith,"
In the slavish humility of ages!
I believe—   510
     not with the kobza
          I believe—not with the lira
I believe that the flame of my heart and my rage
Will serve as my humble oblation
         for the serfs,   515
            for the servants,
               the common man.
This is my offering,
         my humblest of alms.
For somewhere at the bottom of that stygian well   520
Some drops of that water of the blind,
         of the dead,
Anointed my eyes and my heart.
Rebellions and nations!
         Conflagrations and freedom!   525
I crawl down these roads like a wounded stray.
Hungry mouths from across the bare fields
Howl about uprisings and the coming storm.
I'll wear out my legs,
         I'll trample my own heart   530
But I will find my way,
         I will catch up,
With the throngs of the fearless
And as I'm dying give praise
         to rebellions and battles,   535
             and the fires of war …

Я в очі заглянув сліпцю-ненажері,
Сліпий, я побачив сліпецькі серця!
Кінчайся, кумедіє зганьблена ця!
Ведіть до дверей мене! Двері! Де двері?! .

Розділ Другий

На сухому току,
                посеред пилюги,
Каправі й худі міхоноші,
Вмостившись, сваряться за гроші,
За мідні, щербаті шаги.
Сваряться,
          соплять,
                  і потроху
Вминають поцвілі свої
Тяжкі пироги та беркі малаї,
Ковтюхи крупкуваті гороху.
І тліють їх очі, як в тихім огні,
У ніжній сухій золотусі
І сиплються,
            сиплються вії кальні
На щоки при кожному русі.
На теплі й змокрілі повіки ляга
Дрібною, летючою рінню
Золотушна перга,
                сухозлотна перга,
Сліпоти передчасне цвітіння.
Обсипається око, як пух із кульбаб,
Обскубана кулька квітчана.
А рана цвіте—
              бо коли не змогла б
Квітнути плекана рана?
Щоб квітнула рана,
                  щоб око, померши,
Не оживало,—
            сліпцям оддає,

I've peered into the eyes of the insatiable bards,
And though blind I saw the hearts of the blind.
So let's put end to this shame ridden farce.   [539]
Show me the door! The door! Where's the door . .?
[39]

Part II

In the dry village square,
                    in the dust,
Scrawny and scrofulous haulers of sacks
Settle in to wrangle over their hoard,
Of chipped copper pennies.   5
They squabble
                    and wheeze
                              and they slowly devour
Heavy corn bread and moldy old pies
And granular mouthfuls of peas.   10
And their eyes molder slowly in the fire
Of a gentle and dry scrofula,
As their eyelashes shed their ulcerous dust
On their cheeks with each movement.
A minute and airy gravel that falls   15
On their warm and damp eyelids
A golden pollen,
                    a scrofulous pollen—
The bloom of premature blindness.

The eye sheds its substance like a dandelion its fluff   20
And leaves a plucked flowery orb
And the wound blooms
        for how could it not
[40]

When it's so pampered?
For the wound to bloom, for the eye, having died,   25
To never revive
                    the blind man's young guide

Як першу сльозу,

                як засмученість першу,

Зморене око й дитинство своє

Сліпецький водир,

                    поводир, міхоноша,

Що торбу і руку кобзарську несе,

Що стає найдорожча йому над усе

Лебійська засмерджена ноша.

Звикає приймати на гостре плече,

Приречене схнути й хилиться,

Правицю, що душить, лама і пече,

Врочисту кобзарську правицю.

Стенувшись і зблідши, зведеться хлопча

І руки сліпої примари

Покірливо візьме

                  й не скине з плеча

Того п'ятиперстого він пернача,

Тієї руки-костомари.

Обтяжений мудрістю, злом і жалем,

Із серцем голодним і голим,

Стає перед кожним народженим днем,

Перед кожним новим видноколом,

Стає й, тремтячи, прислухається він,

Як за сотні верстов і за тисячі гін,

Минущі і неминучі,

Надходять події прийдешніх годин,

Зустрічі, люди та бучі.

Гогочуть далеко страшні ярмарки

В гопашній, безумній хурделі,

Стліваюсь дороги,

                вщухають стежки,

Розпадаються прахом оселі.

Пробігають і зойки, й огні по юрбі,

Що шляхами,

             здригаючись, лізе.

І багато вогнів заховає в собі

Око каправе та зизе,

Доки закриється в сліпоті,

This hauler of sacks must give his first tear,
           his first blush,
His own tired eye   30
      and his youth and become
The guide
    who shoulders the sack
        and bears the kobzar's hand
And for whom dearest of all is the lebian's stink.   35
He learns to accept on his sharp shoulder blade,
A shoulder condemned to shrivel and bend,
The right hand that throttles and crushes and burns—
The exalted right hand of bardhood.
Quaking and blanching the young boy gets up   40
And humbly accepts
      and doesn't shrug off
The blind specter's hand,
That five-fingered mace,
That skeleton grip.   45
Weighed down by wisdom, regret and malice,
With a heart that is hungry and bare
He gets up before each newly born day,
Before each new horizon,
And as he gets up he trembles and listens   50
Across hundreds of furlongs and for thousands of leagues,
As transient and fated
Events roll out from the hours to come—
Encounters and people and struggles.
And far in the distance the frightful bazaars   55
Roar on their frenzied and senseless carousing.
[41]

The paths grow still,
      and the roads rot away
And settlements turn into dust.
Fires and moans flit through the crowds   60
That shiver and crawl by the roadways
And many a fire will be preserved
        in that scrofulous poor eye
Filled to the brim with its sweepings before
It shuts down in blindness,   65

Наповнившись грузом доценту,
І доки не стануть видющими ті,
Дерев'яні орбіти струменту.
... І вкручуй у пісню,
                         як в плесо,
                                         як в змрок,
Чорториї заюрені мозку!
Співай, як причинний,
                         крутись, як пророк,
Смердючий і злий недоноску!
Не слухай, як глухо скавчать уночі,
Дощату постелю рвучи й гризучи,
Голодні, обкрадені суки,
Віддавши щенята свої в лірачі
Учитись пісенної штуки.
Не слухай, як виють хурделі і пси,
Що вили і витимуть завше.
Пильнуй патериці,
                         торбину неси,
Бандуру від гроз заховавши.
Око, як близну свербливу, віддай,
І котре сліпе й недосліпене котре,
Потовчений в гамуз,
                         покручений вкрай
Безбатченку,
         байстре
                 і лотре!
—Ви, дядьку, до мене?—
                         озвався один.
—Кінчили?
         —Рушаємо звідци?
—Зі всіх пирогів—тільки жменька крихтин,
Бач бо, які ненаситці!
—Пан-отче! .. Рушаймо!
                         Доріг не боюся!
Що я молодий і недужий?
Так що ж! ..
Спитайте, пан-майстре, в оцих міхонош,

And before the instrument's wooden orbs
Will end up all-seeing.
… So spin out into song,
              ripple out into darkness
The turbulent whirlpools of your brain.   70
Sing like a madman;
              whirl like a prophet
You stinking accursed abortion.
Shut tight your ears to the orphaned bitches
That whine hungry into the night, and gnaw at their bedding 75
For abandoning their pups to the lyrists,
To learn the art of the song.
Be deaf to the howling of dogs and of storms
Who've always been howling and will always go on.
Take care of the staff   80
         and carry the sack
And shield the bandura from harm.
Give over your eye like a long-itching sore
Both the one that is blind and the one that's half good,
You bag of scraps,   85
       you contorted freak
[42]

You fatherless
     bastard
        and cheat.
—You talking to me?   90
       asked one,
—You all done? Are we going?
—All of those pies now a handful of crumbs,
What can you do with such gluttons!
—Let's get a move on, Father,   95
         I am not afraid of the road
So what if I am young and a weakling?
        So what …
So, Master, just ask those haulers of sacks

Чи вартий чого я й на що пригожуся.
Ми геть позмітаємо порох з шляхів
І пустимо наші дороги, як змії!..
Промовив якийся, і вії склепив,
Недоброю вільгістю зрошені вії.
—Ти прагнеш, водирю, доріг лірача?
Іч, спрага яка невситима,
Дитино злидарська,
                    лихе потерча
З посохлими й злими очима!
Так нумо ж!—Сліпцям манівців вистача!
Ходім, недоноску, ходімо!
Ходімо,
            несімо лукаве дання,
Найлюбше моє,
                    найдорожче,
Неношене ненькою, скурве щеня.
Ходімо—ганьба нас, як псів, виганя
На зраду, неначе на прощі.
Так згода?
            Рушаємо в мандри удвох?
Тремтиш і лякаєшся, хлопче?
Зважай,
            бо доскочеш таїн багатьох,
Як серце, мов лапоть, протопчеш ...
Мій сину проклятий!
                    Хай ліпше заб'ю,
Ніж візьму за неофіта!..
Як тяжко рушати в дорогу твою,
Двічі зраднику й двічі банито!..
Нехай. ... Добреду! Допалаю. Доп'ю!
Спраго несамовита!..
Ти знову в мені, непоборне страховище,
Плюгава й нудна самоти суєта ...
Ти чуєш?..
            Невже ти б зі мною пішов іще,
Нащадку замучених,
                    утле уровище,

If I am worth my salt and am up to the task.   100
We will sweep the dust from these roads,
We can fly these roads like they were kites …
One of them spoke up and blinked his eyelashes,
That were ominously sticky and damp.
—A guide, craves the roads of the lyrists?   105
What drive, what unquenchable thirst,
In this child of the dregs,
        this unbaptized infant
With eyes that are withered and bode nothing good.
Let's go then—no lack of detours for the blind.   110
Let's go then, you half-baked tyke, let's go then.
Let's go,
      Let's carry the gift of deception.
My lovely, my dearest
Not carried to term, my whoreson pup.   115
Let's go—dishonor drives us on like we're dogs
[43]

On our pilgrimage—to betrayal.
Is it a deal?
        The two of us, off on our mission?
You tremble, boy, are you frightened?   120
Take heed,
      for you will learn many a mystery
When you wear out your heart like an old pair of shoes.
My cursed son!
        I'd rather kill you   125
Than take you on as apprentice …
How hard to set off on your road
For the doubly betrayed and twice banished.
So be it. I'll make it. Burn out if need be. Drink it to the dregs.
What incredible thirst! …   130
You're with me again, you unvanquished horror,
You hideous, nauseous blind alley of solitude.
You hear me?
       Would you really go on with me
Child of the tortured,   135
         you pitiful cast-off,

Голодом вишкрябане з живота?!.
А був би з тобою,
                          як матір із сином,
З загнилим ще в матернім лоні синком ...
Постояв хвилину,
                          й пішов попід тином,
І зник вдалині,
                          вдалині за горбком ...
Скриплять, розриваючи пута з лози,
Насаджені задом на випнуті шкворні,
Рипучі й робучі, чолаті вози,
Неначе скарбівні гонорні.
Роздувши драбки,
      мов огвари, стоять,
Віддавши на ґендлі веселі,
Пахнющу й барвисту, мов райдуга, кладь,
Соки, плоди і зела.
Купи травних і коштовних скарбів
Вивалює, репнувши, бесаг,
Заради пихи
                     і для ґендлю розкрив
Господар, привівши для славних боїв,
Вельможну твердиню на дужих колесах,
Природні клейноди володаря нив,
Державця на луках та плесах.
Стоїть коло возу,
                     в брилі набакир
Величаючись, як в авреолі,
Воєвода з левад,
                     хуторський багатир,
Князь на стожаллі й в стодолі.
Розгортає він груди, як браму, насилу,
Бо м'язень на м'язня берем'я ляга.
Просторо та повно гуляє по тілу
Устояна добре,
                     хазяйська юха.
Розсунувши жили,
                     беруча гамула,

Scraped from the belly by hunger?
I would have been with you like a mother with her son
A son already rotted while still in her womb. ...
He stood for a moment,   140
        then trudged along the wattle fence
And disappeared in the distance,
               far beyond the hill. ...
Creaking and bursting their woven reed trussing,
Imposing their bulk on bulging axles   145
The high-browed and hulking wagons roll in
[44]

Like proud and inestimable coffers.
Exposing gigantic rungs,
        Dilated to the joys of commerce,
Displaying their fragrant and colorful wares,   150
And rainbows of juices, of fruits and of herbs.
Overflowing their bountiful sacks they spill
Piles of edible, succulent treasures
Out of pride
        for display   155
           and for trade.
In his battle for fortune the owner has brought here
His majestic fortress on gargantuan wheels,
And the natural jewels of this prince of meadows,
This sovereign of fields and of ponds.   160
He stands by his wagon,
            with straw hat pushed back
As under a halo he basks,
This voivode of the valley,
          hero of the homestead,   165
Prince of the hayfields and barns.
With effort he puffs out his chest the size of a gate
As his muscles align in great heaps,
And his propertied and ponderous blood pulses
Through his massive body, distending the veins,   170
Suffusing the muscles and flows along the neck,
            and heads for the breast
[45]

Патьоками м'язні гарячі вгорта,—
По шиї спливає,

на груди звернула,
На клубах зачовгала, жирна й товста.
Хазяїн вслухається:

тепло лоскоче
У м'ясо, у сало зав'язаний плин.
Хазяїн м'якого й штудерного хоче—
Чи баби, чи пісні.

Вслухається він—
Стогоном вовчим і клекотом орлим
Сурмить над майданом владущий хосен
У кожне зчорніле, роззявлене горло,
Роз'ятрене з мляви, горілки й пісень.

Ось вона—пісня трактирів і лазень,
Смугастих абахт і товарячих тирл!
Горлай чи лупежник? Лабазник чи блазень?
Мандрьоха базарна чи багатир?
Щоб пісню, як бабу, обм'ять і обсмикать,
Щоб висмоктать пісню, мов пляшку, мов хіть,
Вже рта ворушиться скоцюрблений кікоть,
Що вміє вчепитись, і ссати, і пить.

—А йди-но сюди, галайдацька псявіро!
Заробиш чи гріш чи з товчеником книш.
Музику крути нам,

рипи нам на ліру,
Співай, чортів старче, гучніш і бучніш!
—Та ось вам і пісня, сліпенька зароба!
Гукнули—й почула музика сліпа ...

І напнувся старий,

аж тече з-попід лоба,
З повік, вкритих вразами, жовта ропа.
Заверещала розхитана корба,
І знявся, мов хмарка, над лірою пил,
І смик вереливо поскубує,

And finally finds rests on his hips thick and stout.
The owner is all self-absorption:
                                                as the heat bathes his body   175
Congealing the liquid into meat and to lard.
The owner wants things that are soft and well-fashioned
Whether women or songs.
                                        He's all ears, like a scout,
To the wailing of wolves and the screaming of eagles   180
As avarice trumpets its rule on the maidan
And enters each gaping black maw,
Be it open from vodka, fatigue or from song.
And lo, there they are—songs of taverns and bathhouses
Of striped sentry posts and animal sheds.   185
Are you a crooner or skinner? Miller or clown?
Bazaar strumpet—or hero?
You take the song, like a woman, to handle it, to fondle it
You suck out the song
                                        as you would empty a bottle, or your lust.   190
Already you're moving that stump in your mouth
The one that knows well how to grab, suck and drink.
—Hey you there, you scoundrel, get yourself here,
You'll get you some coins or some knishes or dishes.
Turn out some music, let the lira resound,   195
Sing, you old devil, and do it loud and strong …
—So here is your song—proper toil for the blind ones!
They called for it—and blind music's on call …
And the old man strained
                                        And from under his brow   200
From his eyelids, covered in sores, the yellow pus flowed
[46]

And the handle starts turning and screeching
And a small cloud of dusts settles over the lira
And the turning bow plucks, tweaks and rubs
The instrument's skein of twisted fibers   205
And the wooden box dully resounds
With the pulsating boards and the rhythm of the keys

корпа

Мотуззя костричене й кручево жил.
Ящик дощатий виляскує глухо.
Гунких дощечок верещання і стук.
Ліра рипить—ярмаркова рипуха,
З вереття висмикує зниділий звук.
Ліра рипить—ярмаркова жебрачка,
Жебруча тужільниця,

вірниця скрух.

Бреде, затинається, стогне заплачка,
Стогнеш, заплачко?—
—Ух, ух!
Горільчаний дух
Оковити, варенух, запридух!

Закривайте ярмарки,
Наливайте нам чарки!
Чарко моя, чепурушко,
Тебе вип'ю я, моя душко,
Тебе вип'ю я та не виллю,
Люба чарка мені на похміллю.
Я з тобою, чарочко, погуляю,
Наче біла рибонька по Дунаю,
Бо я хлопець—чарці друг,
Добрий зух,
Ух!
Добрий зух,
І п'янюга, й волоцюга з волоцюг!
Шинкарочки, шинкарки,
Наливайте нам чарки!
Сало смажте, сало шкварте,
Виставляйте калачі,
І горілки повні кварти
Наточи, наточи!
Дай книшів, дай книшів,
Розбивай барила
Для хазяйської душі,
Хазяйського тіла!

And the lira now drones—the bazaar's basic hum
Eliciting sound from a tangle of strings.
The lira drones on—the beggar queen of the bazaar   210
The wandering wailer, the official bearer of grief.
The invocation lament[32] moans in fits and in starts …
Are you moaning my weeper? …
—Hooch, hooch
The spirit of brew   215
Of aquavit, honey vodka, moonshine an' mash
Shutter up the booths
Fill 'em up, fill 'em up,
Oh my lovely shot glass, my little honeycup
I'll lap you up my honeycup and not spill a drop   220
I just love a glass you can dance with
Trip the light fantastic toe
Trippin' through the dew in the moonshine
Love the hooch. Oof!
I'm a guzzler, and a boozer and a tramp …   225
[47]

Oh you lovely maidens, oh you lovely barmaids
Fill 'em up, fill 'em up,
Fry the bacon, fry the bacon
Lay on the puddin' and the pies
And pint after pint of vodka   230
And knishes and latkes
Break open the barrels
Man's got to have
What a man's got to have.

---

32 In Ukrainian: *zaplachka* (заплачка); literally, "starting the weeping," the introductory lament
    with which a particular song or performance would start.

Усі враз, усі враз!

Розгулялись дуки.

Б'ють в підкову, б'ють в обцас,

Садять в закаблуки.

Витинають гопака,

Розривають шати.

Моя ж доля вже така—

Піти й приґравати.

Ух, ух!

Ледь не спух

З тих бенкетів та наруг.

Клята доля, ой недоля, у старцюг!

Доля—злигодні мої,

Чом я десь не дів її!

Доброточки-хазяї,

Люди праведнії, милостивії.

Та простріть же ви руку даящу,

Та згляньтесь на душу пропащу,

Подайте на Отченаш, на обмоленіє,

На своє спасеніе.

Ой, майте ж, моя мамцю, жалість наді мною,

Над моєю нищотою,

Над моїм то каліцтвом довічним

Не бачу ж я, мамцю, як праведне сонечко сяє,

Не бачу ж, моя квітю, як день Божий минає,

Не бачу, мамцю, як вечорок, моя квітю, примеркає.

А заслонило ж мені оченьки, заслонило,

Як кленовим листочком застелило.

Волів би я, мамцю, заробить,

Волів би я, квітю, заслужить,

Гірка моя, мамцю, зароба-заслуга ...

І крутиться корба,

      і ліра рипить,

Ліра рипить—ярмаркова рипуха.

Навколо принишкли,—

      той мріє,

        той слуха,

All together now   235
All together now
Everybody's dancing
Everybody's hoofing it
Dancing fit to burst.   240
Spending every dime
For a wonderful time …
And it's my fate to play along,
Make the music so you can dance.
Oof, oof!   245
I'm fit to burst,
From all these banquets, from all the contempt I get.
Oh this cursed fate, oh the misery of beggars!
Why could I not just leave it behind me!
Oh good gentlefolk all,   250
Kindly extend your hand so generous
Kindly give alms to a soul so fallen.
Give alms for an Our Father, for my prayers
That'll work for your salvation
Oh mother dear have some pity on me   255
On my wretched suffering nature,
On my endless infirmity
For I can't see, mother dear, how the righteous sun shines above,
I can't see, my blossom, how God's holy day passes by,
I can't see, dear mother, how the evening draws to a close,   260
Yes, my poor little eyes were made dark,
Covered as with a little maple leaf
I would rather, dear mother, earn a living as normal people do
I would rather, my dear flower, make my way as normal people do
Bitter, dear mother, is the path of my labors so onerous …   265
[49]

And the wheel keeps on turning
               and the lira keeps droning
And its drone now becomes the *OM* of the market.
The listeners grow silent—
                        this one is dreaming,   270
                              that one is listening

А той, обіпершись об воза, стоїть
Та й засинає поволі.
                    І близько
Присунулась тиша,
                    і чує сліпак,
Як гупає, впавши кудись на билисько,
Цварициним іменем битий п'ятак.
Похнюпився дід і припав до струмента,
Та й слуха, як струни бренять,
                            як із тьми
Спотикаючись, човгаючи чобітьми,
Хтось до нього задумливо плента.
Підійшов.
          Зупинився.
                    Ступив ще на п'ядь.
Поволі схилився,
                й долоня волога
Торкнулась лиця, як уміють торкать
Тільки допитливі руки сліпого.
—Хто це, питаю? . .
                Та хто це, питаю?
Товариш? . .
              На біса товариш мені!
Нехай він деінде ...
                  Бо тут назитаю
І сам на гертиху та кунсо хобні ...
—Я не товариш вам, діду,
                        й не недруг,
Хоч і приблуда сліпий між людей ...
Ні датку собі, ні дівчат товстобедрих
Я не шукаю ...
              Ви, діду, ачей
Не перший десяток вакуєте з лірою
І знаєте добре сліпецькі путі,
Що їх я ніколи не взнаю,
                        не зміряю ...

And the one over there, leaning against the wagon
Is slowly falling sleep.
And silence
Has crept up real close, 275
and the blind coot hears
The thud of the heavy five-kopek coin
etched with the name of the tsarina.
The old man sits hunched and embraces his lira
And senses the throb of its strings 280
and how in the darkness
Stumbling and shuffling his boots
someone is slowly approaching.
He comes up.
And he stops. 285
One more step.
And slowly he stoops
and a moist palm
Touches his face,
that inquisitive touch 290
That bespeaks the hand of a blind man.
[49]

—Who is this, I ask?
So, who is this, I ask?
A friend?
What the hell do I need a friend for! 295
You can go take a hike ...
'cause here
I'll make plate for some bowse and some bingo[33]
—I'm not your friend old man—
but I'm no foe, 300
Just a blind wanderer making my way ...
I'm not here for the scraps or the big-hipped girls
That's not what I'm here for ...
I guess, old man,

---

33 Translator's approximation in English criminal argot of the *lebian* secret language phrase rendered by Bazhan as "Бо тут назитаю/I сам на гертиху i кунсо хобнi"—that is, "For here I can beg for myself some dough for vodka and bread." See his footnote 26.

Діду! Скажи—чи дороги оті,
Замучивши згаймо душі,
                          виводять
Співців та їх вірних в ясний вертоград?
Чи певність та звагу,
                          чи просто—байстрят
Блукаючи світом, бандурники родять?
Чи всохла остання краплина води
В бандурній, лункій та сухій шкаралущі?
Чи, може, вже води могутніші й дужчі
Гримлять об пороги мужицьких твердинь?!
Ти ходиш по світі не перший десяток,
Не на першому стовквищі ницьма лежиш.
І ліра стара та посвячений ніж,
Та, може, ще мудрість і скруха—твій статок ...
Запльований,
                   зганьблений більш над усіх,
Це ж ти—
     найнещасніший з відданих лірі,
І розпач холоне на більмах твоїх,
Одчай, що зневажливу зроджує щирість ...

А лірник мовчить,
               і пливуть,
                          і пливуть
Нерухомо спливають два ока підласі,
Несучи білий мул і гнилу каламуть
З продавлених ям в зашкарублому м'ясі.
А лірник мовчить,
               наче він не зловив
Глухого, мов скрип, шепотіння приблуди.
Навколо сліпців порозходились люди,
Не добравши в тій бесіді глузду і слів.
А лірник мовчить,
               і видзвоню́є муха,
Принаджена соком м'ясистих повік.
Він спить?
          Десь ширяє думками?
                          Чи слуха?

You've been making the rounds with your lira for ages   305
And know all the highways and roads of the blind
Which I'll never know,
        which I'll never measure.
Tell me, old man, do these roads,
While parching the soul, ever lead the blind and their faithful,   310
To the promised land? Do the bandura's bards
Ever bring peace and contentment as they wander the world,
Or do they leave behind them only their bastards?
Did the last drop of water simply dry up
In the sere and resounding husk of the bandura?   315
Or perhaps there are waters much vaster and stronger
That surge at the doorstep of the commoners' castles?
You've been walking this earth for many a year
You have lain in the dust of many a fair.
[50]

Your ancient lira and a knife that's been blessed,   320
And some wisdom and rue, are the sum of your wealth …
And all of it's spat on and rejected by all.
For that's what you are—the lira's unhappy disciple
With despair growing cold on your cataract eyes,
A despair that gives birth to contemptuous sincerity.   325
The lyrist is silent. His eyes, encrusted,
Shed from their orbs a yellowish dust,
A draining of rot from putrescent flesh.
The bard remains silent, as if he had not heard
The incessant drone of the newcomer's whisper.   330
Unable to find any sense in this talk,
Or make out the words, the people around them drift off.
The bard remains silent, and the fly keeps on buzzing,
Attracted by the juice of the meaty eyelids.
Does he sleep? Do his thoughts whirl about? Is he listening?   335
For the man
        there beside him
           keeps at it.

І, поруч, присівши,
                    веде чоловік
Все далі своєї:
                —Я вчився три роки
І очі склепились зогнивши.
                      Отак
Пішов придивлятись до світу,
                     безокий
Мандрований лірник, незрячий жебрак.
Я бачив багато й питаю не вперше,
Востаннє?
         Не знаю.
              Знаю—не вперш.
Ти відаєш, діду,—
             є всякі тверджі,
А сумнів, певне, найбільша з тверадж.
Ламаюся в сумнів, як в браму обвалену,
Розкопую,
       б'ю,
          вивертаю її.
У кожну шпарину,
             у кожну прогалину
Встромляю заюшені пальці свої.
Ти думаєш—так,
            засурмивши у сурми,
Пройдеш крізь облоги, крізь мури й рови?
Ні!
  Треба в страшні і розпачливі штурми
Кидати чорне ядро голови.
Маячня повсякденна,
             шугання думок, наче струмнів,
Що дзвонять у скроні
            та геть одлітають у мить.
Легко зломити голову—
            важко зломити сумнів,
Здолати його і на горло йому наступить.
Порожнеча вирує так боляче й глухо.
              Шалій ти!

—I had studied for three years—till my eyes rotted shut.
[51]

So eyeless I left to observe the world,   340
A sightless beggar, a wandering bard.
And there is much that I saw. It's not the first time I ask
Is it the last?
              I don't know.
                           But for sure not the first.   345

You know, old man,
                 There are all kinds of forts,
But doubt is the biggest of all.
I assault doubt like the ruins of a huge gate
I excavate doubt,   350
              I beat it,
                           I turn it inside out.
Into every crack,
              and every seam,
I insert my fingers—all bloody.   355
You think just like that? By blowing a trumpet
You'll break through, cross the moat, breach the walls?
No!
       In your fierce and desperate sortie
Your head will be the battering ram   360
Butting at everyday madness, the perpetual swirl of thought
That rings in your head and explodes into fragments.
It's easy to break your skull—much harder to break doubt.
To pin it and step on its throat.
The void will gnaw and whirl on in pain.   365
                           So rage on!
[52]

Indecision's circle turns souls into corpses.
So conquer it! Break through! Overcome it! Get out!
Like a man—not a martyr …
                    You hear me?—a man!   370
So give me an answer, passerby …
                    Will I,

Кругойдуче вагання засмоктує трупики душ!
Здолати! Продертись! Пробитися! Вийти!
Як муж, а не мученик ...
                              Чуєш?—
                                        Як муж!
Відповідай, перехожий! ..
                              Невже безсоромно й довічно
По торжищу людському сумнів тягтиму я свій?!
І чоло скривавлено біле,—
                              тільки око кричить дихавично,
Наче здавлений розпачем рот, закам'яніло блідий.
—Що для тебе ганьба?
                              Призвичаївся ти до потали!
Чекаю я, піду,—скажи мені правду на це!
Ти вже так натягавсь
                              і так вже тебе заплювали,
Що плюнути легко й самому собі у лице.
Неважко тобі відказать,
                              спаплюженому жебракові,
Чий строк уже вийшов,
                              чий біль і затих, і засох! ..
Скажи, не лякайся—
                    на площі лишилися вдвох.
Скажи,
        що пророчі сліпці—
                              махлярі й горлаї ярмаркові,
Скажи,
        що козацький співець—
                              кумедний тепер скоморох ...
Я знаю,—
        зміняється світ,
                              і прадавні криваві пожари
На заграву іншу змінились—
                              то смалить кабанник свиней ...

Ever in shame, haul my doubt around the world's market?
The head is silent and only the eye shouts its frenzy
Mouth pale, frozen shut in desperation.   375
What is shame for you? You know what is scorn.
I'm still waiting, old man. Tell me the truth. I'll go soon.
You've schlepped it so long, and been spat on so often
That it's nothing at all to spit in your own face.
Can you, a scorned beggar, now answer,   380
When your time is up, when pain is now muted and over?
Say it, don't be afraid—
          they were now the last ones in the square—
Say it:
          the prophetic blind bards,   385
                    are bazaar conmen and ranters,
Say it:
          The Cossack bard is now a comedian and blowhard …
I know—
          The world's changing   390
                    and the bloody fires of old

[53]

Appear in new guises …
The glow on the horizon is the pig farmer roasting his pigs …
Hey, old man, hey
The Cossack's not bringing back captives from Tatar captivity[34]   395
He's herding meek sheep for the merchants at market …
And sheep wool, and a dog's tail for good measure,
Gets hauled off in carts to the mills, and stores, and estates
By diligent owners—the industrious Cossacks.
They cut stands of oak, centuries old and majestic,   400
They cut the sainted oak from the time of the Hetmans
To use its bark for tanning, for leather, for belts and for boots.
Recycling the Cossack companion—his faithful steed
And the long-horned oxen of chumak[35] lore—
                    they're all flayed alive   405
By Cossacks for profit …
                    The glass for carafes and for goblets

---

34 Central topos in the Ukrainian *dumy*; see TE.

35 *Chumaks* (Ukr.: чумак, чумаки) were traditional salt carters; their profession was particu-
    larly productive for folk song repertoire; see TE.

Гей, діду, гей,
Не татарський ясир, а смердючі отари
Поганяє козак для торгових гостей.
І вовну овечу, ба хвіст навіть песій
Запакувавши в беремища пак,
Везе до вальош, до крамниць, до посесій
Хазяїн уважний, хаптурний козак.
Стинають діброви столітні, прегарні,
Рубають гетьманський освячений дуб,
Корягу дубову везе до чинбарні,
Щоб ремінь чинили, козак-живолуп.
Шкуру та ремінь, на юхт і сап'яни
З лицарського друга, коня-румака,
З волів круторогих, чумацької шани,
Здирає і лупить козацька рука.
Щоб скло для карафок топити, на гути
Предковецькою кров'ю заллятий пісок
З боїща старого, зі схова кісток
Козацтво взялося возами тягнути.
Вивозять і праху дідівського корх,
І тіло внучаче слабе та невкріпле!
Він землю дідів, як пісок, пересипле,
Отой всевладущий, ненаїдний торг!
Я чую—
            реве, роззявляючись, через
І кожен ячить перепроданий морг!
Я чую—
            заходиться лірницький вереск,—
То гонять пісні, наче вівці, на торг ...

—Бодай би не згадувать скрухи і туги,
Бодай би не згадувать муки й гріхи,
Бодай би не згадувать темні шляхи
Великого світу й Великого Лугу!
Путі твої куряні відаю я,
Великий мій Луже,
                        дикий мій Луже,
І вітром твоїм виповнялось недуже

Comes from sand that was soaked in ancestor's blood—
From ancient battlefields, from venerable ossuaries
The Cossacks will export their grandfathers' ashes   410
As well as their grandsons' unformed and young bodies.
The land of their fathers can be sifted like sand
And sold to a ravenous market
I hear—
        the roar of a huge, gaping money belt,   415
And the screeching of each mortgaged acre ...
[54]

I hear—
        the bleating of the lyrists
As songs like sheep are driven to market ...

....

—Better not remember the grief and regrets   420
Better not remember the torments and sins,
Better not remember the dark twisted paths
Of the great outside world and the great Watery Meadow
My great Delta,[36]
        My wild Delta   425
The wind that wafted over you

---

36 The Great Meadow or The Great Delta (in Ukr., Великий луг) are huge territories (over
three hundred square miles) of lowlands and waterways of the delta on the east bank of the
Dnipro river constituting the area of the Zaporozhian Sich, the various Cossack strongholds
beyond the Dnipro rapids; a central geographical and especially symbolic topos of Cossack
lore and identity; see TE.

Серце базарного горлопая.
Ще був водирем,
             і з дідком голомозим
На жебри ходив, на кобзарське вчення,
Коли величався у Глухові Розум,
Оте нерозумне й бучне гетьманя.
Розбито Батурин,
            занедбано Глухів,
Ще куряться кроки сплюндрованих гард ...
Я чув брязкотіння рушниць,
                 алебард,
Тупіт невгавний муштрованих рухів.
Я чув, як ридав недолугий Калниш,
Рвучи на кибитці суху рогожину,
Щоб глянуть востаннє
                  й проклясть Україну,
Й простить Україну, де порох і тиш ...
Я чув, як молився про помсту і звагу,
Над лезом склонившися, Мельхиседек,
Благословивши похмуру звитягу
Залізнякових завзятих дейнек.
Я чув, як багаття гриміли у Кодні,

Still stirs the poor heart of the bazaar singer
Who once was a guide for a balding old man
And accompanied his begging, and learned
his kobzar lore   430
When Rozumovski[37] was lording it in Hlukhiv[38]
That not very smart and uppity Hetman.
I recall how Baturyn[39] was ravaged
and Hlukhiv abandoned
And rafters still smoking in raped Cossack settlements ...   435
I remember the rattle of muskets and halberds
And the endless tramping of marching feet.
I heard the laments of the hapless Kalnysh[40]
Clawing at his cart's wicker screen
To get a last look at, and to curse Ukraine   440
And to forgive Ukraine
Where only silence and dust now remain ...
[55]

I heard the ancient Melkhisedekh[41]
Bowed over the blades, praying
For vengeance and courage, and blessing   445
the grim feat

---

37 Hetman Kyrylo Rozumovs'kyi, 1728–1803 (Hetman, 1750–1764). Note the root word *rozum* means wisdom/knowledge; hence too, it is stressed that he was *nerozumnyi*—not very smart. In historical terms, a puppet, without real power; in the spirit of the Latin *lucus a non lucendo*; see TE.

38 Hlukhiv is a town in northeasternmost Ukraine (Sumy region). From 1708 to 1764 it was the seat of the Cossack Hetmanate; in 1765–1773 it became the seat of the Little Russian (*Malorosiis'ka*) gubernia.

39 Baturyn is a town in northern Ukraine (Chernihiv region). In 1669–1708 and 1750–1764 it was the residence of the Hetman. When Hetman Mazepa revolted against Peter I and sided with Charles XII of Sweden, Baturyn was destroyed and its inhabitants massacred by Russian troops in 1708.

40 Kalnysh, that is, Petro Kalnyshevs'kyi (1691–1803) was the last *otaman* (general) of the Zaporozhian Sich (1762 and 1765–1775). In 1775, he was captured by Russian troops and exiled to the Solovki monastery in Russia's far north. He died there in 1803 after twenty-eight years of captivity. Canonized by the Ukrainian Orthodox church in 2008.

41 Archimandrite Melkhisedekh, in civil life Mathew Znachko-Iavors'kyi (1716–1809) was an Orthodox clergyman from the Ukrainian nobility who actively opposed Polish religious oppression in Right-Bank Ukraine. According to legend (iconically depicted in Taras Shevchenko's *Haidamaky*), he blessed the knives of the *haidamaks* before the uprising of 1768 (the Koliïvshchyna); see TE.

Як репало тіло, узяте в бичі ...
Сьогодні ж ...

             Наслухався добре сьогодні ...
Мовчи, юродива примаро, мовчи! . .
Ти ж, серце нікчемне, старого не згадуй,
Лягай у свій мудрий і зважений лад,
Не втягуй збентежені мислі у зваду,
Вони бо пройшли через тисячі звад.
Мені недалечко лишилось до гробу,
Та мовлю, вмираючи:

               благословен
Більший над чвари козацький хосен,
Господаря чесного чесна зароба!
Бо й справді міняється світ і діла,
Й пасуться отари на вигонах Кодні.
Збирай же, козаче, дари ті природні,
Що їх Україна тобі віддала!
Солодку пшеницю,

               пекучу салітру,
Розсипчасту рибу

               і мед-липовець!
Розкрито країну для доброго вітру,
Що зела заплоджує, втіху сердець!
І радісний вітер, свиріль трудолюбства,
І дощ-теплодай, танцюристий моцар,
Розмиє криваві сліди братогубства,
Розвіє ману недокінчених чвар.
Дивись—

          козаки, трудолюбці смиренні,
Виходять, забувши про чвари й сварки ...
—На торжища йдуть!

             А хіба ярмарки

Of Zalizniak's desperados.[42]
I heard the thundering fires at Kodnia[43]
And the sound of flesh ripped apart on the racks …
And today …   450
      I've heard a lot of things today …
—Be still, you holy fool, be still! …
Your heart's too ignoble to tell us the past
Lie down in your wise and rational order
And let your frenzied thoughts rest in peace   455
For they're all in such constant turmoil …
I'm now just a step away from my grave
And so I can speak, as I die:
              much more blessed
Than ceaseless contention is sheer Cossack bounty,   460
Honest fruit of honest labor.
For the world and its deeds are truly in flux
And herds are now grazing on the fields around Kodnia.
So the Cossack, can rightfully gather around him
All the gifts of nature Ukraine has to offer!   465
Sweet wheat, and sharp calcium salts
Fish that melt in your mouth and linden tree honey.
And the country wide open to a good wind
That fructifies seed and gladdens the heart.
And more joyful wind and the piping of work   470
And the rain that warms and the merriment of dance
[56]

Will wash off the blood and the fratricide
And scatter the madness of endless vendettas.

Look!—the Cossacks, those peace-loving workers,
Come on the scene with minds fully cleared   475
              of battles and conflicts.
—They're going to market!—
              —But aren't the markets

---

42 Maksym Zalizniak (1740–after 1769) was a Cossack who joined and led the Koliïvshchyna
    uprising. He was later arrested by the Russian forces and sent to Siberia.

43 Kodnia is a village in central-western Ukraine (Zhytomyr region) where the Polish authori-
    ties proceeded to execute and torture hundreds of captured *haidamaks*.

Не чесніші за підступи й зради воєнні? . .
Тишина.
       І принишкли сидухи.
                  Ятки ярмаркові
Загрюкали лядами.
             Втишився торг.
—Який то солодкий буде козакові
Зароблений спокій, не взятий на борг!
Незрячий, а бачу—
               імла на покрівлі
Спадає, мов курява з неба тонка.
Щаслива утома,
           догода торгівлі
Вгамує стурбований сон козака!
Утишились рухи земні,
              а натомість
Схвильованим мислям являє свій вид
Єдина справдешня, німа нерухомість,
Ця істина світу,
           цей істинний світ.
Всі рухи безкрайности прагнуть завершень
І, взявшися тільки,
           в собі вже несуть
Передвічний непорух—останнє і перше
Начало всіх рухів, їх міру і суть.
Бо рух—
       як струна, що, найвищим тремтінням
Пройнявшись,
           не зносить його й застига.
Так мудрість приходить,
             знаючість нага,
Народжена безуму лютим кипінням.
Так думка, що в люті нестерпнім шаліє,
Стає, досягаючи мудрости.
           Так
В останнє майбутнє вступає козак,
Здолавши минулого злу веремію.
Подоланий
      вихор минулого
           вщух,

Better than the tricks and deceptions of war? … —
Stillness surrounds them.   480
      The sitters hunch down even further.
                        At the stalls
Shutters were closing.
      The market was over.
—How sweet, for the Cossack, this peace—   485
              honestly earned, not taken on credit!
Though blind I still see
            hoarfrost on a thatched roof
Falling like mist from the sky.
Welcome fatigue   490
      and benefits of trade
Will finally calm the turbulent dream of the Cossack.
The earth's movements turn quiet and violent thoughts
Are slaked by mute immobility,
A verity of the world, the real world as such.   495
In essence all movement just longs for completion
And as soon as it starts it contains in itself
A primal equipoise—the last and the first
The start of all movement, their measure and essence.
For movement—   500
      like a string in the throes of vibration—
[57]

Will resist its lot and finally find rest.
For this is how wisdom arrives, pure, naked knowledge
That's born from the frenzy of madness.
Thus the thought that is roiling in crazed agitation   505
Congeals into judgment and wisdom.
                  Thus, at last,
The Cossack sets foot on the final frontier,
And thwarts the calamitous mess of the past.
The storms of the past are now at an end,   510

І я на дорозі вселюдській співаю
Про ярмарок світу, про діло і рух.
Що вічности силою свою сягає ...
Я бачу—

        сіяє огнем супокою й труда
Козацька ґуральня,

                чумацька ночівля,
Чабанський нічліг, де шумить череда.
Оце переможна й велебна торгівля
Стяги побідні свої викида!
Спокійний спочинок, досягнення борзі
Достойному торжище людське дає.
Аби не забув про козацтво своє
Козак, стоючи на вселюдському торзі,
Хоч він і потрапив у владний полон
Орлових рублів та схизматських корон ...
Капнисте!

      Полетико!

        Знаєте—

              хто ви?
І ти, Кочубею!

      Ревухо,—і ти!

And now on humanity's broad path I can sing
Of the world's market, of commerce and movement
Extending its moment from here to eternity. ...
I see Cossack breweries, Chumak resting places
And countless herds at rest   515
           all lit by the fires
Of peace and prosperity. And victorious and noble trade
Asserting its place in the world. And well-deserved rest—
The fruit of the world's market.
Just so long as the Cossack at this worldwide fair   520
Even while vassal to the Crown or the ruble[44]
Can still know his essence ...
Kapnist[45]
    Poletyka,[46]
        do you know who you are?   525
[58]

And you, Kochubei,[47]
      and you, Revukha![48]

---

44 Both of Bazhan's references here are to Russia, that is, the ruble with the eagle, and the "schismatic" (i.e., Orthodox) crown—although seemingly couched in a Polonocentric mode—not untypical for the Ukrainian late eighteenth century; see TE.

45 Kapnist—most likely Vasilii (Vasyl') Kapnist (1758–1823), a Ukrainian nobleman (of Greek extraction) who was active as a civil servant and a moderately prominent writer in the Russian Empire. He was also an active supporter of Ukrainian rights and autonomy, and specifically wrote on the iniquity of serfdom, in effect slavery, imposed by Imperial diktat.

46 Poletyka—most likely Hryhorii Poletyka (1725–1784), writer and historian active in various Ukrainian and Russian imperial institutions, who constantly worked on Ukrainian history and rights.

47 Kochubei—most likely Vasyl' (1640–1708), although other prominent family members could be implied. From 1687 to 1708 he held high office in the Cosssack Hetman state, led the pro-Moscow faction in the Hetmanate, and denounced Mazepa's impending plans to shift his allegiance to Charles XII and Sweden.

48 Revukha—Wacław Rzewucki (1785–1831); eccentric and prominent Polish orientalist and traveler to the Near East; descended from some of the most aristocratic of Polish families (Rzewuski and Lubomirski); one of the first professional orientalists in Europe. Also known for his great interest in Ukraine, its Cossack traditions and especially its ethnomusicology; along with Arabic pseudonyms, he also called himself "Otaman Revukha"; founded on his Ukrainian estate in Savran (Odesa region) a school for *bandurists, kobzars,* and *lyrists* (*lirnyky*). Joined the Polish uprising of 1830–1831 and died during it under mysterious circumstances. In Bazhan's footnote in the 1931 publication of the poem (p. 59 of the Krawciw edition of 1969) he notes that he, along with Kapnist, Poletyka, and Kochubei, will be discussed in part III of the poem. This continuation has not been found, however.

Ви ж нашого роду, черкаської крови,
В князях та графах, в орденах золотих.
В Петербурґах, Варшавах сидять одуковані
Козацькі краяни, кість наших кісток.
А ти репетуєш—забиті, запльовані!
Та це ж із братерського рота пльовок!
Він чесний, бо ситий,
                        він добрий, бо рідний,—
Плюне земляк, дак і дасть п'ятака ...
А те, що я—лірник мізерний і бідний?!.
Ну що ж!
        Не доскочив!
                    Вже доля така! . .
Та сумнів старого каліку не змарче,
Бо я продаюсь,
            коли сам продаю ...
І він увірвав ту розмову свою.
І озвався молодший, промовивши:
                                —Старче!
Стоїть над нами вік, як чорний частокіл,
І тінь його лягає на дороги,
І тінь, як меч нещерблений і строгий,
Рубає кожен шлях навідмаш і навпіл.
Чудні і трудні ходять оболоки,
Як постріл, пахне порох, дощ і тлінь.
І клоняться ліси—вітри ідуть високі,
І кругами втинають височінь.
Високий вітер править вищий лет,
Він заверта з перейденого кругу,
Накреслює собі свою дорогу другу
І прагне інших, нам незнаних, мет.
І, може, я вернусь, щоб твій зганьбити зір,
Те око виссане, уразище зловіще,
І, може, поведе тебе твій поводир
На голе і глухе, як розпач, гробовище.

You're our own people, of Cherkassian blood,
Transformed into Princes and Counts, encrusted with gold.
Ensconced in those Petersburgs and Warsaws,   530
Sit our newly ennobled, our own Cossack brethren,
Blood of our blood and bone of our bone.
And you say—forgotten, you say—they are spat on?
But if so—it is spit from a brother's mouth.
He's honest 'cause he's fed; he's good 'cause he's family ...   535
He may spit, but he'll still throw you a shilling.
As for me—that I'm poor and a down-and-out lyrist?
What of it?
            Wasn't fast enough.
                          That's my fate.   540
But doubt cannot hobble this cripple,
For I still sell my wares,
                    I can still sell myself ...
And there he broke off his reply.
And the younger man answered by   545
                      saying:
                          —Old man,
Standing over us is an age like a black palisade
And its shadow is cast on the roads and the highways,
A shadow like a honed and double-edged sword   550
Relentlessly cleaving each roadway in two.
The sky is all strange and the clouds are ominous,
There's a smell of gunshot and rain and corruption.
Whole forests bend as powerful winds
Swirl in higher and ever-expanding gyres.   555
[59]

The high wind attains a still higher flight,
The cyclone shifts from its earlier track
As the gale now finds a different path
And seeks out new goals of which we know nothing.
Perhaps I'll come back to refute your vision,   560
Your eye that's sucked out and your festering wound.
And perhaps your own guide will lead you
To a gravesite that's bare and forsaken as despair.

І стане дід, і скаже внук—Дивись:
Глибоку вкопано у землю домовину ...
І дід в онуці не впізнає сина,
Бо й сина був не упізнав колись.
І ляжуть мертвяки, і встануть інші люди,
Бо прийде час новий, і прийде люд новий,
Що в творчій та чудній зненависті своїй
Назве мене—підніжок і заблуда,
А, може, скаже ще—сліпий і тощий скній.
Що людям відповім?
Що темні й упокорені
Були супутники моїх блуденних літ?
Що всі живі шматки,
                всі найдрібніші корені
Мені виривано з моїх пустих орбіт?
Що в зазубнях блукав, коли наскрізь проходив
Дорогами всіма і землями всіма?
Що весь видимий світ,
              земні вагання й подив
Не билися, як птах, на поверхні більма?
Неправда це!
       Бо вишкрябок очей,
Немов жадне зерно, збирає вільгість світу,
Росу усіх доріг
         і зори всіх людей,
І не вгамовує жагу свою неситу!
Неправда це!
       Нема кінця дорозі!
Останнього майбутнього нема!
Невже ж всі ми проходимо сліпма,
Чужі для нас невидимій тривозі?!
Тривого! Земна тривого!
Як не бачить тебе—
        хай почуть,
Слухаючи дороги,
Що перед мене падуть!
Невже ж ти проходиш мимо?
Мої тропи минаєш невже?

The old man will stop, and the grandson will say: look
The coffin is buried deep in the ground ...   565
But he will not see the son in his grandson
Because he once also did not recognize the son.
And the dead will lie down and others will rise up
For a new time will come bringing new people with it
Who in their clever, strange and hateful way   570
Will call me a craven intruder
And maybe blind, emaciated and a wretch to boot.
And how shall I answer?
                    That the companions
Of my blind wanderings were ignorant and crude?   575
That all the living parts, the tiniest roots
Were ripped out from my empty sockets?
Or that I would always founder
Through byways and dead ends and alleys,
And never could see the mystery and wonder   580
Of the living world,
            like the flight of a bird,
                        because of my blindness.
And that is a lie!
                For these aborted eyes
Like a thirsty seed absorb the world's moisture   585
The dew of all the roads,
                    the vision of all the people
[60]

And never fully slake their insatiable thirst.
And that is a lie!
                For this road has no end.   590
There is no final future.
Or do we all just blindly pass on by
Oblivious to the fear that we cannot see?
Fear! Fear of this world!
How can one not see you—not hear you   595
When one listens to the roads
That stretch out before me!
Do you just pass me by? Do you just skirt my tracks?

Невже ж мені сонно і німо
Лежать на дорогах крижем?
Погнити в баюрищах серцю сліпото!
Блукає звалашена й темна земля.
А, може, могили—колиски живого,
Де б'ється в тривозі живе немовля?
А, може, в минулім прийдешнє, дияволе?!
А, може, проклятий,—і це вже повік—
Всі вуха поглухли, всі вуха проґавили,
В могили заритий, майбутнього крик?
Невже збожеволіло наше минуле,
Невже ж всі поглухли, посліпли, поснули?
Невже тільки вічно незрячий блажен?
Й ніхто не вчитає його письмен?
Читати могили, чи гинути в бурях—
Ідем, чортів діду, ідем!
Сліпці умирають на гордих Савурах
Чи під парканами корчем?!
—Помреш, як собака, як вигнаний зайда.
Дограй, юродивий, спотворену гру!
Чого тут розсівся?
                    Підводься і гайда!
А я на базарі своєму помру ...
Молодший підвівся,
                    і одягу помах
Війнув у лице сліпакові здаля
Тим дмуханням запахів, ланцю знайомих—
Плісени, поту, цибулі й гнилля.
Не ворухнувся старий,
                    не поглянув,
І гладила корбу рука лірача,
І десь недалечко водир дідуганів
Сопів, догризаючи шмат калача.
Приблуда руками намацував тропи,
Хитався,
        ставав,
                спотикався,
                        ішов.

Or am I to lie in the road mute and prostrate
And rot in the swamp of a blinded heart?   600
The earth wanders dark and castrated.
Or perhaps the graves are cradles of the living
In which a live infant struggles in its fear?
Or maybe, you devil, the future is all in the past?
Or maybe, God damn you—for now it's forever—   605
(All ears being deaf, all hearing now lost)
It's the scream of the future that's entombed in the graves?
Did our past just go crazy?
Were all of them deaf, or go blind, fall asleep?
Can only he who is blind be the one who is blessed?   610
With no one remaining to decipher his writings?
To read the graves or to die in the storms—
Let's go old man, the devil take you, let's go.
The blind bards are dying on their proud Savur hilltop
Or is it in spasms, and in ditches?   615
—You'll die like a dog, like a banished stranger.
Put an end, you holy fool, to this monstrous game.
[61]

Why are you sitting here?
                        Get up and get going!
And I'll die right here in my own bazaar …   620
The younger one got up
                    and the sway of his clothes
Wafted to the old man from a distance
A bouquet of all too familiar smells:
Of decay and of sweat, of onions and mold.   625
The bard did not stir,
                    did not cast a glance,
His hand only stroked the wheel of the lira,
And somewhere nearby the old man's guide
Wheezed as he gnawed the last of a pie.   630
The intruder was feeling the trail with his hands
He was swaying,
                and stumbling
                        falling
                            and walking.   635

Зашпортувавсь, падав у грузні сугроби,
В ядучі баюри,
              і зводився знов.
Все далі і далі,
           все тихше і тихше,
Й ущухло глухе шарудіння ходи.
І озвався старий, тишину перемігши:
—Вставай, поводирю!
              А йди-но сюди!
Блукають базаром примари непевні,
Пахощі, спогади й тіні самі ...
Чекають на нас у базарній харчевні,
У тихій і теплій, веселій корчмі.
Послухай мене,
           нерозумний нетяго,
Послухай дитино, старого сліпця:
Людині дано найутішніше благо—
Вслухатися в людські спокійні серця.
Ходім поводирю! . .

And stumbling again he would fall into ruts
And large stinking puddles,
                          just to get up once more.
Ever further and further,
                          fainter and fainter,   640
Until the sound of his walk disappeared altogether.
And the old man spoke up overcoming the silence:
—Get up, guide! Come, get yourself here!
Strange specters are roaming around the bazaar,
Vague smells and memories and shadows appear ...   645
But they're waiting for us in the market roadhouse
In the quiet and warmth of that welcoming inn.
[62]

So listen here,
              my naïve waif,
Listen my child, to an old and blind bard: 650
The greatest of gifts that may come our way
Is to listen and hear the peace in men's hearts ...
Let's go then, my guide ...
[63]

Translated by George G. Grabowicz

BIBLIOGRAPHY

Aheieva, Vira. *Vizerunok na kameni: Mykola Bazhan; Zhyttiepys (ne)radians'koho poeta*. Lviv: Vydavnytstvo Staroho Leva, 2018.

Bazhan, Mykola. *Sliptsi*. Introduction by Bohdan Krawciw. Munich: Suchasnist', 1969.

Cherems'kyi, Kost'. *Povernennia tradytsiï: Z istoriï nyshchennia kobzarstva*. Kharkiv: Tsentr Lesia Kurbasa, 1999.

Foucault, Michel. *Fearless Speech*. Edited by Joseph Pearson. Los Angeles: Semiotext(e), 2001.

Makhorin, Hennadii, Serhii Cherevko, and Halyna Shubina. *Narysy z istoriï kobzarstva v Ukraïni: Do 75-richchia vid dnia narodzhennia bandurysta Mykoly Nechyporenka*. Zhytomyr: Vydavnytstvo FOP Ievenok O. O., 2012.

Shevchenko, Taras. *Haidamaky: Poema*. St. Petersburg: Tipografiia A. Sycheva, 1841.

Tychyna, Pavlo. *Chernihiv*. Kharkiv: Literatura i mystetstvo, 1931.

Prose (1927)

Translator's Essay

ROMAN IVASHKIV

Translation is a challenging task not only due to the asymmetries between languages and cultures, but also because it is inherently and simultaneously a decontextualizing and recontextualizing act. In other words, translators not only bring texts from one language and culture to another but must also deal with the changes and differences in time and space, purpose and audience, and, importantly, sensibilities and ideologies. In this light, the translation of "Meeting at the Crossroad Station: A Conversation between the Three" has proven all the more daunting. Written almost one hundred years ago by the three young and brilliant Ukrainian writers—Semenko, Shkurupii, and Bazhan—this work additionally poses the problem of authorship and genre. Was the text indeed coauthored or could it possibly have had a lead author? Is it just a conversation between the three friends as the subtitle suggests? Is it merely an engaging and witty exposition of their aesthetic and political views (and, maybe, disagreements), included at the end of their poetry collection? Or is it also a literary program, a manifesto of sorts (a popular genre in early twentieth-century Europe), which discusses one of the directions in which Ukrainian literature might have gone during those tumultuous revolutionary times if its development had not been so ruthlessly crushed by Stalin's murderous dictatorship?

Even an educated contemporary Ukrainian reader may not find everything in the original version of "A Meeting ..." immediately accessible without some familiarity with the time period, ideas, and people discussed. In the English translation, therefore, footnotes that give some context and provide some background information are inevitable, even though they remain a paratextual element with an explicit educational function, which is nowhere to be present in the original. Explanations of historical and cultural concepts and brief biographical data about Ukrainian writers and public figures come primarily from the *Internet Encyclopedia of Ukraine* (hosted by the Canadian Institute of Ukrainian Studies), one of the most credible and comprehensive yet also concise online sources about Ukraine. Hopefully, however, they are not too intrusive and the text still retains its dynamic flow as a piece that potentially could be performed on stage despite its focus on dialogue and an apparent lack of action.

In terms of language, surprisingly, "A Meeting …" does not seem at all outdated, and the Ukrainian text still reads quite naturally. The translation may draw attention to some peculiar images (like that of the semaphore, for example, which must have been part of the general Modernist fascination with technology, specifically, the train); a few interesting turns of phrase or idioms; several Soviet realia terms, often used as abbreviations or acronyms, which needed to be both spelled out and explained; occasional long-winded, stream-of-consciousness-like syntax; and some idiosyncratic punctuation. But greater translation difficulties have arisen from the work's linguistic playfulness (e.g., instances of multilingual wordplay and impish self-conscious mixing up of Ukrainian and Russian) and its metafictional elements (including self-reflexivity, frequent literary allusions, discussions of other authors, and quotations from and references to other literary works).

Despite these challenges, translating "A Meeting …" was an enjoyable experience, and I hope that together with other translations in this collection mine will help English-speaking readers across the world to discover these great writers, who deserve recognition not only in Ukraine but internationally. I am extremely grateful to Lev Fridman and Graeme McGuire for their thoughtful editing and to Professor Oleh Ilnytzkyj, author of the groundbreaking *Ukrainian Futurism, 1914–1930*, for his feedback and insightful suggestions. Without their help this translation would be impossible.

ЗУСТРІЧ НА ПЕРЕХРЕСНІЙ СТАНЦІЇ: РОЗМОВА ТРЬОХ

Перехресна станція. Рівні й блискучі рейки колій ведуть подорожніх у всі кінці. Тут відбулась зустріч трьох, що їхні колії нарешті знову зійшлися на цій станції.

Там, де колія веде вперед, на грані стиків блищить зеленим вогником семафор у майбутнє. Його поставлено на межі доріг та націй; і лише хоробрі сміливці відважуються вийти за його зелений огонь, бо там починається майбутнє.

Його встановили сміливі конквістадори-піонери як рекордний кордон для всіх подорожніх.

З того часу минуло кілька років; і масло в лямпах семафора вже майже вигоріло, але він ще жеврів зеленим вогником. Багато подорожніх дивилися на цей зелений огонь, та їхні дороги здебільшого вели назад. Конквістадори, що запалили його, роз'їхалися праворуч і ліворуч, проте огонь не погасав. Вони поїхали на розвідку, їм треба було заглибитись у сучасне, щоб у ньому знайти засоби посуватися в майбутнє.

І от сьогодні на цій перехресній станції троє з них зустрілися знов.

Один із них, що обличчя його вміщало в собі риси всіх націй та рас, що його волосся було чорне, як вугілля шахт, а очі блищали вогнем татарських ватр, скитських вогнищ та юпітерами європейських ательє, а кожний сторонній подорожній подумав би, що він з Патагонії, перший вийшов на колію, що вела вперед, і подивився на обрій, де далеко жеврів зелений огонь семафора ...

Цей перший, що від нього пахло морем і далекими шляхами, які перерізують сучасність, попихкав своєю люлькою і задоволено промовив:

—Горить! . .

MEETING AT THE CROSSROAD STATION: A CONVERSATION BETWEEN THE THREE[1]

Crossroad station. Straight and shiny rails take travelers in all directions. This is where a meeting of the three took place when their tracks finally crossed again at this station.

Where the rail tracks go forward, a semaphore[2] on the edge of the joints is flashing its green light into the future. It is situated at the junction of roads and nations, and only the bold spirits dare to go beyond its green light because that's where the future begins.

It was installed by courageous conquistador-pioneers[3] as a record-setting borderline for all travelers.

Several years had passed since then, and the oil in the semaphore signal lamps had almost burned out. It was still glowing with its green light, though. Many travelers looked at this green light, but their paths took them mostly backwards. The paths of those conquistadors who lit it up split as some went right, and others went left, but the light never went out. They were gone on reconnaissance and had to delve into the present to find in it the means to proceed into the future.[4]

And so today, at this crossroad station, the three men met again.

One of them had a face that contained features of all nations and races: his hair was black as coal from the coalmines; his eyes shone with the light of Tatar and Scythian bonfires, reflecting Jupiters from European fashion salons, so much so that a strange wanderer would assume he came from Patagonia. He was the first to appear on the rail tracks, which led forward, and looked at the horizon where the green semaphore light flashed in the distance …

This first man, smelling of sea and faraway paths that crisscross modernity, puffed his pipe and said contentedly,

"It's on!"

---

1   The three men are, respectively, Mykhail Semenko, Geo Shkurupii, and Mykola Bazhan.
2   The image of a semaphore was popular among the Futurists. A literary almanac of Ukrainian Futurists, to which the three writers contributed, was entitled *A Semaphore into the Future: The Panfuturist Apparatus* (1922). In 1923, there appeared another almanac, entitled *Zhovtnevyi zbirnyk panfuturystiv* (*The October Bulletin of Panfuturists*).
3   The image of conquistadors was a particularly popular one with Shkurupii.
4   This conversation is taking place in 1927, a few years after the Futurist movement was interrupted. It foreshadows the immanent appearance of a new literary organization *Nova generatsiia* (*New Generation*). For more detail, see http://www.encyclopediaofukraine.com/display.asp?linkpath=pages%5CN%5CO%5CNovaGeneratsiia.htm.

Другій, що стояв поблизу й показував рукою вдалечінь, чиє обличчя й постать нагадували задумливого мандрівника футуропрерій, з докором відповів:

—Хіба я не попереджав?..

I третій, що великими пальцями правої й лівої руки звужував собі очі, бо він був трохи близькозорий, з породи довгоголових, і що блукав по нетрях провінції, ніби не ймучи віри собі самому,—здивовано промовив:

—А я справді горить!..

I всі троє повернулись обличчями один до одного й простягнувши руки, промовили вголос:

—Це ти, Семенко!..

—Це ти, Шкурупій!..

—Ти, Бажан!..

—Го-го-го!!

—Дай прикурити,—сказав перший, притоптуючи жовтим пальцем у люльці рудий тютюн.

Запахло пивом і тютюном, вугіллям паровозних топок і уборною.

Так пахне комунікація на багатьох станціях нашої країни, що до їхніх перонів мовчазні дядьки, погейкуючи на волів, підвозять збіжжя важке своє й хрумтливий цукор, побоюючись безпритульних та міліціонера.

—На багатьох залізничних коліях стоять семафори. Але хто їх ставить на тупиках?—запитав тоді третій.

Коли б в цей момент до них підійшов один із тих, що так люблять зайцями їздити на потягах нашої літератури, економлячи гроші на підручники версифікації та не жалкуючи їх на пляшку горілки для голови сільського Комнезаму, щоб узяти собі посвідку про безпечне соціальне походження, де б на запитання: «хто ваші батьки?»—не стояла відповідь: «попівський син»—так от цей «заєць з ідеологічних міркувань» підсунув би:

—Ваш семафор—вказівка на коротший шлях до найближчого кафе.

The second man was standing nearby and gesturing into the distance. His face and stature resembled that of a pensive wanderer of futuristic prairies.

"Didn't I warn you about it?" he reproached.

And the third man, from some longheaded species, who used to roam through provincial thickets, was now scrunching up his eyes with the big fingers of his right and left hands because he was slightly nearsighted. As if not believing his own words, he said, surprised,

"Indeed, it's on!"

And all three men turned their faces to each other and extending their hands said loudly,

"It's you, Semenko!"

"It's you, Shkurupii!"

"It's you, Bazhan!"

"Oh-ho-ho!"

"Have a light?" said the first man, packing the red tobacco into the pipe with his yellow finger.

It suddenly smelled of beer and tobacco, of coal from the locomotive firebox and toilet.

This is what communication routes smell like at many train stations in our country, where taciturn men from the countryside, wary of the homeless and the patrol officer, keep bringing to the platforms their heavy grain and their crispy sugar while shouting and yelling at the oxen.

"Many rail tracks are equipped with semaphores. But who installs them at dead ends?" asked the third man.

If at that moment they were approached by one of these free riders who like to take our literary trains so much and who save on versification textbooks but are never short for a bottle of vodka for the head of the village committee for insolvent farmers,[5] a token of appreciation for a certificate, issued by the committee and confirming the holder's appropriate social pedigree rather than stating "son of priests" where it asked about parents, so one of these free riders for ideological reasons would retort,

"Your semaphore is nothing but a sign showing the shortest way to the closest café."

---

5   The Soviet *realia* concept is a portmanteau acronym *komnezam* (*komitet nezamozhnykh selian*). It is spelled out and translated here as "committee of insolvent peasants." The certificate jokingly discussed here is an example not only of Soviet bureaucracy but also, more importantly, of the regime's repression against intelligentsia, the clergy, and the wealthier peasants, later in the text referred to as *kulaks*.

Та цього не сталося.

І третій продовжував:

—Правда, в тих формулах, що за допомогою їх ми роки тому намагалися прокласти нову залізницю в майбутнє, було алгебри й логаритмів не менше, ніж у розрахунках інженера-будівника, але що з того? Найстаранніші й найпильніші бажання довести, ніби 2X2=5, не завжди бувають виправдані.

—Ти став больно розумний,—сказав перший, пихкаючи люлькою й дбайливо псуючи українську мову,—це од тих нерозумних тинів, які ти перелазив за час нашої розлуки. Цей розум дала тобі відсталість, яка оточує нашу оазу і куди ви,—звернувся до другого, що задивився на жовтий дим над шклянками пива, мріючи про веселих дівчат і примхливі рими,—куди ви обоє після вашої зради повтікали. Це—на користь, бо можна й підождати, не все за раз, і коли б ми не зустрілись, то все одно зустріч нашої ідеї, нашокультурної формації відбулася б в цій же кількості, хоч і з другими прізвищами.

—Можна й підождати? Гм, чи не значить це, бува, що папір, де на одній сторінці було виведено чіткі, мов гільйотина, формули смерті мистецтва, треба перевернути, а на другому боці його написати вірш про міську панель і любов на міській панелі? Ти робиш і робив так, але ти не хочеш признатися ...

—Хто його примусить признатися?—промовив другий.—Патентовані слідчі в літературі, що мають мандат на це (від кого?) і горду назву «критики», не змогли притиснути його до стінки. Ох! Я люблю критиків, як алігатор любить пташинку, що колупається в його зубах ...

—Хо!—чи здивувався, чи підтвердив перший.

—Так,—сказав третій,—наші критики нагадують мені дядюшок з села, що по обіді голосно гикнуть і промовлять до своєї огрядної жінки— «оце мені подобається, а оце не подобається». Між іншим—їхні шлунки зовсім не перетравлюють нерозжованої їжі. В них є щось від дегенерата й щось від бугая. Цікава помісь!

—Їх можна класифікувати,—підхопив другий,—в одних—довгі вуса й довге перо, що, мов мітла в руках у пугала, може лякати лише горобців, другі лисі й на голові, й на душі, треті—без усів і без лисини, та в них немає зубів і вони можуть споживати лише солоденьку юшку, куди накришено трохи «революції» та повстань, більше для вигляду, ніж для користі. От!

But since he wasn't around, that didn't happen.

And so the third man continued,

"It's true that the formulae we used to apply in an attempt to build a new railway into the future involved no less algebra and logarithms than the calculations of a civil engineer, but so what? The most diligent and attentive desires to prove that $2 \times 2 = 5$ is not always justified.

"You've become such a whopping smart ass," said the first man, puffing his pipe and carefully corrupting his Ukrainian by using an incorrect modifier from Russian. "This is because of those feebleminded fences that you climbed over during our separation. You got the smarts from the stupidity enveloping our oasis, where you …"—he turned to the second man, who was staring in admiration at the yellow smoke above the pints of beer and dreaming of cheerful girls and whimsical rhyme—"where you," he continued, "escaped after your betrayal. This is for the better, though, because a bit of delay won't hurt. One thing at a time. Even if we didn't meet, the meeting of our idea, of our cultural initiative would still take place with the same number of participants but with different last names.

"A little wait won't hurt, you say? Hm, doesn't it imply then that a piece of paper containing a clear-cut (like a guillotine) formula for the death of art on one side needs to be flipped over so that on its other side a poem could be written about a city street girl and courtesan love? That's what you kept doing all this time, but you won't admit it …"

"Who can force him to admit it?" said the second man. "Even the patented investigators of literature, who have a mandate (issued by whom?) and bear the proud title 'critics,' couldn't nail him to the wall. Oh! I'm as fond of critics as alligators are of little birds picking their teeth."

"Hm," said the first man, in either astonishment or confirmation.

"Yes," said the third man, "our critics remind me of those countryside fellows who belch loudly after finishing lunch and declare to their corpulent wives what is or isn't to their liking. Their stomachs, by the way, can't at all process any unchewed food. They share something in common both with a degenerate and a bull. A curious crossbreed!

"They can be classified into different categories," said the third man. "The first kind have long moustaches and long quills, which like a scarecrow's broom can only scare off sparrows. The second have bald heads and souls. And the third have neither moustaches, nor bald spots, nor teeth, and they can only consume light soups spiced up with a tiny bit of 'revolution' and uprisings, more for show than utility. There, I said it."

Перший випустив од задоволення велике пасмо диму зі своєї люльки, очі йому повужчали ще більше, але він нічого не сказав.

—Вони, більшість в усякому разі, клянуться бородою Маркса,—мовив третій.—Моторні парікмахери! Марксову бороду кожен з них зачісує собі до вподоби. Від цього Маркс у одних нагадує Софокла, в других—романтичного панича, в третіх—нашого шановного Тараса, в четвертих—неголеного дядька з Кибинець, в багатьох—він є копією їх самих. Загадкова ситуація—де ж справжній Маркс?

—А комплект «Плужанина?!»—пискнув би «літературний заєць», коли б підійшов у цю мить. Але не було його, й розмова тривала далі.

—Характерно,—сказав другий,—що за своєю власною пихою вони нічого не бачать. Вони лише з великою охотою сваряться один з одним.

—Чого вас так заїдають критики? Беріть приклад з мене,—промовив нарешті перший.—З самого початку треба плюнути критикові межи очі, щоб не ждати від нього того, чого він по своїй природі не може дати. Тоді ждіть сподіваного, а то ви все, мов якийсь актор од рецензента, ждете несподіваного. Це застрахує від того, щоб ждати якоїсь допомоги від людей, які мусять бути розумніші од вас, а де ж вони візьмуться, ці розумніші од нас люди? Ждіть допомоги й коректив від індустріалізації …

—Значить—пульс сучасности? . .—глибокодумно промимрив другий.

—Його шукати?—запитав третій.—Я не хочу нічого шукати, хоча останнє—дуже вигідно, зручно, безтурботно й навіть приємно. Можливо, що я не намагатимусь всидіти на теплих подушках заялозеної лірики і речі мої перестануть нагадувати убогий і зім'ятий самовар, що в ньому вариться ріденька самогонна юшка рим.

With delight, the first man released a large puff of smoke from his pipe. His eyes narrowed even more, but he didn't say a word.

"They, or the majority of them in any case, swear on Marx's beard," said the third man. "Those nimble barbers! Each one of them combs Marx's beard the way they like. Hence in one version their Marx resembles Sophocles, in another, a romantic young nobleman, in yet another one, our much esteemed Taras,[6] and in yet another one, an unshaven sodbuster from the village of Kybyntsi.[7] For many of them, he is a copy of their own selves. A puzzling situation: where is the real Marx?"

"And what about a set of *The Pluzhanyn*,"[8] the literary free rider would yelp if he came around at that moment. But he wasn't around, and so the conversation continued.

"It's typical," said the second man, "that their own arrogance prevents them from seeing anything. They only quarrel with each other so avidly."

"Why do the critics bug you all so much? Look at my example," said the first man, at last. "From the very get-go you need to spit into the critic's face so you won't have to expect from him anything that by nature he cannot offer. And then expect what's to be expected. Otherwise you always expect the unexpected, like an actor does from a reviewer. Doing so will spare you from false expectations of help from people who must be smarter than you. And where would you find them, these smarter-than-us people? Expect help and corrective reform from industrialization."

"Meaning the pulse of modernity?" the second man mumbled with a wise air.

"The pulse? Is that what we need to be looking for?" asked the third man. "I don't want to stop searching, even though that last option sounds comfortable, carefree, and even pleasant. Hopefully, I won't attempt to keep my snug seat on the warm pillows of hackneyed poetry, and my pieces will stop resembling an old crumpled samovar in which the watery self-made rhyme soup is boiled."

---

6   Taras Shevchenko is Ukraine's greatest poet and the founder of Ukrainian literature, comparable in stature and caliber to Shakespeare in English, Dante in Italian, Pushkin in Russian, and Mickiewicz in Polish literatures.

7   A village in central-eastern Ukraine in the Poltava region and close to the town of Myrhorod. Semenko was born in Kybyntsi. It also has a remote association with the Cossack Hetman Mazepa and with Mykola Hohol' (in Russian, Nikolai Gogol), who will be mentioned further in this text.

8   *The Pluzhanyn* is a literary monthly periodical, published in Kharkiv in 1925–1927. The Ukrainian word *pluh* means *plow*, thus *pluzhanyn* can be translated as *plowman*. Poetically, aesthetically, and ideologically, *The Pluzhanyn* was primarily dedicated to rural issues and rustic themes, which the Futurists opposed.

—Самовар чи сонет?—єхиднувато запитав другий.

—Я не фанатик сонета,—відповів третій .—Просто я люблю добрий вірш. Мені дивно часом, як за римою люди не бачать вірша. Я люблю добрий вірш, і тому я толерантний. Я з любов'ю ворушу сторінки теплих і хороших віршів.

—Глупости ти говориш, любий мій. Що з того, що «Камена» та «Крізь бурю й сніг» наче накрохмалені в добрій пральні,—сказав тоді другий і подивився на першого, що колупав ногтем глибоке чорне дно своєї люльки.—Хіба ти розшукаєш у цих поемах пульс нашої життєрадосності, хіба ти відчуєш у них подих свіжого вітру?

Побожна старушенція, заховавши в облізле хутро свого мерзлякуватого носа, іде крізь бурю й сніг. Хіба їй і направді заборонено там ходити, й чхати, й сякати носа?

Ні! Навіщо ця затхлість, мов пліснявість папірусів з гробниці Тутанхамона? Вони приваблюють тебе формою? Та задушлива їхня форма. Вона, як у зашморгу, втягає молодь, і тоді виходять з неї дідусі з молоком на вустах і з старечим серцем.

—Я не фанатик сонета,—чіплявся за цю фразу третій.—Я люблю добрий і розумний вірш. Я не вірю, що в поета мізок мусить бути схожий на драглі.

—Ти починаєш говорити про поетів?—сказав перший і одверто позіхнув.—Ох, нудно ж. Крім своїх віршів, ні одного не читаю.

Перший підвівся і, склавши ноги свої, мов ножиці, кинув:

—Справді. Краще, ніж читати одноманітне сюсюкання сосюр з маленької літери або видушувати поезію з тичининських поетичних сопляків, розгорнути Пушкіна або Шевченка, але, на жаль, я їх перечитав, коли ще був у першій класі підготовчої школи. Не можна хронічно

"The samovar or the sonnet?" sneered the second man.

"I'm not dogmatic about the sonnet," responded the third man. "It's just that I appreciate a good poem. And it's sometimes surprising how people don't see a poem behind the rhyme. I appreciate a good poem, and that's why I'm tolerant. I leaf through the pages of good, warm poems passionately."

"Nonsense, my dear friend. What's the purpose of Zerov's *Kamena*[9] or Ryl's'kyi's *Kriz' buriu i snih*[10] sounding like they've been starched real good in the laundry?" said the second man and turned his gaze to the first one, who was picking at the deep dark bottom of his pipe with his nail. "Can you really find in these poems the pulse of our exuberance, can you really sense in them a breath of fresh wind? A poor pious old thing, her crinkled cold nose hidden in shabby fur, stumbles through a blizzard. No one is really preventing her from going there, sneezing and blowing her nose, or are they?"

"No," he continued. "Why this mustiness, reeking of mold from Tutankhamun's tomb? Can the form of these poems really be appealing? Suffocating! That's what their form really is. It sucks the young in like a noose, and they emerge as old men with milk on their lips and senile hearts."

"I'm not dogmatic about the sonnet," the third man kept repeating. "I appreciate a good, smart poem. I don't believe that the poet's brain should be like jelly."

"Are you talking about poets?" said the first man and yawned shamelessly. "How tedious, after all! Except for my own poems, I don't read anyone."

He stood up and, crossing his legs like scissors, responded,

"True, rather than plodding through the monotony of soggy sosiura-like[11] poems or squeezing poetry from Tychyna's[12] slime, it may be better to open Pushkin or Shevchenko, but unfortunately I was done with them back when I was a first grader in prep school. One can't live on canned food all the time.

9 *Kamena* is Zerov's 1924 collection of original poems and translations of Roman poets. In Roman mythology, the Camenae were considered prophetic deities.
10 *Kriz' buriu i snih* (*Through blizzard and snow*) is Ryl's'kyi's 1925 collection.
11 Volodymyr Sosiura is a lyrical poet who fought in the Ukrainian National Republic Army, but later also in the Communist Red Army. He was a member of several literary organizations in the 1920s, some of which will be mentioned later. *Sosiukannia sosiury* is untranslatable onomatopoeic wordplay. Verbatim, *sosiukannia* means *baby talk,* but the three characters ridicule the lyricism of his poetry by describing it with a word that sounds similar to his last name.
12 Like Sosiura, Pavlo Tychyna was a brilliant lyrical poet who was later broken by the Soviet regime. His early collections are today viewed as a unique type of Ukrainian Symbolism, Clarinetism.

годуватися консервами. «Укрнархарч» і той дає часом свіжі котлети, а як же тоді бути літературі?

Другий захопився, він мить прислухався до тих нечутних і невидних зворушень, що відбувалися в сірій корці його мозку, потім голосно і дзвінко промовив:

—Так! Невже ніколи я не розгорну свіжої книжки якогось нашого журналу, невже ніколи не знайду на якійсь з сторінок несподіваного, чудесного, нового вірша нової і незнаної досі руки, що безліч приємних новин, надій і несподіванок буде заховано в ньому?

Перший прокотив очі свої від одного з бесідників до другого і хитренько зломив губи:

—Мати надію на випадок—значить мати надію на долю. Мати надію на долю—значить мати надію на бога. Мати надію на бога—значить спродати свої штани, купити біблію українською мовою, піти до відомого поета Вишневого (довідки про цього поета можеш дістати в Миші Ялового) і вивчити назубок літургію. Чудова перспектива: сидіти біля моря й чекати на генія («Невже Україна свого Мойсея» і т. д. і т. д. і т. д. «Не може ж так буть» і т. д. і т. д. і т. д.) ... А ну далі за сонети!—кинув він до третього.

—Сонет—це не спадщина дурнів,—випалив третій, що вже п'ять хвилин тому вигадав цей афоризм і чекав лише на зручний випадок,—а випробований, перевірений, вдосконалений і—не помилюся, коли скажу,—вірний на 96½% засіб пролізти за жилетку людей. Отже, коли й тепер поезія—річ не марна й не непотрібна, то і вдосконалений засіб її—не витребенька профессорів. Потрібен добрий вірш, добрий вірш радянської України, а тому: важливі не запередження, а досягнення. Я люблю ...

—Ну й люби собі, пожалуста! Можеш любити, це є твоя «культурна» база, грунт твого власного творчого пуза ...—перебив його перший.

Третій не вгамувався і перебив першого:

Even the UkrNarKharch[13] society sometimes has fresh meatballs on the menu. So what's to be done with literature in that case?"

The second man got carried away. For a moment, he was carefully trying to grasp those inaudible and invisible movements occurring in the cortex area of his brain. And then he said loudly and clearly,

"Yes! Will I never again open a fresh issue of some local journal and find on one of its pages an unexpected wonderful new poem written by a new and hitherto unknown hand and containing myriad pleasant news, hopes, and surprises hidden in it?"

The first man moved his gaze from one interlocutor to another and cunningly curled his lips.

"To hope for change means to hope for good fortune," he said. "And to hope for good fortune means to hope for god, and to hope for god means to sell your pants, buy a Ukrainian bible, visit the famous poet Vyshnevyi (Mysha Ialovyi[14] can provide more information about him) and memorize the entire liturgy. A wonderful prospect: to sit at the seaside and wait for a poet of genius ('Ukraine will raise its own Moses',[15] et cetera, et cetera 'It cannot be true,' et cetera, et cetera). And again, back to the sonnets!" he said to the third man.

"The sonnet is not the heritage of fools," the third man blurted out. He came up with this aphorism five minutes ago and waited for an opportune moment. "The sonnet," he continued, "is a well-tested, highly reliable, much improved, and—I won't be amiss if I say—96.5 percent effective method to get behind people's vests. Therefore, if poetry is not a futile thing, if it's not unnecessary, then an improved method of writing poetry is not a mere vagary of professors. There is a need for a good poem, a good Soviet Ukraine poem. Thus, what's important is not prevention but accomplishment. I love ..."

"Nobody's preventing you from loving. You can love all you please.[16] That's your personal 'cultural' foundation, the ground of your artistic potbelly," the first man interrupted.

The third man couldn't calm down and fired back,

---

13 *UkrNarKharch* is another Soviet acronym that stands for *Ukraïns'ke paiove tovarystvo narodnoho kharchuvannia*, a Soviet society responsible for food supplies. The comment takes a jab at food shortages, which were a common phenomenon during the early years of the Soviet regime.

14 Mykhailo Ialovyi was a Ukrainian poet, who wrote under the pseudonym Iuliian Shpol'.

15 A line from a famous political poem by Tychyna, in which he expresses hope that a messiah poet-figure will appear in Ukrainian literature.

16 Here again, the Semenko character uses the Russian word for "please."

—Я люблю браму Заборовського й Дніпрельстан. Я люблю органічну, міцну й нефальшовану культуру. Таку культуру Україна знала лише одну: культуру феодалізму, культуру Мазепи, знатиме вона й другу: культуру пролетаріяту, культуру соцбуду. Куркульське селянство, що заповняло прогалини, не здатне творити культури, воно здатне дати лише потенцію культури: «народне мистецтво». Запаморочені проклятим просвітянством XIX віку, що зросло на оцьому самому «народньому мистецтві», ми забули про раніші віки культури й діла.

—Нарбут?—раптово запитав другий, в глибині своїй десь хутко-хутко перебравши нитки тонких і складних інтуїцій, зв'язавши їх у вузол: в слово «Нарбут».

—Так, Нарбут, що був пасеїстичнішим, а міг бути найреволюційнішим графіком України. Йому завадила смерть. Він знав джерело. Брама Заборовського, колишній розпис Печерської лаври, Тарасевич і Зубрицький, ікона Самойловича, Чернигівські гути—невичерпне і творче джерело. Той складний комплекс з географічних, економічних і соціяльно-історичних передумов, що зветься—Україна, сам нап'ється ще раз і всьому людству дасть пити з того джерела, профільтрувавши й очистивши воду ...

"I love the Zaborovs'kyi Gate[17] and the Dniprel'stan.[18] I love organic and robust culture, and Ukraine produced such culture only once: the culture of feudalism, the culture of Mazepa. Now it'll come back the second time: the culture of the proletariat and the culture of building a socialist society.[19] The kulak peasants that were only filling the gaps are incapable of creating culture. They are capable of offering what could only potentially be considered culture: 'folk art.' Giddied by the damned nineteenth-century *prosvitianstvo*,[20] which developed on the basis of this very 'folk art,' we forgot about earlier ages of culture and achievements."

"Narbut?" asked the second man all of a sudden, after going very quickly through the threads of thin and complex intuitions and tying them into a knot, epitomized by the word *Narbut*.

"Yes, Narbut was the most passionate advocate of passéism but he could have become the most revolutionary graphic artist of Ukraine. Death beat him to it. He knew where the source was. The Zaborovs'kyi Gate, the mural painting of the Kyivan Monastery of the Caves,[21] Tarasevych and Zubryts'kyi,[22] the Samoilovych[23] icon, the Chernihiv glasswork tradition—an inexhaustible creative source. That complex network of geographical, economic, and sociohistorical preconditions, which can together be named Ukraine, will drink again from that source, after the water has been cleaned and filtered. Moreover, Ukraine will offer this water to all of humankind."

---

17 *Brama Zaborovs'koho*. For more detail, see http://www.encyclopediaofukraine.com/display. asp?linkpath=pages%5CZ%5CA%5CZaborovskyGate.htm.

18 A part of the hydroelectric station on the Dnipro River in the city of Zaporizhzhia.

19 *Sotsbud* is a portmanteau acronym that stands for "socialist building".

20 *Prosvitianstvo* or *prosvitnytstvo*, literally, "enlightening," is a sociocultural phenomenon that reflects the multifaceted activities of the *Prosvita* societies, originating in western Ukrainian Halychyna in the late nineteenth century. According to the Internet Encyclopedia of Ukraine, *prosvitnytstvo* "laid the groundwork for the establishment of economic co-operatives, educational societies, and other groups that were instrumental in the Ukrainian national movement. In central and eastern Ukraine the development of *Prosvita* societies was stymied by political hostility to the Ukrainian populist ideals that underpinned their work. Nevertheless, the small number of *Prosvitas* established after the revolution of 1905 had a substantial impact on the development of Ukrainian national consciousness. The ground swell of support for the movement following the revolution of 1917 indicated that the societies probably would have developed a mass character if they had not been suppressed by the Soviet regime early in the 1920s" (http://www.encyclopediaofukraine.com/display.asp?AddButton=pages%5CP%5CR%5CProsvita.htm).

21 One of the most famous monasteries in Ukraine, the Kyivan Monastery of the Caves, also known as the Kyivan Cave Monastery was founded in the eleventh century.

22 Both were graphic and engraving artists associated with the publishing house at the Kyivan Monstery of the Caves in the seventeenth century.

23 Ivan Samoilovych was a seventeenth-century Ukrainian Cossack leader.

Перший не стерпів і остаточно перервав:

—Можеш любити. Але, повторюю, хай це буде лише твоєю «культурною» базою, грунтом твого власного творчого пуза. У кожного є це пузо, та не витікає звідси, що треба впадати в стилізацію, реставрацію, ворушити старе барахло, перегортати його й перекладати. Проте все це обумовлює твою творчу індивідуальність. Од безтворчої потенції, або, що те ж саме, од творчої імпотенції всі твої сонети й стилізації під скитів. Це твій занепад як культурного творця, це твоя індивідуальна справа—не роби з цього якоїсь позиції, дивись на це, як на шляхи твого особистого творчого спадання (ти гадаєш—піднесення). І коли ми кожен зокрема самі відповідаємо за свою літературну пику, то, зійшовшись разом, обмірковуючи спільні заміри, мусимо знайти якесь середнє арифметичне, що буде за хребет для нашої групки.

—Так, ми маємо таке!—вигукнув другий.—Спільне єсть: знання роботи, об'єктивне, свідоме знання того, що таке наш матеріял і як орудувати ним, щоб він діяв так, як хоче майстер. Спільне єсть: метод. Спільне єсть: Жовтень. Для нього ми робимо. Коли зможе він,—кивнув на третього,—хай примусить Мазепу служити Жовтню!

—Хай спробує!—з незахованою іронією пробурмотів перший.

Тоді встряг знову третій:

—Признаюся—я склав зброю. Я перестав мріяти про нові форми мистецтва, в тисячу разів упливовіші, міцніші й величніші за давні. Я перестав вірити, що завтра або позавтра замість камерного, кишенькового, свійського мистецтва (свійська худоба!) прийде нове мистецтво юрб, площ, демонстрацій і штурмів. Ждати—так ждати,—сказав я і почав лоскотати собі ніздрі соломинкою. Але за таким приємним ділом я не забуваю про ненависть. Я ненавиджу!.. Перераховувати, що я ненавиджу?

—Перераховуй, коли це не буде надто довго,—сказав перший і запалив свою люльку, що була загасла.

The first man couldn't take it anymore and interrupted one last time,

"You can love all you want, but again, keep it only to yourself, this 'cultural' foundation and this ground for your artistic potbelly. Everybody has their own potbelly, but it doesn't necessarily imply a relapse into stylistic imitation, pastiche, and recreation, or retrieving some old junk by rereading and translating it. However, all of this defines your artistic individuality. All your sonnets or imitations of the Scythian style derive from your artless potency or artistic impotence, which is the same thing. Your decline as an artist, as a creator of culture, is your own problem. Don't turn it into an ideological stance. Look at it as a way of personal and artistic decline (or ascent, as you think of it). If each of us is individually responsible for their own literary phiz, getting back together and considering common goals, we must find some arithmetic mean that will serve as a backbone of our little group here."

"Yes, we do have such a thing!" exclaimed the second man. "We do have something in common: we know our task. We are objectively and consciously aware of what our material is and how to handle it so that it would behave exactly as the master wishes. Another thing we have in common is method. And one final thing we have in common is October.[24] October is our ultimate goal. And if he can," the second man gave a nod hinting at the third man, "let him make Mazepa[25] serve October!"

"Yes, let him try!" mumbled the first man with unhidden irony.

"Okay, I'll admit it: I've laid down my arms. I stopped dreaming about new forms of art that are a thousand times more influential, robust, majestic than the old ones. I stopped believing that tomorrow, or the day after tomorrow, private, petty, domesticated art (like in the collocation 'domestic cattle') will be supplanted by a new art of mobs, streets, demonstrations, and uprisings. 'If what we need is to wait, I'll wait,' I told myself, and started tickling my nostrils with a little straw. But while indulging myself with this pleasant tickling, I can't forget the hatred. I hate …! Should I enumerate what I hate?"

"Go ahead if it's not going to take too long," said the first man and lit his pipe, which had just gone out.

---

24 A common Soviet metonymy for the revolution.
25 Ivan Mazepa (1639–1709) was a Ukrainian Cossack Hetman who fought with the Russian emperor Peter I against the Turks, but eventually sided with the Swedish king Charles XII to form an anti-Russian coalition. For more detail, see http://www.encyclopediaofukraine.com/display.asp?linkpath=pages%5CM%5CA%5CMazepaIvan.htm.

—Я ненавиджу кобеняк хазяйновитого дядька, я ненавиджу туган-баранівську кооперацію, я ненавиджу хуторянські масштаби, я ненавиджу УНР, що з хуторянства логічно витікає. Потім ще—вишивану сорочку, пасіку, «Просвіту» (байдуже, якого коліру), письменника Гринченка, оцю українську Чарскую в матні та вишиваній сорочці, автокефальну церкву …

—Гм! . . В ненависті ми теж можемо зійтися!—сказав другий, а перший тоді встав і виголосив таку промову:

—Невідомо, що дасть нам ця зустріч. Можливо, що нас буде більше. Але зараз треба яскраво виявити себе на кілька років і організовано йти вперед, не давати завмирати тим творчим комбінаціям, які повстають у наших жвавих, живих і безконкурентних головах. Ми постоїмо біля Семафора, але мені здається, що в майбутнє таки дійсно один шлях, і всі стають у чергу біля Семафора. Ви ж знаєте добре, що ми все-таки перші, і всі ті, що підуть за нами,—перші. Треба висадити наш десант на цьому безнадійно порожньому, закинутому на власне самоз'їдення березі. Треба кинути наші бумеранги, а головне—працювати й показувати, як треба працювати. Висадимо десант і підемо українськими преріями вносити електрифікацію на хутори й перешкоджати знищувати ті індустріяльні надбання, які ми принесли в українську культуру. Невже подібними станемо до тих старих поетичних калош, що, видряпавшись із символістичного багна, вибралися на широке революційне море і кумедно тут намагаються не захлинутися і не потопнути? . .

Після патетичної і голосної промови, передихнувши трохи, сказав раптом перший:

—А чи чули ви про останню літературну подію?

"I hate the capuche worn by those thrifty Ukrainian peasants. I hate Tuhan-Baranovs′kyi's[26] concept of cooperativism. I hate the scope of the Ukrainian homestead mentality. I hate the Ukrainian National Republic, which logically stems from this homestead mentality. Other things I hate? The embroidered shirt, the apiary, the 'Prosvita' Society (no matter the political hue), the writer Hrynchenko,[27] this Ukrainian Charskaia[28] person wearing baggy pants and an embroidered shirt, the autocephalous church …"

"Hm …! Hatred can unite, can't it?" said the second man, after which the first man stood up and delivered the following speech:

"It's unclear how we'll benefit from this meeting. Maybe we'll be joined by more people. But at the moment we need to vividly manifest our agenda for the next several years and move forward in an organized way. We should not let those creative combinations that arise in our agile, lively, and unrivaled minds lay dormant. We'll stand here near the Semaphore, but it seems to me that there's only one path into the future, and right now everybody's lining up near the Semaphore. You are well aware of the fact that we are, after all, the first. We need to deploy our airborne forces to this hopelessly empty forsaken shore that is otherwise doomed to devour itself. We need to throw our boomerangs and, most importantly, to work and to demonstrate how good work must be done. Let's deploy our forces and go into the Ukrainian prairies to start electrification in farmsteads and to prevent the destruction of those industrial accomplishments that we brought to Ukrainian culture. Are we indeed going to assimilate with these old poetic galoshes that have barely scrambled themselves out of Symbolist sludge, struggled into the broad revolutionary sea, and now are comically trying not to sputter and drown? …"

Catching his breath a little, after that emotional and loud speech, the first man said suddenly,

"And have you heard about the latest literary event?"

---

26 Economist, sociologist, and theoretician of the cooperative movement. For more detail, see http://www.encyclopediaofukraine.com/display.asp?linkpath=pages%5CT%5CU%5CTuhan6BaranovskyMykhailo.htm.

27 A more appropriate transliteration of his last name is Hrinchenko. But it is misspelled in the original. Hrinchenko was a nineteenth-century Ukrainian writer and public figure. For more details, see http://www.encyclopediaofukraine.com/display.asp?linkpath=pages%5CH%5CR%5CHrinchenkoBorys.htm.

28 Lidiia Charskaia (real name Churilova) was a Russian actress and writer.

—У городі бузина?—вирячив очі третій.

—Ні, у городі Харкові—нова літорганізація,—поважно промовив перший.—На установчих зборах після промови основоположника, ідеолога і критика, коли на всі лопатки остаточно було покладено всіх ворогів, коли шляхи було до революційної літератури цілком розчищено, коли знову дим пожеж і боїв мусив розлягтися над літературними нивами, коли останню цеглину було вкладено в підмурівок соціялістичної культури і останній кілок осиковий було вбито в могилу «тих, що по той бік», тоді спинився промовець, обвів очима потомлену в пень авдиторію свою і сказав: «Я скінчив. Чи є в кого якісь питання?» І підвелася тоді над юрбою худенька і волохата рука, стискаючи новенький членський квиток, і хрипкенький голосок запитав: «А чи скоро будуть видавать обмундіроваиіє?»

Понуро схилили голову троє.

«Чижило жить на єтом свєтє, господа!»—як сказав наш земляк Коля Гоголь.

—Що?—встало тверде волосся першого дибки—Унивать?

—Ні!. . Ні!. .—поклялася решта.

Перший, заспокоївшись, продовжував:

—Пошукаємо хлопців, що з нами підуть, дехто сам пристане. Там, у Харкові, десь запрезідентився Шпол, треба витягти його до Семафора. Сил наших досить, щоб розпочати рух. Треба вивести культуру з того бездарного самозадоволення, в яке вона зараз попала. Коли вже комусь треба гуртуватися, то хай собі гуртуються, але вже по принципу якости і по творчій псіхиці, а не під гаслом «український письменник». Треба знову йти до «ізмів», а не до «рідної хати, де мир і тишина».

"What? Elderberry blossoms in the village?"[29] said the third man with his eyes wide open.

"Not in the village—in the city. … A new literary organization has started in the city of Kharkiv," said the first man solemnly. "Its founder, ideologist, and main critic delivered a speech at the constituent assembly. And when all the opponents were downed, when all the paths towards revolutionary literature were cleared, when the smoke of fights and fires spread again across the literary cornfields, when the last brick was laid in the foundation of socialist culture, and when the last aspen stake was nailed into the casket of 'those who ended up on the other side,' then the speaker paused, looked around at the dead-tired audience, and stated, 'I'm finished. Any questions, anyone?' And then a thin hairy hand, clasping a new membership card, went up above the crowd, and a wheezy little voice asked, 'Will they start giving out our uniforms and equipment any time soon?'"

Dispirited, the three men bowed their heads.

"Harduous it is to live in this world," as our fellow countryman Kolia Hohol' used to say.[30]

"What?" said the first man, his hair standing on end. "Despondency?"

"No way, no way!" the others vowed.

Collecting himself, the first man continued,

"Let's find the lads who'll go with us now. Some others will join us later. There, in Kharkiv, Shpol[31] has taken up his presidential post, and now we need to get him closer to the Semaphore. We have enough momentum to start the movement. We need to lead culture out of that talent-short complacency in which it found itself. If anyone needs to unite and create organizations, let them do so, but in that case let them be governed by the principle of quality and by their creative psyche rather than under the slogan of 'a Ukrainian writer.' We

---

29 This is part of a Ukrainian saying, "U horodi buzyna, a v Kyievi diad'ko" (verbatim, "Elderberry in the vegetable garden, uncle/sodbuster/old man in Kyiv"). A variation of that saying has "devil/demon" instead of "uncle/sodbuster/old man." While in contemporary Ukrainian the saying is used to refer to a non sequitur situation, according to some etymologists, it can also be interpreted in the context of elderberry's property to repel evil forces. Here, however, the characters use it for the sake of wordplay, because the Ukrainian word for "kitchen/vegetable garden" and an old Slavic word for "city"—*horod*—are homographs, only differing in the stressed syllable.

30 Kolia Hohol' is informal (e.g., Nick) for Mykola Hohol' (or Nikolai Gogol in Russian). The final line from his *Tale of How Ivan Ivanovich Quarreled with Ivan Nikiforovich* reads, "skuchno na etom svete, gospoda" (verbatim, "it is boring [to be/live] in this world'). In various published translations it ranges from "It is a depressing world, gentlemen!" to "It is gloomy in this world, gentlemen." Here, the line is not only misquoted but also given in a transcribed Ukrainian version of Russian.

31 Iuliian Shpol is Mykhailo Ialovyi's pseudonym. See footnote 15 for more about Ialovyi.

—Де це «мир і тишина»? Співробітництво потрібне! От у ВАПЛІТЕ ...—крикнув другий.

—У ВАПЛІТЕ? О, там: did t-e-la passe, baba l'on bié, sam pan sil très a-ge úo prive!—як кажуть французи.

—Ох, упрів Яловий, добре ж таки попрів!—зітхнув третій.

—Треба виходити на широкий шлях світових творчих завдань, а не грузнути в своїй юшці,—скрикнув перший.—Треба позбутися провінції, яка знову починає огортати нас своїми трухлими тротуарами й підсліпкуватими гасовими ліхтарями. Інакше ми, не провінціяли, задохнемося або втечемо. Тікати нікуди, значить, висаджуй десант! Полоскочимо пузо літературних самозадоволених куркулів. Хай знову блисне полум'я самовідданих конквістадорів, що йдуть до комуністичного майбутнього не за страх, а за совість!

Так, значить, десант?

—Десант!!!

—Дайош!

—Дайош?

should get back to 'isms' and not to the 'native home' where 'peace and quiet' rule."[32]

"Where did you see 'peace and quiet'? Collaboration is what we need! Look at those guys in VAPLITE[33] ...," shouted the second man.

"In VAPLITE? Oh, as they say in French, a garçon Garry à la campagne drank champagne et managed crème de la crème ... with his fingers ... what a faux pas, je ne sais quoi, what a shame, what a cliché."[34]

"Oh, Ialovyi must have sweated bullets!" sighed the third man.

"We need to embark on a major international journey of artistic tasks instead of getting bogged down in our own watery soup," shouted the first man. "We need to get rid of the provincial, which again starts enveloping us with its moldering sidewalks and weak-sighted kerosene street lamps. Otherwise we, the nonprovincialists, will either suffocate or escape. There's nowhere to escape though, so let's deploy our airborne forces! Let's tickle the potbellies of self-satisfied literary *kulaks*. Let that flame shine again! The flame of selfless conquistadors headed to the communist future not because of fear but because of conscience!"

"Ready to deploy?"

"Deploy!!!"

"Let's go!"

"Let's go?"[35]

Translated by Roman Ivashkiv

---

32 "Peace and quiet" is a line from a famous song from Ivan Kotliarevs'kyi's play *Natalka-Poltavka* (*A girl from Poltava*), which to the Futurists was an example of the "homestead mentality" that they opposed.

33 VAPLITE (full name: Vil'na akademiia proletars'koï literatury [Free Academy of Proletarian Literature]) [was] a "writers' organization which existed in Kharkiv from 1925 to 1928" (http://www.encyclopediaofukraine.com/display.asp?linkpath=pages%5CV%5CA%5CVaplite.htm).

34 In the original Ukrainian, it is a string of words describing a countryside scene and peasants at work. To a Ukrainian ear, it is intended to sound like French but also to capture the irony of high and low (e.g., peasant work) explained, allegedly and jokingly, in French. This is a parody of Khvyl'ovyi, who tended to use foreign phrases; his VAPLITE group was seen as pretentious by the Futurists.

35 A transcribed Russian verb *davat'*, "to give," in the second person singular (that is, "you are giving" or "are you giving" as a question). In Soviet times, it was used a slogan of encouragement for action and productivity.

Afterword. From the Whirlpool of Creativity to Living on the Edge of a Psychological Abyss: Mykola Bazhan in the 1920s and 1930s

ELEONORA SOLOVEY

In late May 1935 Mykola Bazhan and Pavlo Tychyna[1] gave a poetry reading in Kharkiv. The city was no longer the capital of Ukraine. All literary life was run from Kyiv, or, more precisely, from Moscow, where in September 1934 the first Soviet Writers' Congress announced Socialist Realism to be the one and only method of composition acceptable in Soviet literature. The poets who arrived at the Kharkiv Assembly of the Union of Soviet Writers were probably eager to meet representatives of their literary milieu, to get a nostalgic glimpse of the colorful life that had either already passed or radically changed. One of the poets blended well with the audience; like everyone else, he listened with

---

1   Pavlo Tychyna (1891–1967): a leading Ukrainian Symbolist of the early twentieth century, who created his own style of *kliarnetyzm* (clarinetism). Starting early 1930s, Tychyna capitulated to the regime, consequently producing poetry collections in the Socialist-Realist style. However, there is no consensus among the scholars of today as to the intended meaning of those poems. They can, however, be read as a way to skillfully mimic the party line and create ambiguity around seemingly monosemantic phrases—*Translator's note.*

admiration and applauded with passion. That poet was Volodymyr Svidzins'kyi.[2] These three equally great poetic figures were the most important representatives of the Modernist movement. Their fates can help us gain understanding of that complex and contradictory epoch.

Let us zoom in on Bazhan, one of the characters in this trio. The youngest of the three, he never renounced the creative principles of his youth. Unlike Tychyna, he did not sacrifice his talents to fear; he escaped the kind of rebirth or, rather, personal deformation which many artists went through if they managed to survive the purges intact, be it because of a lucky coincidence or by betraying their principles. At the same time, he did not become an internal émigré like Svidzins'kyi; he did not choose "loneliness, work, silence"[3] as his foundational values. Nor did he stash his works in the drawer of his writing desk with no hope of ever seeing them published. Fate played a curious trick on Bazhan. Having survived the attacks of his critics during the loud public trials and soundless night arrests, and having endured the grueling wait for his own arrest, Bazhan suddenly found himself admitted to high office. He had become an important functionary.

Let's remember, however, to be careful in our evaluation of those times and those lives. With our current knowledge of how law enforcement agencies extracted confessions and what circles of hell the accused had to go through, we must leave final judgements for the future. What we can be sure of, though, is that the work of the young Bazhan, like Tychyna's early writing and Svidzins'kyi's entire oeuvre, testifies to how Ukrainian poetic Modernism, interrupted as it was by the purges, never fulfilled its promise.

Even with all the challenges he met in his life, Bazhan was rather favored by fate. He was lucky to be born into a good family and raised in the atmosphere of love and care. His early life impressions, so important in forming his personality, were connected to the city of Kam'ianets'-Podil's'kyi. The city, unique in its beauty and multilayered culture, preserved the traces of being under the rule of Kyivan Rus', Poland, Lithuania, and the Ottoman Empire. When Bazhan's family eventually moved to Uman', they found that the new place had a similar aura; it boasted a rich cultural history, and its Sofiïvka Park,[4]

---

2   Volodymyr Svidzins'kyi (1885–1941) was a Ukrainian poet and translator destroyed by the Soviet system. Attempts were made to erase his name and his work from the literary history; despite this, his works received deserved attention again in the 2000s.

3   This is a line from Volodymyr Svidzins'kyi's 1932 poem: "I have three joys I can't be deprived of: loneliness, work, silence."

4   A park and arboretum in Uman' built by the architect I. Metzel for the Polish count Stanisław Potocki in 1796–1800.

with its fascinating past and the colorful characters it attracted, was another Ukrainian place of power.

Bazhan managed to survive the rather peculiar adventures of his youth: as a gymnasium student, he recovered cultural artefacts for the local museum—artefacts which had been stolen by impoverished locals raiding the destroyed manors of Polish landowners. Bazhan's lifelong interest in art can be traced back to those early experiences. Later, as a university student, Bazhan miraculously survived a trip from Kyiv to his hometown, which he undertook while gravely sick, burning with typhoid fever.

He was also lucky in his education: despite all the destabilizing factors, such as the Bolshevik Revolution of 1917 and the resultant civil war, he had a chance to receive some homeschooling and later to attend a gymnasium. Even though subsequent study at a trade school left Bazhan dissatisfied, he still pursued self-education. Importantly, in the city of Uman' the young Bazhan met Les' Kurbas, an outstanding theatre director and reformer; this encounter proved to be momentous for Bazhan's biography.[5] In the early 1980s, the elderly Bazhan shared a moving memory of Kurbas in an essay about the time,[6] the publication of which facilitated the decisive rehabilitation of the director's work in Soviet Ukraine.

Kurbas' Theatre Studio in Uman' helped Bazhan connect to the broader avant-garde and influenced his early creativity. Let's keep it in mind that the Ukrainian avant-garde of the period was about to carry out an aesthetic takeover, produce a complete paradigm change. Vira Aheieva, a contemporary literary historian, makes the following astute observation regarding Bazhan's generation: "the pandemic exaggerated soft-heartedness of the Ukrainophile lyrical poetry was perceived by this generation as definitively outdated. Avant-garde urbanism brought about a break from the disgraced passéism and rusticity."[7]

Nevertheless, the inevitable self-defensiveness of certain movements within Ukrainian literature slowed the radicals' advance. Despite the superannuated themes and exhausted techniques of the literature they sought to demolish, the avant-garde still faced an enormous challenge. For example, the dark, autumnal, mid-1920s city in the poem "An Indistinct Sound"—with its "slums, ... brothel's frightening shadows," breweries, and prostitutes, "flames of the city, flames of the swamplands"[8]—is both brutal and disconsolate, alive

---

5   Kurbas and his troupe stayed in Uman' for the entire theater season of 1921.
6   Mykola Bazhan, "U svitli Kurbasa" (In the light of Kurbas), *Vitchyzna* 10 (1982): 118–150.
7   Aheieva, *Vizerunok na kameni*, 60–61.
8   See Amelia M. Glaser's translation of "Indistinct Sound" in the present volume.

and exhilarating. This kind of writing was shocking and perverse in the context of Ukrainian literature.

Bazhan managed to self-actualize fully as a poet during that brief moment of relatively unrestricted national and cultural development, creative freedom and experimentation. Iurii Lavrinenko states in his anthology *Executed Renaissance* (1959) that it was precisely Bazhan who "during the short five minutes before 'midnight' (1928–1931) managed to become a poetic hero of our century."[9] Two of Bazhan's early collections saw the light of day even before the period referred to by Lavrinenko: *The Seventeenth Patrol* (1926) and *The Sculpted Shadow* (1927). Rounded out by the 1929 collection titled *Edifices*, Bazhan's poems were personal and original reflections on the character of the epoch.

An adequate rereading and reinterpretation of Ukrainian literature, especially work written under Soviet rule, in many ways still remains to be done. For instance, Bazhan's poem "The Trooper's Song," one of the signature poems in *The Seventeenth Patrol*, has been read until recently as an expression of the "poet's romantic worldview."[10] Nowadays it is more appropriate to view it as a glorification of violence, with "class struggle" being hailed above all as imminent and necessary. Futurism was naturally integrated into this discourse, as evident from "Ruhr-March," "Imobe from Galam," and other poems written between 1923 and 1925.

The early Bazhan absorbs the music of his time in a very sensitive and, perhaps, somewhat indiscriminate manner: he produces uneven rhythms, dissonance, and a Tychyna-like *enharmonic* voice typical of that era of tectonic political and aesthetic shifts. Bazhan's style of the 1920s can be described as Expressionist-Baroque-Romantic; however, even this complicated definition is not quite broad enough. His celebration of brutality, against an ubran backdrop, and the poet's attempt to defeat his own inner humanism are reminiscent of the French *poète maudit*. One can discern the influence of Ukrainian and European modern art; and the nascent cinematographic traditions of Europe and the United States played their role, since Bazhan himself was involved in filmmaking. In late 1920s through through the early 1930s, he worked at the

---

9   Iurii Lavrinenko, *Rozstriliane vidrodzhennia. Antolohiia 1917–1933. Poeziia—Proza—Drama—Esei* (*The Executed Renaissance: An Anthology, 1917–1933. Poetry—Prose—Dramatic works—Essays*) (Kyiv: Smoloskyp, 2004), 316.

10 Natalia Kostenko, comments and footnotes to the chapter "Poetry," in *Mykola Bazhan. Vybrani tvory v dvokh tomakh* (*Mykola Bazhan. Selected Works in Two Volumes*), vol. 1, ed. Dmytro Pavlychko (Kyiv: Ukraïns'ka entsyklopediia, 2003), 555.

All-Ukrainian Administration for Photo and Cinema (VUFK) and edited the journal *Kino*; he also wrote a number of film scripts. His output in all genres was complicated by the general hardships of the postrevolutionary years, as well as his personal difficulties. Bazhan's poem "To My Friend" displays marks of intense emotionality: it is a self-addressed meditation on the difficulties of the creative process, his inability to render those feelings hidden deep inside himself and the overall resistance of life to representation in words.

At the same time, the young Bazhan's poetics resonated with people whose understanding of modernity was summarized in the slogan "*Ad fontes!*" ("Back to the sources!"). Even though it is now commonplace to talk about Bazhan as a Futurist and an avant-garde author, a number of his sonnets, such as "Fern" and "Lovage," a triptych titled "Love Potion," a diptych titled "The Night of Zalizniak," and the tetraptych "The Infinite Road" display a poetics related to that of the Kyiv Neoclassicists. One can recognize the same intentions, richness of vocabulary, and historical allusions that help restore connections between various periods, "images and centuries," to borrow an expression from the title of a collection of sonnets by Mykola Zerov. "Fern" echoes the work of the young Ryl's'kyi and of Zerov:

> This bog-star moon is like an ancient trove,
> These white and foamy clouds—ancient dreams.
> I see the pagan night in restless twitch
> Descend to shroud the pitch-black grove.[11]

There is, however, one significant difference: Bazhan's sonnet refers to pre-Christian culture and not the antiquity so loved by the Neoclassicists.

Even though Bazhan followed the tenets of Futurism consistently only for a limited time, and was never wholly convinced by it because of the movement's fascination with destruction, receiving the Futurist "inoculation" opened him to avant-garde aesthetics. This revealed itself in the poet's commitment to the kind of creative exploration and technical flexibility which would soon have to be concealed.

By the early 1930s, when fabricated trials and denunciations made it seem as though no place was safe because "even walls had ears," cultural and ideological dictatorship started to dominate both public and private life. Old relationships were severely tested, and Bazhan was affected by this to the full. The

---

11 Quoted from this volume.

16

dramatic story of his friendship with a talented Ukrainian writer Iurii Ianovs'kyi is now well known.[12] When Ianovs'kyi was being harshly criticized for his novel *Living Water*, Bazhan, in the fall of 1947, and by then a high official serving as deputy head of the Council of Ministers, was forced to publicly denounce his friend. Both Bazhan and Ianovs'kyi suffered greatly because of what transpired. In 1979, when Ianovs'kyi was no longer alive, Bazhan wrote *The Master of the Iron Rose*, a memoir dedicated to his friend, in which he openly repented for bringing the friendship to its end.

Mistrust and fear broke apart countless married couples, on occasion leading to pathological behaviors, such as spying and denunciations. Some stories came to light after archives were opened, yet many more left no traces. Only recently could the disparate fragments about Bazhan's friendship with the film producer and writer Oleksandr Dovzhenko[13] be pieced together. It is as if the epoch itself, not that remote yet so incomprehensible, speaks to us through the dramatic collisions of the personal and creative relationships of artists.

Bazhan became friends with Dovzhenko and Ianovs'kyi in the mid-1920s. They all lived in Kharkiv, enjoying the creative audacity and achievement still possible there. The triumvirate of talented young artists could have posed for a group portrait that captured the era at its peak. Working together on the development of Ukrainian cinema brought them even closer as friends. Bazhan frequently reviewed Dovzhenko's films; he gave *Zvenyhora, Arsenal,* and *The Earth* particular praise. In 1930, Bazhan published an essay on Dovzhenko—Bazhan found that the original poetic cinematography of *Zvenyhora* and *Arsenal* corresponded to his own aesthetic sensibility especially well. It was Bazhan who identified Dovzhenko's tendency to synthesize genres, blending visual arts, music, theatre, literature, and journalism together.

However, during World War II, while suffering from the brutal attacks of his critics, Dovzhenko imagined that Bazhan had joined his enemies. It is hard for us to imagine how warped life was under Stalin. Even at the height of being harassed, Dovzhenko was convinced his audience with the dictator in 1933 had

---

12 Iurii Ianovs'kyi (1902–1954) was a Ukrainian Neoromantic poet and novelist, whose works were criticized and banned by the Soviet regime.

13 Oleksandr Dovzhenko (1894–1956), Ukrainian film director best known for his Expressionist masterpieces *Arsenal* (1929) and *Zemlia* (*The Earth*, 1930). His film novel *Ukraïna v ohni* (*Ukraine in Flames*, 1943) was banned from publication. On Bazhan's relationship with Dovzhenko, see Volodymyr Panchenko, "'Vzhe ia ne Dovzhenko, a chort': Do vzaiemyn kinorezhysera z poetom Mykoloiu Bazhanom," *Filolohichni dialohy. Zbirnyk naukovych prats'* 5 (2018).

saved him from being arrested. In a November 1943 diary entry, he wrote that he "owes his life to him [Stalin—*OR*]."[14] This account of the leader's "miraculous" intervention in Dovzhenko's fate rhymes with the story of Bazhan's translation of Shota Rustaveli's rendition of *The Knight in the Panther's Skin*, a Georgian national epic composed circa 1220. Allegedly, in the days when Bazhan spent every single night awaiting arrest, Stalin himself wrote Bazhan's name in the list of award recipients for his translation of *The Knight*. Inevitably, those tales became myths adding to Stalin's personality cult and the widespread erroneous belief that the great leader was simply not aware of the scale of the purges, the number of innocent victims, and the unfair trials.

In the early 1930s, critics writing about Bazhan changed their tone towards him. In the same way that every important Soviet author was scrutinized, Bazhan's political loyalty and "ideological purity" were questioned. Tensions grew, the process of Ukrainization got curtailed,[15] the purges spread, and storm clouds began gathering over Bazhan's head. Critics bluntly inquired: "Where is Bazhan heading?" An article under such title appeared in the journal *Krytyka*.[16]

In this atmosphere of terror, which established itself in Ukraine earlier than in the rest of the Soviet Union, Bazhan wrote his first panegyric to Stalin. It helps to remember that no writer was able to avoid this task. For instance, Svidzins'kyi had to do the same thing when he worked for the *Literary Journal*. Failure to behave slavishly in those days meant not only losing a job, but risked a sentence. For that reason, Bazhan continued to fight "abstract humanism"[17] with genuine passion; one was required to do so in keeping with the ideas of class morality. His poems "The Death of Hamlet" (1932) and "The Trilogy of Passion" (1933) are evidence of this struggle. He mercilessly tortured himself for having poetic talent; he tried to suppress his own grave doubts and complicated questions, and made desperate attempts to keep revolution, class, and nation in harmony with one another. Somehow, incomprehensibly, he managed to remain a true poet.

---

14 Oleksandr Dovzhenko, *Shchodennykovi zapysy: 1939–1956* (*Diary Entries: 1939–1956*) (Kharkiv: Folio, 2015).

15 Ukrainization: a period of a temporarily favorable attitude of the regime toward the Ukrainian language and culture in the 1920s. Ukrainization constituted a part of the *korenizatsiia* (Nativization), aiming to involve the local manpower in the process of strengthening the Soviet state throughout the immense multinational union.

16 See Selivanovs'kyi, "Kudy priamuie."

17 "Abstract humanism," a term from the 1930s, was employed during the massive purges orchestrated by Stalin. The term was coined to condemn traditional ideas about humanity and anthropocentric philosophy that privileged personal freedom.

Fate was especially merciful to Bazhan in his old age: he was able to once again be his former self, so to speak, and to let his guard down. He no longer had to renounce or be ashamed of his old books (such as *The Sculpted Shadow* and *Edifices*), or his old poems (like "Ghetto in Uman'," 1930, and "Blind Bards," 1930–1931. However, "Immortality" (1937), "Mother" (1938), and "Father and Sons" (1938), as well as a number of poems written after World War II ("English Impressions," 1949) indicate that party ideology, forced pathos, and forced allegiance to "the only correct" creative method pushed poetry in a trap, a dead end. Bazhan was one of the few poets who managed to get out of the trap before reaching the point of no return.

Even in his early works Bazhan employed whimsical and crafty techniques pertinent to the aesthetics of the Ukrainian Baroque. However, his turn to Baroque "ode writing" yielded Stalinist pathos-filled poems which strike us, his readers, with a sense of dark irony. One example is Bazhan's notorious, widely disseminated, monumental poem "A Man in the Star-Bearing Kremlin ..." (1932). Subconsciously, Bazhan was looking for a way to flee from the ideological dictatorship; that was why he turned to the rich cultural traditions of other Soviet ethnicities and started to translate literary works from other languages.

The second half of the 1930s were the hardest for Bazhan. In 1935 a criminal investigation was opened in which the poet was named as a member of an underground "Ukrainian Military Organization." Ianovs'kyi and Ryl's'kyi were listed among other members of the nonexistent group. (The organization was fabricated by the security services.) Under pressure, Bazhan continued to glorify Stalin's industrial projects and became engaged in the fight against "bourgeois nationalism." However, those in power were still not convinced of his loyalty. The scope of his creative personality prompted the security services to keep compiling a dossier that implicated him in working with an "anti-Soviet group" of Russian writers, as well as with Georgian "nationalist poets." In truth Bazhan, a man ahead of his time, demonstrated another gift—a gift for conducting cultural diplomacy and engaging in wide-scale humanitarian projects. Contact with the West was decreasing, and within a short time most of the world would disappear behind the Iron Curtain. Yet the Soviet Union was made of republics which boasted distinctive ancient cultures. Literary translations offered a possibility to earn a living and take part in the process of cultural development. Bazhan liked complex work; he translated the poetry of Alisher Navoi (1444–1501) and Davit Guramishvili (1725–1792), and numerous works by Georgian, Belarusian, Polish, Bulgarian, and Russian poets. During the last two decades of his life, as the Ukrainian school of poetic translation blossomed, Bazhan continued to create his own anthology of translations, from Dante to Rilke to Celan.

The roller-coaster nature of Soviet reality left its mark on Bazhan's personality. Under Stalin's rule an artist was either doomed or compelled to undergo a transformation, sometimes a drastic one. We encounter the following description of Bazhan's new personality proposed by a contemporary scholar:

> [He was] harshly beaten up in the 1930s, reserved, careful, with all buttons tightly fastened (since he was a high-level functionary—a Deputy of the Council of the People's Commissariat of the USSR!). A vigilant internal censor has been residing inside him, taking care of all checks and balances. He had an emotional personality, too; however, Bazhan's passions resembled magma seething in some unimaginable depths.[18]

From time to time, drops of that magma found their way to the surface. As testified by the denunciations that have now become public, even in the most dangerous of times Bazhan expressed imprudent opinions in an attempt to protect the Ukrainian language and culture.[19] Those opinions, duly written down by the agents of the state security, are striking in their courage and contradict the image of a strictly buttoned-up, ever-vigilant man.

World War II had not come to an end yet, its ashes still smoldering, when Bazhan stepped forward with his poem "Ravine" as part of the *Kyivan Etudes* (1943–1945). It was written before its subject, the Babyn Yar massacre became taboo.[20] It was brave to write something like that; two other important Ukrainian poets of Jewish background, Leonid Pervomais'kyi (1908–1973) and Sava Holovanivs'kyi (1910–1989), also wrote about Babyn Yar at the time. Holovanivs'kyi's poem did not survive. It is believed that he destroyed it, even though legends about it still circulate, and attempts to locate the text are still being made. Perhaps Semen Lipkin,[21] the author of the poem "Union," risked less than Bazhan, since in metropolitan Russia a writer could take more liberties than a colleague in the favorite colony strangled in the "brotherly embrace" of Stalin.

---

18 Panchenko, "'Vzhe ia ne Dovzhenko, a chort,'" 57.
19 See https://www.ukrinform.ua/rubric-society/2505348-arhivi-kgb-akademik-bazan-ocima-donosikiv.html.
20 See http://www.yivoencyclopedia.org/article.aspx/Babi_Yar.
21 Semen Lipkin (1911–2003) was a Russian poet, translator, and fiction writer. A native of Odessa, Lipkin wrote impressionistic poetry about the events of the Holocaust in his home city (see *Metropol': literaturnyi al'manakh*, ed. V. Aksenov et al. [Moscow: Ardis, 1979]).

Bazhan did what he thought was right according to his conscience as a humanist and a patriot. He could not have foreseen that the next wave of purges was imminent, and that the fight against "rootless cosmopolitans" (who in practice were singled out on the basis of the fifth line in their passports) would be more intense in Ukraine than in any other region.[22] Pervomais'kyi and Holovanivs'kyi, the two poets who went through World War II, who were wounded and decorated, who wrote war reports and editorials, poems and songs, could not have imagined the humiliation of the forthcoming campaign either. It was an advance offensive; now those authors could not anticipate any possibilities of getting published, of heading writers' unions, or even of having any moral authority. Instead, those who waited out the war far away from the battlefields got their chance to act.[23]

And act they did. They instigated a disgraceful campaign, which proved a disaster for Ukrainian culture and an assault on the military reporters whose work had been paid for in blood. The euphemism "cosmopolitans" failed to mislead anyone. Rumors about Bazhan's Jewish background circulated, and he never tried to disprove them, since the truth about his family could have caused him even more trouble. (His father was a military cartographer, a lieutenant colonel in the tsarist army, later in the army of the Ukrainian National Republic [1917–1920]. Bazhan's mother was from the old aristocratic family of Porzecki.)

Even though Bazhan was known for his remarkable composure, the prewar and postwar challenges did cause him suffering and pain, as witnessed in Sava Holovanivs'kyi's memoirs:

> I would never forget our evening strolls in the city [Kyiv—OR], during those first years after the war. My situation at the time was worse, Bazhan's was more complicated. Very recently we had been fighting a common enemy … and yet now I was among those on whom the critics poured mud almost daily, and he was among those who were if not carrying out the campaign, at the very least had to support it. It is not difficult to imagine what was going on inside of him.[24]

---

22 The fifth line in applications and passports in the USSR listed ethnicity. The campaign against the "rootless cosmopolitans" was aimed at Jewish writers, artists, and other members of intelligentsia. In order to disguise the nature of the campaign, about every tenth victim had to be Slavic.
23 During World War II, many Ukrainian writers with families, as well as museum collections, libraries, and numerous academic institutions were evacuated to the city Ufa, located in the Ural region in western Russia.
24 Sava Holovanivs'kyi, *Memorial: Spohady* (*Memorial: Memoirs*) (Kyiv: Radians'kyi pys'mennyk, 1988), 43.

The death of Stalin and the dismantling of his personality cult, as well as other social processes known as the Khrushchev Thaw, brought about some changes, perhaps not seismic, but certainly irreversible. Together with his colleagues— poets of the same generation—Bazhan experienced incredible elation and excitement, although he also remained cautious. Like many others, he went through a "third blossoming." One gets the impression that the poetry collection *Near the Savior's Tower* (1952) was written by one person, while the following works, such as *Meetings in Italy* (1964) and the poem *Flight through the Storm* (1964), were written by someone else. Clearly, this was not the early Bazhan anymore; by now a mature master, he was happy to feel the power of harnessing words again, to see order prevail over chaos and violence again. The metaphysical motifs of the early poetry stayed in the past; instead, Bazhan now contemplated major existential issues. This more philosophical work exhibits a harmony between the intellectual and the emotional, an accord between thoughts and words.

Memories of Uman': Poetic Novellas appeared in 1972, a year notorious for a new wave of arrests that rounded up members of the Ukrainian intelligentsia who opposed the regime dissidents. One of Bazhan's poems, "Debora," was cut from the collection by censors after it was published in a journal in 1968. In his letter to Raisa Ratova, to whom the poem was dedicated, the author complains about the "hapless, torn-apart *Memories of Uman'*," and expresses his hope that the "worrywarts would finally stop."[25] Bazhan remained optimistic; however, the next time this poem saw print was in 1988, after the author's death. It did not even appear in the original Ukrainian but in translation, published in Moscow in the Russian edition of Bazhan's *Short and Long Poems*.

Despite some forced abrupt reversals, Bazhan's creative trajectory shows a gradual return to where things started, which is evident even in his choice of words. In "Amusement Park Elegy" (1927), a poem filled with expressive paradoxes and oxymorons, the word "mark" (*karb* in Ukrainian)[26] appears to carry a special importance for Bazhan; it becomes endowed with a high status. It shows up again in Bazhan's symbolic metaphysical poem "Blind Bards" (1930–1931):

> The sign,
>> and greatness
>>> and mark of blindness ...[27]

---

25 Quoted from Kostenko, comments and footnotes to the chapter "Poetry," 593.
26 The Ukrainian noun *karb*, a mark, is related to the verb *karbuvaty*, to engrave. The nuanced connection is lost in English as the word "mark" does not allude to the process of engraving— *Translator's note.*
27 Quoted from this volume.

The Sculpted Shadow is also an oxymoron. Sculpting can be understood as carving, engraving a drawing, or a design on hard surface. Sculpting a shadow might be a reference to the sophisticated and whimsical nature of drawing, ever fleeting and vanishing. The critics, once incredulous and harsh, now pronounced Bazhan a "master of engraved words."[28] *The Marks* (1978) was Bazhan's last poetry collection. It is late Bazhan on the verge of saying farewell, an author who truly left a mark with his magnum opus.

Did the older Bazhan composing his farewell think of his early poetry? Yes, those poems might have emerged in his memory. Despite the complexities of his creative journey, now the circle was complete. The poet came back to himself in a poem from the above-mentioned collection, "… entering the endless lanes/Into the eternity of outstretched silence."

Translated from Ukrainian by Oksana Rosenblum

BIBLIOGRAPHY

Aheieva, Vira. *Vizerunok na kameni. Mykola Bazhan: zyttepys (ne)radians'koho poeta.* Lviv: Vydavnytstvo staroho leva, 2018.
Bazhan, Mykola. "U svitli Kurbasa." *Vitchyzna* 10 (1982): 118–150.
Holovanivs'kyi, Sava. *Memorial: Spohady.* Kyiv: Radians'kyi pys'mennyk, 1988.
Kostenko, Natalia. Comments and footnotes to the chapter "Poetry." In *Mykola Bazhan. Vybrani tvory v dvokh tomakh,* vol. 1, edited by Dmytro Pavlychko, 554–573. Kyiv: Ukraïns'ka entsyklopediia, 2003.
Lavrinenko, Iurii. *Rozstriliane vidrodzhennia: Antolohiia, 1917–1933. Poeziia—Proza—Drama—Esei.* Kyiv: Smoloskyp, 2004.
Panchenko, Volodymyr. "'Vzhe ia ne Dovzhenko, a chort': Do vzaiemyn kinorezhysera z poetom Mykoloiu Bazhanom." *Filolohichni dialohy. Zbirnyk naukovykh prats'* 5 (2018).
Ryl's'kyi, Maksym. *Kriz' buriu i snih (Through blizzard and snow).* Kyiv: Slovo, 1925.
Shevtsova, Svitlana. "Arkhivy KGB: akademik Bazhan ochyma donoshchykiv." https://www.ukrinform.ua/rubric-society/2505348-arhivi-kgb-akademik-bazan-ocima-donosikiv.html.
Zerov, Mykola. *Kamena.* Kyiv: Slovo, 1924.

---

28 In 1964, a book titled *Maister karbovanoho slova: Statti do 60-richchia z dnia narodzhennia Mykoly Bazhana (Master of Engraved Words: In Celebration of Mykola Bazhan's 60th Birthday)* was published by the Soviet Writer Publishing House (Sovetskii pisatel') in Moscow. Memoirs about Bazhan later appeared under the title *Karbovanykh sliv volodar: spohady pro Mykolu Bazhana (Lord of Engraved Words: Memoirs about Mykola Bazhan)* (Kyiv: Dnipro, 1988).

Editors, Translators, and Contributing Writers

Halyna Babak is a scholar and editor in chief of the Czech journal *Navýchod*. She received her PhD in Slavic literatures from Charles University, Prague (2020). Her research focuses on Ukrainian and Russian avant-garde literature and Ukrainian interwar literary theory.

Lev Fridman is a Russian-born speech-language pathologist based in New York City. He writes and translates (from Russian to English) and facilitates translation projects and publications. His work has appeared in publications by *Ugly Duckling Presse* and the *Odessa Review*. Most recently, he has written on the literary legacy of Mykola Bazhan.

Dr. Amelia M. Glaser is Associate Professor of Russian and Comparative Literature at the University of California, San Diego, where she directs the Russian, East European, and Eurasian Studies Program, as well as the Jewish Studies Program. She is the author of *Jews and Ukrainians in Russia's Literary Borderlands* (Northwestern University Press, 2012), the translator of *Proletpen: America's Rebel Yiddish Poets* (University of Wisconsin Press, 2005), and the editor of *Stories of Khmelnytsky: Competing Literary Legacies of the 1648 Ukrainian Cossack Uprising* (Stanford University Press, 2015). She is the coeditor, with Steven S. Lee, of *Comintern Aesthetics* (forthcoming 2020, University of Toronto Press). Her most recent book *Songs in Dark Times: Yiddish Poetry of Struggle from Scottsboro to Palestine* is forthcoming from Harvard University Press.

George G. Grabowicz is the Dmytro Čyževs'kyj Professor of Ukrainian Literature at Harvard University. He received his PhD in comparative literature from Harvard (1975), where he was also Junior Fellow in the Society of Fellows (1971–1974). He was one of the founders and president (1991–1993) of the International Association for Ukrainian Studies and president of the Shevchenko Scientific Society in the US (2012–2018). In 1997, he founded, and since then has been editor in chief, of the Ukrainian monthly *Krytyka* (http://www.krytyka.com), a leading intellectual journal in both Ukraine and Eastern Europe. Professor Grabowicz has written on Ukrainian, Polish, and Russian literature, as well as on literary theory. A full bibliography of his writings (up to 2015) is available online at http://faculty.slavic.fas.harvard.edu/files/george-grabowicz/files/grabowicz_-_festschrift_-_bibliography_-_hus32.pdf. Since the 2010s, he has been actively translating Ukrainian poetry into English.

Dr. Yuliya Ilchuk is Assistant Professor at Slavic Department at Stanford University. Her major research interests fall under the broad heading of cultural exchange, interaction, and borrowing between Russia and Ukraine. She has published articles on contemporary Russian and Ukrainian culture and society and translated contemporary Ukrainian poetry.

Dr. Roman Ivashkiv is a lecturer in Slavic languages and literatures and the language program coordinator at the University of Illinois at Urbana-Champaign. His research interests include translation studies and comparative literature. His current research focuses on transmesis in Slavic film and fiction. With the Canadian writer and translator Erín Moure, he translates Ukrainian poetry into English.

Anzhelika Khyzhnya is a scholar and journalist. She holds an MA in Slavic languages and literature and is a PhD candidate at the University of California, Berkeley. Her research interests include linguistic aspects of early nineteenth-century Russian and Ukrainian prose, Ukrainian poetry of the 1920s, and the relationship between literature and the visual arts.

Ostap Kin edited an anthology *New York Elegies: Ukrainian Poems on the City* (2019), translated Serhiy Zhadan's collection of poems *A New Orthography* (2020; with John Hennessy), Yuri Andrukhovych's collection of poems *Songs for a Dead Rooster* (2018; with Vitaly Chernetsky), and Vasyl Lozynsky's chapbook *The Maidan After Hours* (2017; with Ali Kinsella).

Dr. Roman Koropeckyj holds PhD in Slavic languages and literatures from Harvard University. He is Professor of Slavic Literatures at the Department of Slavic, East European, and Eurasian Languages and Cultures at UCLA. He is the author of two award-winning books on Adam Mickiewicz, as well as numerous articles on Polish, Ukrainian, comparative Slavic, and Little Russian literature.

Svetlana Lavochkina is a Ukrainian-born novelist, poet, and translator, currently residing in Germany. She was runner-up in the Paris Literary Prize, and finalist in both the Tibor Jones Pageturner Prize and the Million Writers Award. Her work has appeared in *AGNI*, *New Humanist*, *POEM*, *Words for War*, *The White Chalk of Days*, and elsewhere.

Seán Monagle is a poet, translator, playwright, and librettist. His poetry has appeared most recently in Manos Sucias/Dirty Hands, a collaboration with painter Greg Slick and poet/printmaker/book artist Paulette Myers-Rich, which was released in January 2019. He has collaborated with Roman Turovsky on translations of two poems by Zbigniew Herbert "Mr. Cogito's Soul" and "The Poet." He lives in Beacon, New York.

Ainsley Morse is a scholar, teacher, and translator, primarily of Russian and former Yugoslav literatures. Her research focuses on the literature and culture of the postwar Soviet period, particularly unofficial or "underground" poetry, as well as the avant-garde and children's literature. She teaches Russian language and Russian/Eastern European literature at Dartmouth College.

Bohdan Pechenyak was born and raised in Lviv, Ukraine. He immigrated to the USA in 1998 and graduated from Arcadia University (BA, Sociology) and Temple University (MSW, MPH).

He believes in interdisciplinary approaches and attempts to balance activism, scholarship, and creative pursuits. His interests in the arts include film, writing, and translation.

Oksana Rosenblum is a Ukrainian-born art historian and translator residing in NYC. She studied cultural anthropology at the National University of Kyiv-Mohyla Academy, Jewish studies at the Oxford Center for Hebrew and Jewish Studies and Jewish visual art at the Jewish Theological Seminary in NYC. Oksana's projects have included visual research for the newly created museums of Jewish History in Warsaw and Moscow. Her poetry translations from Ukrainian have appeared in *Kalyna Review* and *National Translation Month*.

Dr. Myroslav Shkandrij is Professor of Slavic studies at the University of Manitoba. He has published and edited several books that deal with Ukrainian literature and art, nationalism, and Soviet cultural politics.

Iryna Shuvalova is an award-winning poet and translator. Her work has been published internationally, and her first book of poetry in English is due in 2019 with Lost Horse Press. She holds an MA in comparative literature from Dartmouth College and is currently a PhD candidate at the University of Cambridge.

Dr. Eleonora Solovey (Honcharyk) has a doctorate in linguistics and specializes in literary theory and comparative literary studies. She is a professor emerita, a member of the Ukrainian Writers' Union and the International PEN-Center. Her research focuses on the history of Ukrainian and Russian literature. Dr. Solovey has authored six monographs and edited the complete works of Serhii Yefremov (2002) and Volodymyr Svidzins'kyi (2004). Her book of selected poems by Svidzins'kyi was published by the Canadian Institute of Ukrainian Studies Press in 2017. In 2007, she received the Vasyl Stus Award.

Roman Turovsky studied art at the Kyiv Art Institute and New York's Parsons School of Design. His multimedia work includes video-installation, photography, and music. Turovsky's poetry translations from Russian, Ukrainian, and Polish have appeared in *Cardinal Points*, *The Germ*, and *Odessa Review*.

Mykyta Tyshchenko is a scholar of Russian and Ukrainian literature. His interests include postcolonial, postrevolutionary and post-Chernobyl art and culture. He holds a BA in English and Germanic studies, applied linguistics, and the history of European literature from Kyiv National Linguistic University, Ukraine. For the past two years, he has worked as a Russian Language Resident at Pomona College, California, teaching classes in Russian and East European studies.

Illustrations

Figure 1. Mykola Bazhan's cover design for Oleksa Slisarenko's *Poemy* (Poems) (Kyiv: Panfuturysty, 1923).
(Private collection of Bohdan Tsymbal, Kyiv, Ukraine)

Кембрідж. Масс.
США

Вш.П.О.Пріцакові

Вельмишановний Пане Професоре:

Я глибоко зворушений Вашою увагою до мене. Однак мушу висловити свій сумнів у **реальності** і вчасності Вашої ініціативи щодо висунення Вами моєї кандидатури на здобуття Нобелівської премії. Я цілком розумію, яке глибше і значно ширше та важливіше за мою скромну особу значення Ви вкладаєте у цю свою акцію, бажаючи і таким чином привернути увагу західно-європейської та американської громадськості до явищ української літератури. Проте не без підстав побоюсь, що моя кандидатура для цього не надається. Якби там не поцінювати мою літературну працю, але на Заході про неї (заслужено, чи не заслужено - це вже інша річ) мало знають. Десь під час війни і невдовзі після неї друкувалися переклади моїх поезій англійською, французькою, німецькою мовами, але й було їх мало, і якість перекладів була сумнівна. Я їх навіть не зберіг і тому мушу на Ваше прохання надіслати бібліографію перекладів моїх творів відповісти, що такої бібліографії не маю і навіть не знаю, чи останніми роками в Європі чи Америці (окрім країн соціалістичного табору) переклади такі з'являлися.

Разом з цими щирими словами подяки хочу надіслати Вам свою працю, яка забрала в мене кілька років і яка дещо зоігається з тією галуззю людинознавства - тюркологією, де Ви є одним з найбільших у світі знавців. Висилаю Вам свій переклад поеми славетного староузбека Алішера Навої "Фархад і Шірін". Прийміть цю книгу на знак моєї сердечної поваги.

Микола БАЖАН

2 лютого 1970 р.
м.Київ, вул.Репіна, 5, кв.5

Figure 2. Mykola Bazhan to Omeljan Pritsak, Kyiv, February 2, 1970. Typescript. (Omeljan Pritsak Memorial Library, Archival Collection, National University of Kyiv-Mohyla Academy, collection 10, file 983, 101–118).

HARVARD UNIVERSITY
COMMITTEE ON UKRAINIAN STUDIES
1737 Cambridge Street, Room 208
Cambridge, Massachusetts 02138
Tel. 868-7600, Ext. 653 or 235-9238

Omeljan Pritsak, *Chairman*

Members:
Horace G. Lunt
Richard E. Pipes
Ihor Ševčenko

Кембридж, 17-го лютого 1970 року

Високоповажаний Пан
Академік Микола Бажан
Київ,
вул.Леніна 51 УРСР

Високоповажаний Пане Академіку!

Мені надзвичайно приємно було одержати Вашу відповідь. З великим нетерпінням очікую одержання Вашого перекладу поеми нової " Фаргад і Шірін ", яку я особисто дуже люблю і не раз читаю зі своїми учнями на семінарах середньо-тюрської літератури. Прошу прийняти мої вислови щирої подяки за цей прекрасний дарунок. Жалію, що не можна було мати бібліографії перекладів Ваших творів на Західні мови, але це в основному не найважніша справа. Шведська Академія звернулась до мене про мою думку, а я зі своєї сторони серйозно обдумавши і простудіювавши справу, прийняв своє особисте рішення, яке я і переслав тим, хто мене питали.

У прилозі залучую копію цього мого листа,який прошу задержати у Вашому приватному архіві. При тій нагоді хочу поінформувати Вас, що у нас вже почали діяти Катедри української історії і української літератури. Вас може зацікавить факт, що на семінарі із нової української літератури бере участь 17 слухачів,між ними майже половина не українського походження. Професор Тарановський у цьому семінарі веде спеціяльний семінар про поему "Гайдамаки" Шевченка, в якому беруть участь 9 студентів. Ми почали теж видавничу справу і я дозволю собі в скорому часі післати Вам тематичний план наших видань на рік 1970-й.

Також в міру того, як вони будуть виходити Ви будете діставати один примірник кожного видання.

З правдивою пошаною
Ваш
Омелян Пріцак

Figure 3. Omeljan Pritsak to Mykola Bazhan, Cambridge, MA, February 17, 1970. Typescript.
(Omeljan Pritsak Memorial Library, Archival Collection, National University of Kyiv-Mohyla Academy, collection 10, file 983, 101–118).

The Nobel Committee of   January 29, 1970
the Swedish Academy
Börshuset 11129 Stockhom

Dear Sirs,

    In replying to your gracious invitation to nominate a
candidate for the Nobąl Prize for Literature for 1970, I have
given much thought to possible candidates in literatures with
which I am acquainted. I have come to the conclusion that the
most deserving author whom I could unreservedly support is the
Ukrainian poet Mykola Bazhan(born Sept. 26/Oct.9,1904). There-
fore I nominate Mykola Bazhan as candidate for the Nobel Prize
for Literature for 1970 on the basis of his poetic works. I will
now now explain to you the reasons for my choice.

    The generation of poets which appeared on the Ukrainian
literary scene in the 1920's found the normative canon of established
schools abd trends of Ukrainian modernism constraining rather than
inspiring. While formally belonging to one literary association or
another, they put individual style aboue "group loyalty" and
often derived most significant lessons from the work of their
literary opponents. This synthesis of poetic methods, so charac-
teristic of the twenties, was most fully achieved in the art of

Figure 4. Omeljan Pritsak to the Nobel Committee, January 29, 1970. Typescript. (Omeljan Pritsak Memorial Library, Archival Collection, National University of Kyiv-Mohyla Academy, collection 10, file 983, 101–118).

Mykola Bazhan, which transcend the narrow framework of the
established contemporary styles and, at the same time, transform
creatively the most interesting elements of both the Ukrainian
and the European poetic traditions.

Bazhan began as a futurist, and the influence of Majakovskij
and the Ukrainian aspanfuty Semenko and Shkurpij is strongly
felt in his early verse(Bazhan began to publish in 1923: his first
book of poems, The Seventeenth Patrol, appeared in 1926). The
rhythmic originality of Bazhan(who was a pioneer in the development
of the Ukrainian tonic verse), the rich sound texture and the strik-
ingly complex metaphor of his mature style undoubtedly owe a
great deal to his early futurist experiments.

However, the narrow scope of Semenko's experimentation and
the eclectic Russian neoromanticism of Tixonov, which was fashion-
able at the time and had left its imprint on Bazhan's early
ballads, soon ceased to satisfy the poet. Bazhan seeks complexity,
precision, and a perfect balance between all the elements and
levels of poetic structure. He turns to M. Zerov and M. Ryl's'kyj,
the two greatest representatives of the so-called Ukrainian
"neoclassicism", and, through their mediacy, rediscovers the
French Parnassians, in particular, Heredia.

The "panfuturist" Bazhan becomes a master of polished
sonnet,although in a quite different manner than either of his

Figure 5. Omeljan Pritsak to the Nobel Committee, January 29, 1970. Typescript. (Omeljan Pritsak Memorial Library, Archival Collection, National University of Kyiv-Mohyla Academy, collection 10, file 983, 101–118).

two neoclassical masters. His metaphor is unhampered by the neoclassical restraint, his syntax is involved, his imagery is grossly sensual, and his meaning enigmatic and ambiguous. The wealth of his poetic vocabulary surpasses that of any of his contemporaries. He has no peers in modern Ukrainian poetry as the explorer of previously untapped strata of dialectal speech. Collecting rare Ukrainian words is his passion.

A poet whose gift is predominantly epic, Bazhan treats his favorite historical themes in the spirit of the Ukrainian baroque tradition, with its profusion of grotesque emblematic details, extended metaphors, often enigmatic metonymies, and an approach which is at the same time furiously sensual and icily detached.

The collection A Carved Shadow(1927) marks the end of Bazhan's years of study. He returns to the genre of epic meditation, his youthful romanticism now tempered by irony. In his famous triptych "The Buildings"(1929) he challenges the historical and artistic concepts of the neoclassics, approaching the cultural heritage of the Old Ukraine(and the Baroque, in particular) with a typically baroque ambivalence: a mixture of admiration and revulsion, aphoristic precision and fanatical passionateness. The rhetoric of enlightenment permeating his other masterpiece, " The Ghetto in Human"(1929) is based on the stylistic devices

Figure 6. Omeljan Pritsak to the Nobel Committee, January 29, 1970. Typescript. (Omeljan Pritsak Memorial Library, Archival Collection, National University of Kyiv-Mohyla Academy, collection 10, file 983, 101–118).

of a religious sermon. This poem is the most characteristic
specimen of Bazhan's "neobaroque" style.

In the long poem "Hoffman's Night"(1927), Bazhan tackles a
theme which had deep personal implications. He explores the nature
of the conflict between the poet and the philistine state as a
grotesque confrontation between E.T.A.Hoffman and his personages
drinking together in a nightmare inn "gaping like the sour mouth of
a drunkard".

In the climax of Bazhan's literary path is his long poem The
Blind Singers(1930-1931), of which only some parts were allowed to
be published. Here the force of Bazhan's poetic invective can be
compared only to that of Shevchenko (and,indeed, it was Shevcheno's
Perebendja th t inspired the poem of Bazhan). The conflict between
poet and society, so pertinently exposed in "Hoffman's Night" and
The Blind Singers, has caught up with Bazhan himself. For decades,
the demands imposed by this conflict have been crippling the gift
of Bazhan. During that time he published little that could stand
comparison with his earlier poetry, such as The Ghetto in Human'
and The Blind Singers which, indeed, have not even been republished
in the most recent two-volume edition of his works (Kiev, 1965). His
best achievements during those years are his translations from Georgian
and from Russian. Fortunately, the poems published by Bazhan
after 1953 (Mickiewicz in Odessa /1956/, Italian Encounters /1962/,
Four Tales about Hope - Variations on a theme from R.M. Rilke /1967/)
testify to the unexhausted wealth of his poetic talent. His place

Figure 7. Omeljan Pritsak to the Nobel Committee, January 29, 1970. Typescript.
(Omeljan Pritsak Memorial Library, Archival Collection, National University of
Kyiv-Mohyla Academy, collection 10, file 983, 101–118).

among the five or six greatest modern Ukrainian poets is un-
contested. He influenced not only the Ukrainian poets of the
younger generation, but also such Russian poets as Bagrickij and
Antokol'skij(both produced excellent Russian translations of
his works).

Bazhan's poetic work, although impressive when judged even
by the highest European standards, remains largely unknown out-
side the Soviet Union, due to the absence of qualified translators
and popularizers. He has much to offer, not to the Ukrainian reader
alone but also as a unique representative of the European experi-
mental style. His poetics also combine elements of neoclassicism
and baroque neo-romanticism providing an unparalleled insight into
the literary evolution of our time.

I hope that this presentation may be of use to you in your
very demanding search.

Respectfully yours,

Omeljan Pritsak

Figure 8. Omeljan Pritsak to the Nobel Committee, January 29, 1970. Typescript. (Omeljan Pritsak Memorial Library, Archival Collection, National University of Kyiv-Mohyla Academy, collection 10, file 983, 101–118).

CPSIA information can be obtained
at www.ICGtesting.com
Printed in the USA
JSHW031426111120
9509JS00007B/73